THE MOTIVATION TO ACTIVELY CARE

multitude of organizations populated with all sorts of compelling personalities to keep the reader interested. Those familiar with Dr. Geller's work will find the usual discussion of solid organizational development and motivational theory combined with a page-turning storyline.

This scholarship by Dr. Geller and Mr. Veazie offers something for anyone involved or interested in continually improving his or her occupational or even personal life. These internationally-respected organizational consultants have delivered an excellent resource for us, whether the user is the chief executive, the first-line supervisor or someone in between. Even a small-business owner looking to surpass the competition will discover many keys to establishing a top-performing operation hidden in the pages. I have my fingers crossed there will be a third installment!"

—**Scott Bowers**, Safety and Risk Manager,
Colorado Department of Human Services

"This enlightening and entertaining storybook struck so many chords that Bach would be impressed! I felt like the pages were speaking directly to me. So many of Joanne's experiences and emotions mirrored my own that I half-expected to discover I'd been secretly spied upon as research for the book. Countless times, Joanne's struggles resurrected flashes of similar events and feelings from my own life. Her thoughts, her words, her perceptions…they all felt like mine. At times, I even felt vindicated knowing that someone else out there saw things exactly the way I do. If Joanne had a cheering section, I would be in the front row. I truly enjoyed that while I was being entertained (and hooked!) by the story, I also learned several useful skills I can put into action.

The questions at the end of the book are wonderful tools for reflection and discussion. I envision them as being part of a training module on self-motivation. I identified with Joanne so much that I actually broke down and cried when she opened the letter from Doc and read it. I also got teary-eyed when she called her Dad to thank him for everything. I now feel compelled to do the same thing… with *all* of my parents (i.e., Mom, Stepdad, Dad, and Stepmom). There are so many other elements of this book I could gush about, but what I really want to do is ask the Leadership in my company to read every word in it and seriously discuss its relevance to our organization. Perhaps it would spark the positive change we so desperately need."

—**Teresa Reinwasser**, Safety/Environmental Manager, Romeo RIM, Inc.

"This is an inspiring tale for the times. It comes complete with the adversities, stresses, pain, loss and uncertainties we know too well from current economic hardships. But it shows how courage, determination, family, friends and mentors can all help us keep on keeping on, stretch our abilities, and realize aspirations we thought beyond our reach."

—**Dave Johnson**, Editor, *Industrial Safety and Hygiene News*

"Read this book and you will discover a wealth of information about developing caring relationships even under the most difficult circumstances. Dr. Geller gets to the root of motivating actively caring for people leadership. Pass it on!"

—**Douglas R. Hole**, Colonel USAF (Ret.)

"This book is an easy read, with a poignant message, embedded in a great story. Unfortunately, I found myself in the story, along with others in our organization. But fortunately, the story had a happy ending because it gave me the tools to fix ours."

—**Anthony D. Carter**, CSP, El Paso Corporation

"One of the greatest treasures in life is friendship. When you are blessed with friends who are wise, your treasure is even greater. I treasure those moments in my life when my friend, Scott Geller, has shared his wisdom with me. Now you can enjoy a great story and learn the skills to make a difference in the lives of your employees. Discover the power of self-motivation. Scott and Bob know how to take research-based information and teach it to you effectively and in an entertaining way. To sum it up I would like to say, 'thanks' and after reading this book you will say the same."

—**John Drebinger**, Certified Speaking Professional,
John Drebinger Presentations

"A small group of researchers has been saying for years that this is the crux of the matter in organizational effectiveness: *How do we motivate people to actively care for people?* Dr. Geller and Mr. Veazie are on the forefront of this new wave of individual and group success by dealing with this critical issue.

Geller and Veazie accurately identify one of the principle problems in organizational management today: that companies repeatedly make the mistake of thinking rules or mandates can substitute for culture. The study of behavior management has proven time and time again over the last 50 or more years that this way of thinking will not produce the results companies desire.

I love the story-style of this book. It makes the learning so easy that you don't even know it's happening!"

—**John Austin, Ph.D.**, Managing Consultant, Reaching Results

"Geller and Veazie have written a compassionate, easy-to-read book that holds one's attention throughout, yet provides invaluable information about developing self-motivation and human relationships. This is an essential read for any person interested in effective life improvement—both professionally and personally. This book should be a standard for corporate Human Relations personnel."

—**Joe Ferrari**, Professor of Psychology, Vincent DePaul Distinguished Professor & Editor, *Journal of Prevention & Intervention in the Community*

"The Motivation to Actively Care is such an inspiration! This book deals with many real-world situations that businesses and families are dealing with right now, crafted in such a way that you can visualize the situations, issues and solutions, and apply the self-motivation lessons to your own life."

—**Tara D. Henderson**, CSP, CHST, STS ,
Safety Analyst, Fairfax County Government

"Geller and Veazie have done it again by making it exciting to read this emotionally-engaging and uplifting story. This book helps readers develop resilience when faced with life's challenges both on and off the job. It is packed with some of the most insightful questions you could ask in order to discover hidden opportunities that uncover not just the symptoms, but the underlying factors that help organizations achieve their goals and live up to their values. Thank you for continuing to Make A Difference by teaching us how to respond to requests for help, without anger but with compassion."

—**Kevin Figueiredo**, Group SH&E Manager,
Woolworths Limited, Australia

"Dr. Geller and Bob Veazie continue to unravel the string ball of academia and organizational development theory so it is no longer elusive, but describes cultural development to benefit the bottom line of business. They reveal practical ways to empower people to overcome their individual paradigms that impede willingness to change and work interdependently to build and sustain an actively caring for people culture."

—**Joe Bolduc**, Division EHS Manager—Fibers Industry

"I found myself totally enwrapped in the characters and story-line in this book as it taught me how to be a better person at work and at home by Actively Caring for People. The fiction becomes my life as I see myself in the position of Joanne with anger at myself and my work culture for not doing more to bring the best out of myself and others."

—**Gary Pierce**, Process Operator, ExxonMobil Baton Rouge Polyolefins

"This enjoyable easy-to-read storybook convinced me self-motivation is the key to success at all levels of an organization and it taught me practical ways to make this happen within myself and others."

—**Sean Barker**, Global VP of Information Technology,
Ingram Micro Corporation

The Motivation to Actively Care is a wonderfully engaging story that's full of heart, and yet the research-based lessons about leadership, communication, getting the best from your workforce, and defining and living your values, are still clear. Without doing the legwork, the reader gains valuable perspectives by walking in the shoes of management, supervisors, workers, and those who are tasked with helping them all continually improve. I look forward to sharing this book and my take-a-ways with co-workers, colleagues, and friends.

—**Kathy Doyle**, Safety and Environmental
Protection Manager, Waste Management Inc.

The Motivation to Actively Care reminds us that true motivation comes from within. To be sustainable, motivation needs to come from a personal desire to perform—not from the fear of not doing so. Dr. Geller and Mr. Veazie bring this important principle to life through an engaging story using real-world scenarios and practical applications.

—**William Yates**, President/CEO,
W. G. Yates & Sons Construction Company

"Self-motivation is the key to opening the door of actively-caring-for- people leadership. With an understanding of Geller and Veazie's new book, self-motivated leaders emerge from this doorway, more prepared to effectively lead others, and ultimately, to help them lead themselves."

—**Brian M. Kleiner, Ph.D.**, Professor, Department of
Industrial & Systems Engineering, Virginia Tech

In their first book, *The Courage to Actively Care*, Scott Geller and Bob Veazie broke new ground in the safety world (and I suspect the world of organizational psychology) by wrapping the principles and applications from years of research into a fictional novel. In this follow-up scholarship, *The Motivation to Actively Care*, Scott and Bob turn up the amps. Our AC4P hero, Joanne, faces a myriad of new issues that challenge her values at the personal, family and organizational level.

The result is an engaging, fast-paced story laced with leadership lessons, but is not overloaded with technicalities and psychological jargon. For those with a penchant for self-reflection, the opportunity to enhance the knowledge and applications from the story by working through a series of questions at the end of the book will add even more value to the read.

Scott and Bob may have opened a new genre of writing, psych-fiction. Geller and Veazie enable scientific research to be taken to the masses. This book thumbs its nose at pop-psychology and says '*here is the new benchmark; lift your game.*' Bob and Scott, I admire your genius.

—**Martin Ralph**, President, International Network of
Safety and Health Practitioner Organizations

With AC4P self-motivation, Scott Geller and Bob Veazie produced a work of inspiration and elegance, painlessly bringing the power of behavioral science to the messy and fascinating worlds of organizational culture and personal living. In the current climate, sustaining organizational morale, community, and effectiveness is particularly challenging. The story told here leads the way through these trying times. Perhaps even more importantly, *The Motivation to Actively Care* inspires the reader toward a life of courage and humility, supporting values essential to justice and human survival. You really need to read this book!

—**Mark Mattaini**, DSW, Professor, University of Illinois at Chicago,
Editor, *Behavior and Social Issues*

THE MOTIVATION TO
ACTIVELY CARE

How You *Can Make it Happen*

E. SCOTT GELLER, PH.D
BOB VEAZIE, M.B.A

NEW YORK

NASHVILLE • MELBOURNE • VANCOUVER

THE MOTIVATION TO ACTIVELY CARE
How You *Can Make it Happen*

© 2017 **E. SCOTT GELLER, PH.D & BOB VEAZIE, M.B.A**

Published in New York, New York, by Morgan James Publishing. Morgan James is a trademark of Morgan James, LLC. www.MorganJamesPublishing.com

The Morgan James Speakers Group can bring authors to your live event. For more information or to book an event visit The Morgan James Speakers Group at www.TheMorganJamesSpeakersGroup.com.

ISBN 978-1-68350-472-6 paperback
ISBN 978-1-68350-473-3 eBook
Library of Congress Control Number: 2017902558

Cover Design by:
Rachel Lopez
www.r2cdesign.com

Interior Design by:
Bonnie Bushman
The Whole Caboodle Graphic Design

In an effort to support local communities, raise awareness and funds, Morgan James Publishing donates a percentage of all book sales for the life of each book to Habitat for Humanity Peninsula and Greater Williamsburg.

Get involved today! Visit
www.MorganJamesBuilds.com

DEDICATION

Dedicated to the Actively Caring for People (AC4P) club and the Center for Applied Behavior Systems (CABS) at Virginia Tech (VT), both student-led organizations apply the self-motivation and leadership lessons exemplified in our story to cultivate an AC4P culture on the VT campus, and beyond.

The more than forty years of research by the graduate and undergraduate students in CABS was critical to developing and verifying the principles and procedures illustrated in this storybook. The current coordinators of CABS are Ashley Underwood and Brian Doyle, whose AC4P leadership has enabled the applied experimental research and scholarship of five graduate students and fifty Bachelor of Science students in the VT Department of Psychology.

TABLE OF CONTENTS

PREFACE

At times, most people need an external accountability process to keep them motivated. Psychologists call these "extrinsic motivators," and managers use them to keep employees on track. But sometimes people develop self-motivation within the context of an external accountability system. In other words, it's possible to establish conditions that facilitate self-accountability and self-motivation. This book teaches practical ways to make this happen within ourselves and among others, as gleaned from research in the behavioral and social sciences.

The storyline for this narrative approach to education follows from our prior storybook—*The Courage to Actively Care: Cultivating a culture of compassion.* However, you don't need to read our first book in this series to understand, appreciate, and apply the evidence-based leadership lessons presented here.

The situations and character interactions are based on authentic events. In fact, it's likely every reader has experienced life-changing episodes similar to those displayed in our story. Indeed, the disparaging circumstances we disclose happen all too often in the business world, but the research-based solutions we offer to these human-relationship issues have been applied successfully to alleviate these problems.

Unlike our prior storybook, this Preface is relatively brief and we have not included a Foreword. Furthermore, the Acknowledgements are given at the end. Why, because readers of the first publication of *The Courage to Actively*

Care indicated the excessive introductory material delayed their engagement in the enjoyable and educational read. Since the real-world drama in this book is also a page-turner, with more human development lessons than in our prior book, we urge you to begin reading Chapter 1 as soon as possible. If you have time to read on, we bet you will. Besides being entertained by the dramatic representation of realistic accounts to which you will certainly relate, you will learn at least the following:

- How to increase the self-motivation to actively care for people in yourself and others.
- The meaning of self-determinism and the factors that influence this motivational state.
- Practical distinctions between a priority and a value.
- What it means to feel empowered and why this person-state is important.
- What it takes to initiate and sustain an actively caring for people (AC4P) culture whereby people regularly go beyond the call of duty to contribute to the health, safety, and welfare of others.
- The meaning of competence, choice, and community with regard to an individual's degree of self-motivation.
- How perception surveys can be used to diagnose cost-effectively before intervention.
- Practical connections between empathy, compassion, actively caring, and self-accountability.
- Five modes of communication and how these facilitate versus inhibit the cultivation of an AC4P culture of self-motivated participants.
- Practical distinctions between transactional and transformational leadership.
- How the alignment versus misalignment between values and behavior determines people's self-motivation to perform AC4P behavior.
- De-motivational problems with the typical performance appraisal process used in many organizations and how to fix them.
- Why the standard outcome-based incentive programs used to motivate employees are ineffective and can do more harm than good.

- How to develop and implement performance-appraisal and motivational systems that help rather than hinder the bottom line.
- Why it's more realistic and functional to claim competence leads to self-motivation rather than the reverse.
- How to set individual and group goals that increase both self-motivation and goal attainment.
- How equity theory can be used to diagnose and alleviate personal feelings of disparity, imbalance, and unfairness in relationships at home and at work.
- Why the prevalent ranking systems in business and academic settings often do more harm than good.
- Practical applications and ramifications of the maxim: "Pay it forward."
- The real-world meaning and benefits of "inclusion" and how to attain this all-important determinant of self-motivation at work and at home.

TWENTY EVIDENCED-BASED and practical leadership lessons are interspersed throughout the text as each becomes relevant from a particular episode in our true-to-life story. Then at the end of our book, we provide several questions for each chapter, designed to stimulate your personal reflection and interpersonal conversation about the real-life ramifications of the leadership and motivational lessons revealed throughout our narrative. We hope you will use the questions to make these research-supported improvement lessons and strategies relevant to your personal and professional lives.

Please start with the premise that leadership is not reserved for the select few who hold top hierarchical positions of control in the public or private sector. Rather, anyone can be a leader and help bring out the best in others, regardless of his or her position in an organization, government agency, community, or family, and thereby benefit from the teaching/learning experiences of our story characters.

We hope you enjoy learning the life-enriching lessons revealed in *The Motivation to Actively Care: How you can make it happen* while you watch our story unfold. More importantly, we wish you the best in reflecting on your own behavior and becoming intentional about arranging situations and contingencies to augment the self-motivation to actively care for people within yourself as well as among your family members, friends, teammates, and work colleagues. The result: An enriched culture of people—empowered and self-motivated to actively care for the well-being of others—not because they have to but because they want to.

CHAPTER 1

"Success is never final and failure never fatal.
It is the courage to continue that counts."
—Winston Churchill

I BLINK AGAINST THE late morning sun (*late morning, of course it looks strange, you're never out here at this time of day* comes the unbidden thought) and I force myself to concentrate on the dark green Honda in the half-filled parking lot dead ahead. My arms clutch the cardboard box blindly to me and I thinks maybe I can count steps, here, nothing to it, twenty steps to go, maybe less, blink, bright sun, blink, (*don't cry don't cry,*) fourteen steps now, the dry sound of the asphalt under my heels, ten steps, kid stuff, nearly there, come on (*don't you do it, don't you dare cry, don't, don't*) three, two one…and with a loud exhale I allow the box to drop onto the roof of the small car.

The small, hollow movements from within the box serve as a bitter reminder of how few things it actually holds. Twenty-two years, and the physical evidence of my time on the job doesn't even fill a single, small box. My coffee mug. The three small plaques from the consecutive years in which my team had exceeded the corporate safety goals. My signed copies of Doc's last two books. The framed picture of Keith and our kids, smiling out, Mother's Day 2008, the frame says, "We Are So Proud of You!" and, and (*don't cry don't do it not here not where they can see*)

…and would they be proud today, of this, not likely…

Fumbling my keys out of my purse, the key ring slips from my fingers, and in twisting to catch them my shoulder brushes against the box and now *it's* falling, it's that kind of day, there it goes, sliding in slow, inexorable motion down the side of the car, the lid falling open, the contents tumbling, tumbling… I half lunge, my hands groping to try and catch something, anything, missing everything, the dull crack of ceramic on asphalt, and a higher-pitched, crisp >TIK!< and I know, even before I look, the glass covering the picture of Keith and the kids…yep. A big crack, forking and reforking into a tiny splintering web in the corner.

I pick it up gingerly and a large piece falls out, tinkling into smaller pieces as it hits the pavement below and somehow that's it, that's the last straw; I know distantly that for perfect cornball irony the picture should have been something of me working happily at my job, *what* job Jo, right, *former* job, my past, cracking into sharp and cutting splinters but here, "We Are So Proud Of You!" broken, which is exactly the way I feel…and it's stupid, I know it's stupid but I can't help it, the tears come and my breath shudders into heaving sobs and I sag against the car, bereft and so alone.

After only a moment I start to feel the wall of blank, corporate glass staring down at me from the other side of the parking lot. I imagine eyes on the other side of that glass, watching, whispering, *who is that, is that Joanne Cruse, did you hear what happened, oh no…*It's more than I can take; in quick, jerky movements I sweep my things into my box, noting absently when the sharp edge of the chipped mug catches my knuckle and the blood starts to flow, fine, might as well leave a little blood on the ground while I'm making my getaway, stride around half blindly to the driver's side, toss the box over to the passenger seat and climb in, stabbing the key into the ignition and twisting it savagely, feeling the little engine catch before I smash the accelerator, revving it and then dropping it into reverse, lurching backward out of the spot, braking hard, shove the gear shift forward, stomp on the gas, the tires chirping as my little car hurtles out of the parking lot, swerving wildly onto the access road.

ONCE I'M ON THE ROAD I calm down a fraction and ease off the gas. No sense getting killed. The headlines would be too perfect: "Award Winning Safety Director Killed Doing Sixty in a Twenty-Five." Just as I achieve a more safe and sane speed, tinny music blares from my cell phone: Bette Midler singing "You Gotta Have…Frriieeee-eennnnddss." I smile, Jeff.

Jeff's more than a friend. He's an advisor and a confidante and a defender and a wingman. If he weren't gay I'm certain we would have generated enormous amounts of office romance gossip. (Who knows, maybe we did anyway.) He's a rare combination of no-nonsense, bottom-line assessments mixed with sly humor, and he runs the Quality Division of Perfect Plastics with cool efficiency.

He's also the first person in the company I turn to when I have a problem. A couple of years ago I had a huge problem with our old General Manager (*stop saying "our" Jo, it's "their" now*), and Jeff hadn't known me very well at the time but he had seen someone being wronged and just like that, he stepped in to help. We've been good friends ever since, and I've always hoped I'd get to return the favor someday. Seems less likely as of about two hours ago.

I grab the phone and thumb the button, "Hey Jeff."

"Joanne!" His voice crackles with cell phone static but his concern is still audible. "I just heard something insane; tell me it's not true."

I try to laugh. "Depends on what you heard. If you heard I no longer get the employee discount in the cafeteria, you heard right."

"Oh honey…I'm so sorry…"

The pained sympathy in his voice makes my eyes brim full again. It's the kind of friend he is—when you're happy, he's happy, and when you're hurting, he's hurting. Thin attempts at humor are pointless, he'll just see through them to the pain underneath. I blink quickly, trying to clear my vision.

"Listen Jeff, I'm on the four-sixty bypass and the cell phone is trying to squirt away from my ear, lemme find a place to pull over and call you right back."

"I'm right here, doll." I hear the beeps of the disconnect and I toss the cell phone onto the seat next to me. More ironic headlines: "Ex-Safety Director Drives Blind While on Cell Phone." Sub-headline: "Began Defying Death Upon Exiting Office for Last Time."

Yeesh. Get a grip, girl. There we go, Kwik Stop, that's exactly what I'll do, stop real quick…I grab the phone and punch speed-dial. Jeff picks up immediately, "You at the Kwik Stop?" he asks and I have to laugh. "What's so funny?" he asks, mock-wounded, "It's the only logical stop in the first seven miles from here." A head full of trivia, that's our Jeff. (*their Jeff*, whispers the devil who's been living in my brain for the last couple of hours, *he's not yours anymore* and I feel a stab of pain. Will I wake up in six months to discover this friendship ended the same day as my paychecks?)

"Jeff, we're not gonna fade out of each other's lives, are we?" I hear myself asking anxiously. "We won't let this be an excuse to fall out of touch, will we?"

His voice is soft and soothing. "I am wayyy harder to get rid of than that, and I'm not looking for any excuse to fall out of touch, now listen, I need you to take a deep breath and just…tell me." Such an easy request. So hard to perform. The deep breath makes some of the sobs locked in my chest break apart and start to dissolve. It feels good. I do it again. Now for the "Tell me" half of the equation.

A third deep breath and then "I got called in to see Kathy Miller right after our morning meeting…" In telling it, my mind travels back. Allllll the way back to two hours ago. It feels like a lifetime. In a way, perhaps it is.

I had come into work today feeling upbeat and happy, the way I usually feel. I loved my job; I loved the people I worked with and I loved the fact that my job actually made a difference. We saw to it that people working in a dangerous environment went home whole. Perfect Plastics had the same hazards as any manufacturing operation, but had significantly fewer injuries and no fatalities on my watch—ever. Not one. These men and women went home every night to their families and took care of themselves and each other every day, and as Director of Safety I played a big role in that. It felt good.

We'd had our normal meeting this morning. It's just a chance to share observations from the previous day's work, bring up any topics that need attention. One of the reasons our record is so good is that the workers own the process; they all feel personally responsible whenever *anyone* is injured. These morning meetings are part of how that ownership is ongoing.

We wrapped up and I was on my way to check some figures for a study which had asked permission to use our plant as a baseline model for excellence in safety—flattering to be asked, but I wanted to make sure their numbers were accurate. But before I could get to my desk, our floor receptionist Melissa said "Joanne, Kathy Miller wants to see you up in the Tower right away."

The Tower: The top-floor office with huge, tinted windows which oversaw the plant floor on one side and the administrative floor on the other. It was the traditional roost of the plant's GM and it held a certain sense of foreboding. Trips to the Tower were never fun. In fact, Jeff and I had met and bonded over an experience which began with the Tower's previous inhabitant, who had moved on two years ago and left in his place the icily-quiet Katherine Miller.

Jeff interrupts my reflecting, "Did you have any idea what she wanted?"

I sigh, "No. I mean, it's the Tower, she's not having me up for tea and crumpets, but I figured she wanted to emphasize the importance of some upcoming benchmark or something, you know?"

"Mmmm" Jeff agrees. If you don't know him, he might sound as though he's not paying full attention, but I know it's the opposite—he's so dialed in he's got nothing left for chatter. Listening as hard as he can. Hoping he'll hear something he can do to help.

As I'm telling him, I can't help thinking about how dreamlike the whole episode feels, especially my memory of the elevator ride. I had pushed the top button and felt the same sense of increasing dread I had felt anytime I found myself in this dark, wood-paneled compartment. Some people compare it to an elevator to your dentist for root canal, some people say it's actually a trick and you're traveling down ten-thousand feet to a subterranean lair, but no matter what stories we tell each other afterward, it's never a fun ride.

"Before I knew it, Katherine was gesturing me into a chair and telling me she was sorry, she was going to have to keep things brief, she was sure I was aware of the challenges facing the company with profits being eroded from overseas competitors and fewer manufacturer's placing the kinds of advance orders that keep our cash flow viable, and while I tried to think of something hopeful to say she pushed a Work Force Reduction package across her desk at me and said, "I'm afraid we're out of options."

Jeff stops me again. "Hang on," he says, as though seeking some hidden punch line. "She WFR'd you? Like *that*?"

"Oh, no it gets better," I answer him, a small, bitter laugh escaping me.

"I just stared at the package, you know, it was just jamming in my head, Work Force Reduced, me, today, now, no, it can't be, and I asked her something like 'but what will happen to the Safety Program, you can just pitch it' and then she waved her hand, *waved her hand*, okay, like some petty little duchess who didn't like her dessert, and she says 'That will fall under HR now—the program is so smooth, it practically runs itself.' "

I can hear Jeff's mental gears grinding. "Wait, slow down, she—she said your program, *your* program, doesn't *need* you?"

"That's right. And then she kinda smiles like we're pals and she says, 'I guess if you hadn't done such a good job we wouldn't be able to trim your office.'"

"Oh Good Heavens…" I can hear from his voice that Jeff has actually tipped his head back, away from his phone's mouthpiece.

There's a weird masochism in it for me now, a fascination with exactly how badly I can make it hurt, like poking at a sore tooth, and I tell him the *coup de grace:* "But Jeff listen, she sits there after she says this and can see me, like, just, you know, system failure, blue screen, I can't process any of it, and I feel her staring at me, kind of intrigued, right, like I'm some bug in a science project and she asks, 'Are you surprised?' "

"NO!!" He's aghast. I can't blame him. I am too, actually; I've just had a few more minutes to get used to the idea.

"Yup," I nod, as though he can see me, and then I can feel my voice wavering again. "It was like she was almost…amused, you know? Like I'm a story she's gonna tell to all the other executioners later, like how could she not *know* it was *coming,* what a *moron!*"

"Jo, how could you have ev—?"

"*I FEEL LIKE AN IDIOT!!*" I shriek, and I'm not shrieking at Jeff really, I'm shrieking at the whole universe, I'm shrieking at any world that could let a thing like this happen. "*I HAD NO IDEA! IT'S LIKE I RAN OUT INTO TRAFFIC, LIKE SOME STUPID kuh…kuh-kuh-KID…*" and just like that, I'm crying again.

Because he's exactly that kind of friend, the perfect kind, Jeff understands. He lets it go on for a bit, doesn't tell me things I already know, doesn't tell me I'm not a moron, doesn't tell me he's sorry. He has a big enough heart to give me exactly what I need right this second, which is the space to scream and cry like a child.

After a moment, when I've gotten some measure of control, he asks, "What did you figure on doing the rest of the day?"

Rest of the day. Such a weird phrase. But he's right—it's not even lunch time. "I don't really know," I say. "I should point out, I *was* given the option of finishing out the month, if I liked, or if I preferred I could leave immediately, the severance package is the same either way, one week of salary for every year with the company. Which for me is twenty two. Almost half a year of pay. I guess some people have it worse."

"Remind me again, what number were you?"

He's asking about when I joined the company. Those of us who have been here long enough are sometimes referred to by numbers. Like the founder, he was Employee Number One. His partner who put up the rest of the money was Employee Number Two. I tell Jeff I was Number Seventeen. "Seventeen," he repeats with a kind of wonder. "The seventeenth Perfect Plastics employee ever, and they do you like this."

"Well, I did take a little small-minded pleasure in saying, 'No, I would *not* finish out the month…' but the Snow Queen smiled like this was fine with her and she shoved a couple of extra papers toward me for me to sign, and then… oh, it's just so weird, it's like remembering a dream, she punched a button on her phone, and before I knew it, someone from Protective Services was standing there and the next thing I know we're both at my desk and everyone is looking and he's watching me fill this little cardboard box with my personal belongings and then he's walking me to the door and they ask me to hand over my ID Badge and… here I am.

"I take another deep breath, wondering at how surreal I feel telling this story. Then I add, "Which is a really long way to say I haven't the faintest idea what I'm doing for the rest of the day."

I can hear someone talking to Jeff away from his phone and I hear Jeff tell them he'll be right there and then he's back and he says, "Listen, Jo, why don't you turn around and come back, I've got to spend a couple of minutes explaining our addendum to last week's report, it'll be quick, by the time you're back I'll be waiting in the lobby and I'll take you anywhere you say for lunch, what do you think?"

I think if I see that building I might start crying all over again is what I think, never mind all the people inside. "I don't know, Jeff," I say slowly, "I mean, I'd feel kind of weird, and I don't really like the idea of people staring at me and muttering to each other; I hate the idea of oiling the gossip machine, you know?"

Jeff laughs, "Honey, that's all you and I have *ever* done is oil *that* machine." I laugh along with him and then he seems struck by a thought: "Hey, I don't suppose you've called your friend Dr. Pitz have you?"

I'm surprised by the question, but I remember that Jeff met Doc and knows how important he is to me, it would make sense that I would seek his counsel in times of trouble…but as I say to him now, "I haven't had the chance to call *any*one, Jeff, I haven't even…" and the sentence dies in my mouth as it hits me that I haven't even called Keith yet. It's such a strange thought that I turn away from it, almost physically turning in my car seat.

I hear an impatient voice in the background of Jeff's call and I hear him call "All *right*," and then his voice is back. "Come on, Jo, come back, you won't even have to come in, I'll meet you right out front and we can have a big old They-Don't-Know-What-They're-Losing Lunch, okay?"

I know if I said I'd rather be alone, he'd understand. But I don't want to be alone. In fact, right now, being alone sounds like the worst thing in the world. "Okay, I'll get turned around and head back your way."

"Then hang up the phone and be safe!" he orders with elaborate strictness, making me giggle. I can almost hear his answering smile. "I'll see you in a few," he says, and then he's gone.

PULLING BACK INTO the company parking lot strengthens the feeling that everything earlier was a dream, I'm only now arriving at work, there's my spot, right where I left it, all is well…but I see the cardboard box on the seat next to me and I know all is not well, I consider sitting in the car and waiting for him, but that feels too cowardly to bear. This has been my place for twenty-two years. A relationship doesn't vanish just because one side gets signatures.

I take a deep breath and then get out of my car and walk briskly to the front entrance. I push through the front door and see Barney, one of my favorite security guys, in his normal seat behind his desk. I always greet Barney with a smile and he always grins back and says something like, "I feel safer already," but right now he's not smiling—he's got a distinctly uncomfortable look on his face and he's rising to his feet rather more quickly than I would expect for a casual greeting… and now he's moving purposefully on a line to intercept, his hands up. "Hang on a second Miz Cruse…"

He probably thinks I've come back to throw some kind of downsized-employee fit, I don't blame him for being careful. "Don't worry, Barney, I'm not wearing a bomb or anything I'm just meeting Jeff for lunch, he said he would be—hey!"

This last sound is because Barney has in fact placed himself squarely in front of me, and I have to stop suddenly to avoid running into him. "Barney!" I say, my astonishment and hurt vying for equal time in my tone.

He looks miserable, but he doesn't budge. "I'm sorry Miz Cruse, you're not allowed past this point."

I stare at him. "Past this point? Barney, there's nothing past this point except a water fountain and Ricky's catalogues of office supplies—is someone worried I'm gonna swap in new Staples fliers for all the old Office Max fliers?"

He shakes his head, as steadfast as a mountain and almost as large. "It's policy ma'am."

"Barney!" Jeff's voice from down the hall, approaching quickly, and if Barney looked miserable before, he's doubly so now. Everyone who works at Perfect Plastics has heard Jeff get wound up at someone on at least one occasion if not a dozen, and they would all agree it is nothing one wants to be on the wrong end of.

"What are we doing now, our best version of the Nuremberg Defense, you're just following orders, Barney, you *know* this woman! If she had never worked here there would be no Perfect Plastics, and if there's no Perfect Plastics you don't get to do your Gestapo act in front of everyone, is that what you'd prefer?"

I have to hand it to Barney. I can see a dozen less polite answers ripple across his face before he settles for "What I'd prefer, sir, is for you to take a step back and let me do my job. And Joanne," he says, turning to me, a quiet urgency in his eyes, "I'd prefer if you'd wait for him on one of the benches over there."

"One of the benches???" Jeff's hitting fourth gear now and I try to raise a hand to stop him. Barney's right. He's just doing his job. But one of Jeff's colleagues beats me to it, coming from behind to tap his shoulder and say something quietly.

Jeff's eyes get even wider, and he says, "I explained it twice already! The second time I drew pictures! What do they—you know what, never mind, tell them I'll be there in one second."

He comes closer to me, walking toward the benches after throwing a dirty look back toward Barney. "The world doesn't want us to have lunch today Joanne. I'm really sorry. I'll phone you just as soon as I can, okay?"

I'm suddenly so tired. The day is catching up with me and the idea of putting my feet up at home is sounding better all the time. "You're sweet to have tried," I say, giving him a quick, hard hug. "I think I'm going to head home. There's a bubble bath there with my name on it."

Jeff grins, "SO jealous," he says, and then he's moving back toward his office. His work. The tasks he performs which have been found to have value. Those are the things I don't have anymore…

No. I won't go down that road. I have value. If this company doesn't see it, that's their loss. I walk out the same way I had walked in, with a brisk pace and my head held high.

IN MY CAR, I see the cell phone I had tossed into the passenger seat. I can't bear to call Keith. Not now. Not about this. This is something which should be done in person. But I *am* feeling the urge to tell someone, and I remember Jeff asking if I had been in touch with Dr. Pitz yet. It's a half-tempting, half-scary thought.

Doc will see things I don't see, that's for certain, but he's not much for small talk or kind-hearted commiseration. I remembered being his graduate teaching assistant and the two of us walking past two young coeds comparing bad boyfriend stories. Doc hadn't even broken stride as he barked at them, "Get on with your lives!"

Still…I'm holding the phone, my thumb moving over the keys lightly. When it chirps I nearly scream and throw it. My nerves are shot. But then I have to smile as I see the caller ID and the ring tone plays through my car—the old Patsy Cline song, "Crazy."

As usual, Dr. Pitz is a step ahead of me.

CHAPTER 2

"In the middle of every difficulty lies opportunity"
—Albert Einstein

THE RING TONE FEATURING Patsy Cline's "Crazy" is assigned to only one caller. Of the 284 contacts memorized by this tiny device, only the internationally prominent Professor of Applied Behavioral Science, Dr. B.F. Pitz, merits this kind of irony. It's my own little joke on a gentleman

I would argue knows more about human behavior than any living person, and yet is perfectly capable of overlooking social cues the average 8th grader would recognize.

He *is* a little crazy.

But it's this crazy of passion, of deep, deep commitment and total focus that often make the rest of the world simply nonexistent for him. Of course, this is what makes it so special when he *does* notice you; when you become aware that almost super-human attention is focused one hundred percent on *you*. It can be a wonderful feeling, and I experienced it many times when I worked as his research assistant while working for my Master's in Applied Behavioral Science. But I also experienced the opposite end of that spectrum during my very first class with him in my sophomore year as an undergrad.

I was a student in his large "Intro to Psychology" survey course, one of more than five hundred. Most of the tenured faculty exempted themselves from these sorts of classes, preferring to work with smaller groups, seminars and roundtables, leaving the oversized intro courses to the graduate teaching assistants and the lower tier of instructors and untenured assistant professors.

Dr. Pitz was tenured. He was also published, multiple times, in internationally prominent journals, as well as having two popular textbooks to his credit. He was among the four professors on our campus who could most easily insist on teaching only small, exclusive groups of eager aspirants. The only thing preventing this was his fundamental nature; as he explained to me once we knew one another better years later—he had not come to the university to *avoid* teaching. He had come to help as many people as he could, imparting his own ideas with a kind of missionary's intensity. It was holy work to him, and the larger the "congregation," the better.

Of course, as a sophomore all I had known was that this was a huge survey course taught by one of the most celebrated members of the University's faculty. The waiting list for it was even larger than its roster. (Years later I joked to him that he should simply request the use of the football stadium for his lectures, and he got a faraway look and asked, utterly serious, "You think they'd let me?" But then he murmured to himself about bad weather and coats, and I assumed he'd figure out sooner or later I had been joking.)

On the day in question, the school year was only two or three weeks old, routines had been established, and of course there was that inevitable cockiness which imbues all sophomores—we're no longer intimidated, we know our way around, we're cool, we can ride this horse. Not for nothing does sophomore translate to "wise fool."

I'd had at least ten or fifteen minutes to loiter in the large lobby of the lecture hall, and some distant part of my mind knew I should go to the bathroom. But some friends of mine and I were eagerly working out the logistics for attending a party at one of the off-campus fraternity houses. ("She can drive?" "You can't wear that, it's *my* turn to wear it!" and so on.)

When the chimes pinged to signal the start of class, I made my way to a central seat, and almost immediately I began to understand the simple math of X minutes of bladder tolerance during a lecture is sure to last at least four times X. The facts were inescapable, and while I struggled to focus on the lecture topic, which seemed to be something called "self-determinism," all I could really think about was the struggle to not stand up in the middle of his lecture—a struggle I knew I was about to lose.

After a few minutes, I surrendered, rising as quietly as I could and excusing myself past the half dozen students between me and the aisle. Dr. Pitz surely saw me the instant I stood, but he waited until I was approaching the exit before booming out, "Was it something I said?" I heard a ripple of laughter behind me, mercifully silenced as the fire doors closed behind me.

I completed my journey as quickly as possible, thinking only of how best to avoid further disruption. I'll sit on the aisle, yes, not even worried about a seat, just slip in the door and ease down right there. Maybe I'll apologize to him after class…

But before I had even completely re-entered the lecture hall, I heard his jolly baritone ring off the back wall. "Welcome back Miss Sanders! Could you step down here for a moment please?"

I glanced around, attempting to see whether I'm the only one not in on the

joke, but my fellow students' faces were curious—whatever was about to happen was a mystery to them too, and somehow that made it okay. I walked down the aisle, and for some reason I remembered my father telling me that a difficult task is best begun quickly, so I said "Dr. Pitz, I'd like to apologize to you and to my classmates for disrupting the session; it was thoughtless of me."

His eyes widened in a moment's surprise and he smiled broadly. Without missing a beat he asked, "And tell me what makes you say that."

I was confused by the question. "What… makes me, I'm sorry, what?"

He was nodding, looking at me eagerly, the full weight of his attention suddenly almost more than I could stand. I felt myself beginning to blush and my heart was pounding and he asked again, "What makes you say that? What is driving you to make this very kind apology right here and now in front of everyone?"

I blink, and do my best to follow him. "Making me, nothing is *making* me, I just felt that…"

He stepped closer to me, his eyes bright, "Nothing? Nothing is making you, nothing at all? There must be something; is it perhaps a religious belief?"

A titter from my fellow students and I can't tell whether I'm being made fun of, but I'm definitely beginning to feel picked on and I don't care for it. "No professor, it's not a religious belief, I think it's what most people would call 'courtesy.' "

"Courtesy!" he called out loudly, turning away from me in a slow pivot. "Courtesy," he said again, as though testing the flavor of the word.

"And how does this thing you call courtesy make you deliver your fine speech? Is it connected somehow to the speech centers of your brain, or is it more mysterious than that, some sort of—"

"No, of course—I'm sorry Professor Pitz, but it's nothing like that."

He peered at me, "God didn't make you say it?"

God? Why is he asking…"No sir."

"Are you perhaps aware of hidden cameras; you're trying to be on your best behavior?"

I shook my head, "No sir."

He stage whispered, "Alien mind control?"

The class laughed and I had to smile myself, "No sir, I just figured, you know, basic courtesy, I thought I should say something, so I—"

He stepped back and pointed in triumph, "*YOU* thought!"

What had I said? "Um... yes sir..."

He circled me slowly, still speaking loudly enough for the entire hall. "*You* thought. *You* believed courtesy was called for, *you* decided to speak, *you* chose your words, and all based on what *you* believed was correct."

I nodded, "That's right."

He beamed, "It *is* right. Thank you Miss Sanders." He extended his hand, and when I shook it, somewhat confused, he went on. "You've just provided the best possible example of self-determinism. You acted in a manner consistent with your own values, your own beliefs about what

LEADERSHIP LESSON 1

What you do when no one's watching or holding you accountable is self-determined or self-motivated.

you feel is important, and you weren't daunted by the presence of your peers nor by the fact I might be cross with you. You made a decision based upon personal values and you acted upon it."

I looked around nervously, "Is that, like, some kinda big deal?"

His smile became even broader, "My dear Miss Sanders—in my well-considered opinion, it is the very biggest deal of all."

INDEED, DOC'S CAREER has carried him through a range of fascinating explorations of this particular aspect of human behavior—the ways in which we make personal choices, the many varied ways in which we struggle to integrate those choices with the world around us.

After working in his Center for Applied Behavior Systems (CABS) for two years, I requested to be his research assistant when I began graduate school. Two more years, makes it four years we worked closely together. In the subsequent decades we stayed in close contact, professional distance having long ago morphed into friendship and deep affection.

And now he's calling me, out of the blue.

I take a deep breath, flip open the phone and say, "Hi Doc."

His voice is warm and familiar, even through the static of satellites and cell towers. "Joanne! Have I caught you at a bad time?"

The irony of the question makes my response lodge in my throat for a moment like a fish bone, and I dislodge it with a dry bark of a laugh, "You might say that."

I fancy I can feel twenty percent more of his attention turn to me. "What do you mean? Is anything wrong?"

I take another deep breath, trying to steady myself. I do not want to play the tearful victim scene, lost cub turning to papa bear for help, but I'm still unable to keep a slight quaver out of my voice as I say, "Perfect Plastics let me go, Doc."

There is a brief pause and then his confused voice crackles through the earpiece, "Let you go, let you go where?"

Bless his heart; geniuses are always the slowest on the uptake. "Let me go as in fired me, gave me the boot, showed me the door, and please don't ask why I needed to be shown a door, it's an expression, I am no longer employed by my old firm." There is silence, and not trusting the cellular connection I double check, "Hello?"

His voice returns, "I understand Joanne and I'm aware of what a difficult transition this will be for you, but you need to understand that in every difficulty there inheres the positive energy necessary for the next phase of life—every transition is an opportunity and the measure of our character. It..." and he continues, measured and wise, but unfortunately for him, I'm not in the mood for measured wisdom just now.

"Doc!" I interrupt him, and he falls silent. "Look, Doc, I know all of that is true and everything, but I bet one of your books has some kind of grief chart in it, and I can promise you, the third hour is too soon for the spiritual pep talk, you know? I just found out and I'm really shaky, and I know I'm being a bitch but I just...can't hear a lecture right this second, 'kay?"

I can practically see him cocking his head and factoring in these new variables. I never have to worry about hurting Doc's feelings, he always knows more about what I'm doing than I do anyway—in fact, that's maybe his only weakness. He's usually so far ahead of the conversation that he has to work very hard to engage us mortals at our own pace. At length he says, "I'm sorry, Joanne, you're quite right, of course, my intentions sometimes outrun reality, please forgive me."

Another deep breath, "It's okay Doc."

He continues, "But Joanne, I must say, there may truly be an opportunity to be seized here."

I shake my head at his astonishing capacity to *not get it*. "Doc, seriously, I can't—"

"I'm not speaking generically, Joanne. If you'll think back a minute or so you'll recall it was *I* who phoned *you,* yes?"

Hmm. He had me there. "Yessss…?" I venture.

His mild rebuke is almost automated as he repeats one of his oldest rules, and I don't mind this one—my skin thickened against this genre of lecture long ago and it's so familiar that it's almost a comfort: "Observe, Joanne, objective and reliable observation is the cornerstone of all science. Its omission is the hallmark of a lazy mind."

"Bless me Doc for I have sinned. It has been three hours since my last employment, now why don't you enlighten this poor girl. Why'd you call?"

"I called because I wanted to ask you whether you had time to meet with me on Monday."

I chuckle ruefully—time is something I suddenly have an abundance of. "Lemme check, Monday, Monday, Monday, yeah, I'm looking, I think I can squeeze you in on Monday…"

"Good, that's good; could you come by my university office midday? We could grab a bite to eat."

I can't tell whether he's ignoring my little joke about squeezing him in or whether it just flew right over his head. I almost tease him about objective observation to see how he likes it, but that would probably fly over his head too.

With Doc you always have to be careful about the five-second joke which requires five minutes of explanation, so I settle for, "I'd really like that Doc, thanks. Can you tell me what it's about? You said something about an opportunity…?"

He laughs. "If I tell you now, we'll have nothing to talk about on Monday. I have to go, Joanne, have a good weekend and I'll see you on Monday. Bring an open mind!"

And just like that, he's gone. I stare at the phone for a moment, and then look up. I'm startled to realize I'm still in the Perfect Plastics' parking lot. For some reason, I had felt I was already long gone from there. Maybe I am.

AS I APPROACH OUR HOUSE it's only a little past noon, and I'm surprised and then worried when I see Keith's car already there ahead of mine. Is he sick? Is something wrong with one of the kids? Or, good heavens, did he somehow hear about me getting fired and he's here to comfort me, wondering why I haven't called him. I had been counting on a couple of hours alone in the house to gather myself and try to get a handle on the day...but that plan's done.

I roll into the driveway, hyper-aware of the sounds my car makes—the tires crunching loudly over the rough surface, the vibrato of the engine suddenly dying...the crisp sound of the car door slamming...I know what these moments sound like when heard from within the house. I imagine Keith, either looking up in surprise and sudden worry, or else preparing, with a kind of weary sorrow, to hear what he already knows...and to wonder why he had to hear it from someone else first.

With a kind of sick knot of dread in my stomach, I make my way into the house. As the front door opens, I'm able to catch a whiff of Keith's Chicken Kiev. He's a professional chef, and he enjoys surprising me with dinner every now and then. This is why he's home early. But has he heard about my job since getting home...?

Once I'm through the door, he's there, coming out of the kitchen with a look of alarm on his face. "How come you're home, angel, are you okay?"

I can't lie, but I can't just dive right into it. So I settle for "Hey, boyfriend..." and I turn to hang up my purse. I realize the box is still in the car. Oh well, It's not going anywhere.

In the absence of any signs of real distress, Keith relaxes into a kind of exasperation, "You know, I wish you'd give a holler if you're going to come home early, I mean, there's not really much of a surprise now..." and seeing his disappointment, knowing I've let him down with this small thing and in a moment he'll know about the really *big* letdown…it's all too much and I start to cry again, very softly, standing in the middle of the front hall.

I hate it. I hate crying like this, as a matter of fact I'm *tired* of crying like this and it just keeps happening and I hate it, and that just makes it worse.

"Hey, hey, Jo, baby, hey shhhhh what is it, come here…" and Keith is moving toward me swiftly, opening his arms and pulling me in to his broad chest. He holds me and whispers softly, gently, helping me know it's okay, *making* it okay, just by being here. I soon calm and after a moment I hear in his chest as he murmurs, "Tell me what's going on baby."

I give him the whole lousy story and it's amazing how short it is. How much damage was wrought in just a few minutes? How much history was cast aside? How much commitment was betrayed?

When I finish, Keith is a model of indignation, proclaiming the company is run by "fools" and predicting a rapid bounce-back in my career. Upon getting home, our kids, Matthew and Jessica, quickly rally to the cause, affirming Perfect Plastics is a "bunch of stupid dorks" and pledging never again to purchase anything made of plastic.

Their protective care of me and my feelings is sweet, but I have mixed emotions, for there are a great many people at the company whom I care about, who are good people. My experience doesn't mean every good person there needed to be tarred by the single brush of poor management.

So while I do try to smile along with their good spirited "scorn" of the new "enemy," my smile is wistful. They're trying to convince me the company isn't worth my sense of loss, that I'm better off; but I've got too many good years invested in that place for that to be an easy thought.

It's unsettling. There's now a new picture. In this picture there's still a place called Perfect Plastics, but I don't work there anymore. It's a picture I can't quite fit into my head yet. Maybe because it's just too frightening.

LATER THAT NIGHT, lying in the dark, Keith says softly, "I wish you'd called me when it happened babe. You know?"

I sigh. He's right. I turn over on my left side to face him. "I know. I'm sorry. I just…it felt too big for the phone. Like, I wouldn't tell you I have cancer over the phone, you know?"

Keith chuckles, "Well this isn't as bad as all that…"

"I don't know." I roll onto my back, staring up into the shadows.

"Hey…" Keith's voice is incredulous. "I know you loved that job, Jo, and this sucks, and they suck for doing it, but that's kinda my point—I never yet saw the job that loved you back, you know?"

"If you want to believe that, fine, but there were a few years in there where we shredded that old saying. I believe that."

"For awhile, maybe," Keith allows.

"Yes," I agree. "For awhile."

Keith pushes up onto one elbow, "But not lately."

I have to sigh, "No, you're right. Not lately."

"So…?" I know without being able to see him that his palm is up. "It's bad. But we'll be okay."

I can feel my lips tightening of their own volition. "We've got to come up with about sixty grand a year of 'okay' pretty quick…"

I feel his weight shifting as he relaxes back onto the mattress. "It'll be okay baby. You've got the severance; I can pick up a few more hours at the restaurant…"

I'm feeling oddly distant from my body as I hear my mouth laugh and say, "You think a few more Thursday dinners are gonna cover the gap? Is that your plan?"

I hate the harsh tone of my voice. The hurt and angry part of me is picking a fight with the one person who does the most to take care of me; I should stop, but I'm on some kind of sad, savage autopilot. It's as though I'm looking at the remnants of a house after a storm, and rather than being brave and picking up the pieces, I just want to set the whole thing on fire.

Thank goodness Keith knows a thing or two about how I am at times like this, how I deal with bad news, and he knows when to let things go.

"It's a setback," he says conclusively. "But I don't think it's bigger or better than we are. We need to sleep, and in the morning we'll start to think about exactly what we need to do."

He turns to kiss my shoulder and then rolls over. Within moments his breathing has changed and I know he's asleep.

I stare up into the darkness for a long, long time.

THE WEEKEND PASSES in a kind of surreal blur. On one level everything is normal—errands, yard work, driving the kids here and there. (I reflect at one point that my kids' combined social calendar is far busier than my professional one.) We have meals. We have family movie night—a horribly silly monster movie. At one point Keith turns down the sound and he and the kids invent their own dialogue to replace the awfulness onscreen. A typical pleasant weekend.

On a deeper level, there's disquiet. I apologize to Keith for the way I had spoken to him Friday night, and he just hugs me and tells me I'm allowed to be scared.

Good thing, too.

Keith and I talk into the nights. Plans. Counterplans. What-if's. Should I take a temp job? Are we prepared to relocate? What's the least money we could make it on *without* relocating? I can see Keith growing more and more worried. I've always made more money than he does, and it's never been an issue between us; he used to joke about having been a successful gold digger—that he married me for my riches.

He has worked his four nights a week as a chef and then he has taken care of a majority of the domestic chores, from grocery shopping to kid-shuttling. It has worked very well…but with over two thirds of the household income suddenly gone, I can see him weighing possibilities he has never had to worry about before.

And of course I feel pressure too. I was the breadwinner. My income was the difference between the goodwill store and the mall; between fresh croissants from the cafe and three-day-old rolls from the bakery thrift.

Keith began saying things like, "You know, in global terms we're still filthy rich" which is how you *know* he's worried—when he's not worried, he never mentions money. Knowing he's worried makes me feel worse, too, like I'm letting the team down.

I mention my Monday meeting with Doc to him, and he becomes very excited. "Maybe he's going to offer you something!" he bubbles, and for some reason this irritates me.

Doc's a friend; he's not an employment agency. Pinning my career hopes on a semi-random phone call from Doc feels absurd, and I find myself even more irked when I realize Keith's hopes have infected me; I, too, am hoping Doc will have something to offer. This is *not* how I want to think about him. So I put the whole thing out of my mind. Monday will come when it comes. We'll know when we know.

AND OF COURSE MONDAY *does* come. Two decades of work have my internal alarm clock more or less auto-programmed. I'm never able to sleep in until the last couple of days of any vacation, and in any case I want to feel a part of the life of the household. It would be too easy, and too self-defeating, to simply roll over and go back to sleep and let my family forge ahead into the week without me.

So I put on my robe and get breakfasts and lunches together. Keith has to meet with a caterer who's planning a menu for a special event at the restaurant, and so he and the kids form a typical-seeming procession at the doorway, kissing me goodbye as they exit, and wishing me the best for my meeting with Doc.

And then, suddenly, here I am, in a very empty house on a Monday morning. The aftermath of the bustle is odd, and I feel vaguely like an intruder in my own home, as though the house is watching me, disturbed by my unexpected presence.

Enough. I am not idle. I am awake and alive. I have a meeting.

After a short time, the strangeness starts to fade and I'm able to relax enough to enjoy a cup of coffee and the morning paper. A flash of movement catches my eye, and I see two young mothers power walking with their space-age strollers. Most days I'd never see them; I'd be gone long before they passed.

So strange, how many different kinds of daily life there are to be found in my neighborhood—all sorts of rhythms and patterns, most of which remain invisible if you stay locked into your own routine.

I shake my head to clear it and proceed upstairs, beginning a fairly leisurely version of my getting-ready process. When necessary, I've learned I can do the entire thing, from alarm clock to last swipe of mascara, in eighteen minutes. Now, with no reason to rush, I take my time, luxuriating under the hot shower, pampering myself.

I spend time going through my wardrobe, forcing myself out of the rut of the normal rotation of seven or eight business outfits. I find a nice dress I haven't worn in a while, and I'm ridiculously happy when it fits as well as ever.

I regard myself in the mirror. I will not grow sluggish and fat. I will not sit on the couch with only Oprah and cheese puffs for company. I will not feel sorry for myself. I will go out into the world. I will do things.

As I adjust my dress, I remember having heard or read some advice for the recently unemployed—it recommended that you continue dressing for work every day, not only to be ready for the unexpected interview, but more importantly to keep your own head in the game, to keep yourself feeling like a profession. I can definitely relate to this concept. I feel active. I like it.

BY THE TIME I PULL into the guest parking next to Doc's office at the University, I'm actually starting to feel happy—happy to see him, happy to hear whatever it is he wants to tell me. If it's a work opportunity, terrific—if not, still terrific. My friend and mentor has something he wants to talk to me about, that's really all I should require for a good mood.

I spot him waiting for me on the front steps of old Williams Hall and he meets me and gives me his patented bear hug. Then, smiling at me he says, "Come on, lemme take you to lunch." I'm pleased and curious, but of course it comes as no surprise when our short walk carries us not into a quiet oaken room of linen napkins and expert waiters, but into one of the university's cafeterias.

I have to smile—only Doc would consider this as "taking a guest to lunch." Convenience and efficiency rules.

After pleasant inquiries about my kids and Keith, we've gotten our trays of food and we find an empty table. Once we're settled, Doc says, "I don't want to sound overly Pollyanna about things, Joanne, but I've been thinking about it rather deeply and I hope you know your departure from Perfect Plastics is a good thing."

Whatever Doc thinks deeply about has been thoroughly mined and mapped. "Okay," I say. "Tell me why."

As he digs into his salad, he says, "Over the last eighteen or so months, whenever we've spoken about Perfect Plastics, you've had a new piece of news about some movement further and further away from the values which had at one time made it such a good fit for you."

I try to remember the specific points made during recent phone calls, but Doc is ahead of me. "Eighteen months ago you told me they had done away with the Employee Newsletter, declaring it a waste of resources. The Newsletter was something in which your co-workers had taken pride and pleasure, it had helped to unite them as one team with one mission and in terms of cost per month it was a fraction of a fraction, in terms of man-hours and actual direct costs. Management deemed those pennies to be of greater value than the solidarity engendered by the Newsletter."

I nod. Now that he said it, I remembered telling him about it, and about how disappointed some of the staff were. I'm astonished he would remember it with such detail though. "You don't have, like, audiotapes of those calls or anything do you Doc? Anything from the Richard Nixon School of Archiving?"

He stares at me in utter bewilderment, "Richard Nixon?"

I have to giggle at the expression on his face. "Never mind, dumb joke, what else?"

Doc continues, "Fourteen months ago you told me about a new campaign to try and re-brand the management structure within the company. Top-Down Leadership, or something like that?"

"That's right," I tell him, taking a bite out of a surprisingly good club sandwich.

Doc opens his palms as if appealing to the heavens for support, "Top Down? It's not exactly an inclusive message, is it? It screams authority, control, hierarchy, pecking order. It's a wretched slogan and I daresay a wretched idea. Then, eight months ago, they forced you to change the safety slogan displayed around the plant floor."

This was a clear and painful memory. After establishing a truly remarkable safety record, we had decided to change our "Safety is a Priority" slogan to "Safety is a Value We Can't Compromise." We were proud of our strong, no-excuses approach and it made good sense to us.

"Eight months ago management had decreed our new slogan was: "Safety is a Condition of Employment." I murmur now to Doc, "Yeah, the guys didn't take long to start calling it, "Be safe, or we fire your ass."

Doc nods, "Threats. If they work at all, they only work for a short while, and really, we know they don't work even then because they're doing personal damage while appearing to be working."

"Like radioactive waste," I offer, and he nods.

"Good!" he smiles. "Yes, and then, just a few weeks ago, you told me about the results of the most recent employee perception survey, indicating the workers' sense of being included, of having a voice in the policies and directions of the company, had dropped radically in just one year. The problem was clear: employees don't feel included. So does management seek a way to include them?"

I grin, "Nope, management formed a study team to look into it and make recommendations. This could have been done in about a minute by looking at the survey results and then saying, 'Ummmm, maybe, wild guess, include 'em more?' "

Doc is waving his fork like a baton, conducting some inner symphony of thought as he says, almost absently; "Inclusion can't be legislated. It doesn't happen by mandate. It's a behavior, and behaviors can be adjusted by internal adjustments in motivation and understanding. Inclusion issues can't be discussed or studied away."

I'm nodding vigorously, "You're saying it's as though they found out the secretaries were all starving, and formed a group to do a six-month study on the caloric intake of secretaries, instead of just sending back some pizzas."

He laughs out loud, drawing startled glances from several students and faculty in the room. I see a few of them smile, however, clearly accustomed to Doc's unedited outbursts. "Perfect! But I was *not* saying that Joanne, I only *wish* I'd been saying that, this is one of your great gifts you know—simplifying academic language for public consumption."

I'm not sure how to respond to this compliment. "Well, that's, thank you, I…"

"I have a proposition for you." He is leaning forward and regarding me intently. It's another of those rare moments when I have his fullest attention, and it's a bit like a laser beam.

He continues, "The situation at Perfect Plastics, this drift from core values, is not unique. I'm afraid it's more common than rare. All over the globe, businesses exhibit day-to-day behavior which is randomly and grotesquely inconsistent with their stated values. If these businesses were individual people, we would say these people are displaying very weak character."

Businesses as people…people whose character can be assessed. This is a new idea to me.

"What is character?" Doc continues, getting wound up into full lecture mode and I have to smile, knowing we could easily still be here when they try to close if he really gets going.

"Character is nothing more or less than the presence of a consistent pattern of choice. Those people who act with the greatest self-determinism display the strongest character—if their core values are known, their behavior becomes highly predictable, because they consistently honor those values."

I chew my sandwich as I chew this idea. "Okay, fair enough. But," I ask musingly, "That doesn't automatically equal behavior we'd call good, right? If I understand your definition, serial killers are *loaded* with character, they just happen to value some horrible things."

He is grinning around his salad, "Precisely. Character and self-determinism do not de facto lead to any particularly virtuous or sinful behavior, except for the virtue of being true to one's self."

"To thy own self be true," I offer, adding, "That's not me by the way, Doc, that's Shakespeare."

"Yes," he agrees dryly. "But, it's fine advice, and far too many businesses have no idea how to follow it. They are unable to assess what their true self *is* you see. If they can't articulate their core values accurately, they certainly can't enable employee behavior consistent with those values. They need help. They need guidance. They need the assistance of career experts in the field of behavioral science—people who are capable of noticing subtle elements within—"

"Doc," I interrupt, and then point briefly at him at the corner of my own mouth. After a moment of blinking incomprehension, it clicks, and he lifts his napkin to wipe away the large blob of salad dressing which had been there. I nod approval, grinning, "Good. You were saying?"

"I formed a company a few months back. A consulting firm called Make-A-Difference. The difference we attempt to make is in helping companies create and maintain an actively-caring-for-people culture. Actively-caring-for-people workplaces consist of employees who *all* understand the company's mission, and who *all* understand the ways in which each worker's tasks relate in some way to that mission.

"If you work at an actively-caring-for-people business, you not only know your job is important—and let's be frank, even that would often be an improvement—but you also understand that *every* job is important. There's mutual investment in overall success which then manifests in a desire to nurture the value-consistent efforts of one's colleagues."

I smile, "You're saying people look out for each other."

He smiles back, "Yes, again, well done." He studies me for a moment and then says, "I believe Make-A-Difference and Joanne Sanders Cruz could be a very nice fit."

My heart leaps, but I sit hard on my inner three-year-old. Don't get excited. Find out what he's talking about. "That sounds pretty wonderful, Doc. Can you tell me a few of the things you think I bring to the party?"

He cocks his head as though wondering if I've been paying attention. It's a look which never fails to leave me feeling slow witted. "You've been demonstrating it throughout lunch. Make-A-Difference is rooted in strong behavioral science, verified and applicable, but it's sometimes difficult for our clients to understand what we're getting at, because the language can be formal

and dusty sounding. You could perhaps be a highly effective bridge between the science itself and the practical understanding of the people attempting to integrate it."

"You're saying I could be your Rosetta Stone."

He's nodding and smiling, but not done, "Yes, good, but not just that. Your work in the safety field demonstrated consistent skill in identifying and codifying workplace behaviors, improving it through feedback, and then designing policies and procedures that augment the good behavior and eliminate the bad. And you did it in easy-to-follow language."

I have to look away; his approval is almost as intense as his disapproval. "That's very nice to hear Doc, and it's a lot to think about, so why don't you tell me the downside?"

He sits back, a small sigh escaping him. "There's a lot of travel, and it could be hard on your family. We make observations and recommendations, but we're not always believed, and we sometimes return home without having won the opportunity to help. It can be frustrating."

I nod, "It sounds like it has something in common with a sales job."

His head bows fractionally at the appropriateness of the analogy. "Fair enough, and as you know, there are many people who are not cut out for a sales job."

I begin to say something meant to indicate interest but he rides over it with, "I'd like to ask you to come back to our offices with me and meet my partner, Michael Vasquez. He's had a great deal of real-world practice implementing our philosophies in real-world circumstances. He works with most of our clients directly, and I think he's uniquely positioned to answer any questions you might have. Could you do that, for perhaps another hour?"

I spread my arms, "I seem to be available."

It's as though I've said, "Yes, let's go at once." He stands abruptly, saying "Good" and begins walking. I have to scramble to get to my feet and catch up; he's almost out the door by the time I'm at his side again.

"If after speaking to Mickey—that's what we call Michael, Mickey V—after you speak to Mickey, if the work seems to align with what you think you'd like to do with this new phase of your new life, I would propose we try a one-month trial, and revisit things at the end of that month. If after, at the end of a month, everyone is happy, we'd take you on permanently. What do you think?"

I'm too busy smiling to think much of anything. I answer as simply as I can, "I think that may turn out to be one of the most valuable ten-dollar lunches I've ever had!"

CHAPTER 3

*"You can't measure everything, sometimes you
just do it because it's the right thing to do."*
—W. Edwards Deming

'M CONFUSED THAT WE SEEM to be taking a different route back,
until I realize we aren't going back to Doc's academic office. "Yes, Make-A-
Difference leases space from the University up here on the Upper Quad. Not
a good idea to run your own business out of your academic office."

"Especially if your business is about values," I add and Doc chuckles.

We enter the ancient brick building, maintained by the University since its early days as an all-male military school, but surprisingly nice and modern on the inside—abstract paintings in the cool hall as we move down and then come to a door with a modest logo and lettering for Make-A-Difference, Inc. Doc gestures for me to enter.

Inside is a very comfortable, large area which feels more communal than any single office. There is a large table with a high-tech conference speaker phone in its center, and a couple of smaller workstations in corners. One wall is dominated by a dry-erase calendar with a large side-bar section for notes.

I take all this in at first glance, but my eye snags and stays on the dark gentleman rising from the table to meet us, his Armani suit moving well over his obviously fit frame. His teeth flash in a blinding smile as his dark eyes sparkle, and the hand he extends is large; when I take it in greeting, I feel not the soft hand of an office worker but the hand of a man who has done hard work in his life and isn't afraid to do more. The quick dry pressure is over in a second, and I'm distantly aware that my own hand feels stunned, taken by surprise and wanting one more chance.

"You must be Joanne, I'm Mickey," the smiling mouth says, and the northern accent is clear.

"Brooklyn?" I ask and his eyes widen a little bit and he replies, "Hey, not bad, missed by a little though, Syosset, Long Island."

"But you've been down here for awhile?"

He nods, "Almost eleven years now."

"Well then," I smile, "Your time among us has diluted your accent, so it's not my fault."

He laughs, "You were right Doc, she's a pistol!"

Now it's my turn to laugh, as I glance at Doc. "He called me a pistol?"

Mickey shrugs a little, "I paraphrase slightly. He said something like 'she's an excellent example of self-determinism across a wide spectrum of manifestations.'"

We both turn grinning at Doc, who looks sheepish, "My meaning was clear," he pretends to grumble.

"Anyway!" Mickey is still smiling, and he pulls a chair out for me. "Please, Joanne." Something about this small touch of old-world courtesy is supremely flattering, and I take my place in the chair with a smile of gratitude as Doc and Mickey find their own seats; there is then a small silence before Mickey speaks again.

"Doctor Pitz told me about his hopes for interesting you in our work Joanne, and I have to say, my fingers are crossed too. Our business is growing like a weed, and we need help…but it's not as though we can just go out on the street and find someone who truly understands the work we do and can help us deliver."

"Well," I give a small laugh. "I'm not sure yet *I* understand the work you do. And maybe that will take a little longer than we have right now. How about instead of that you tell me why you think your business is growing as fast as it is?"

I feel almost like a journalist, starting with a basic question for an article I'm writing. Never mind that this could be my whole future we're talking about, as casually as if it were baseball standings or the weather…

Mickey spreads his arms, "In a lot of ways they're the same question. We're growing so quickly *because* of what we do, because what we do is unique among consultants."

Doc chimes in, "There are any number of consultants who visit a business and provide various extrinsic structures for the necessary scaffolding to build toward improvement, and while these structures do bear a certain short-term weight, they don't represent capital improvements of any reasonable longevity."

I look at him for a long minute and then I say, "You mean they do some good but not enough."

Mickey throws his head back and laughs, "*Pistolero!*"

I smile, trying to seem like handsome exotic men throwing their heads back and roaring approval of me happens every day. Doc just smiles indulgently like a parent watching two precocious children. I point at Mickey, "*You* tell me."

He is still grinning, but he leans in, clearly wanting me to understand the point. "You're from big industry Joanne, so you know. Most businesses don't run as well as they could. The world is full of consulting firms whose employees are smart enough to go into a place, identify some structural weaknesses, and provide guidelines for repair. New procedures. Adjustments to processes. Usually these are written out like prescriptions, and when the company follows these prescriptions, they *do* work. Somewhat. For awhile. Yes?"

I nod. I had certainly seen it happen.

"But!" Mickey continues, "The improvements tend to decay quickly, because the structural issues were never more than symptoms of cultural issues, and if you don't fix the culture, new problems pop up pretty quickly."

"Make-A-Difference fixes the culture?" I ask, and I'm suddenly aware of how relaxed I feel, interrogating my mentor and a stranger about their life's work—I sure don't sound like a girl who's hoping for a lasting placement with a firm. I'm lucky they like me.

"Even the culture is a symptom, Joanne, or perhaps I should say a byproduct," Doc answers. "The culture emerges as a function of the interaction between expectations and realities, between internal values and external demands."

I think about this for a moment, and both men watch me. It suddenly feels much more like the traditional job interview. "And so..." I speak carefully, "You help them identify those values and those demands, and then you identify the gaps...and then you help create ways to close or bridge those gaps?"

Both men beam at me as though I'm a particularly bright child reciting a difficult poem.

Mickey says, "Exactly, very nice. The bottom line is this: No matter what the business is, all employees need to know a few things as certainties. They need to know their own values. They need to understand how the company's mission aligns with those values. And lastly, they need to understand how the things they do on a day-to-day basis contribute to the company achieving its objectives—which, if we've set things up correctly, becomes the same thing as helping employees achieve objectives that line up with their own."

Doc jumps in, "Your motivations and your energies will come from within if you understand why you're performing a task and how that task fits into the big picture."

Mickey again, "And motivations from within are one helluva lot more dependable than the ones which come from outside, like fear of punishment or whatever, you know?"

I nod, "Self-determinism again. They don't just show up for work because that's what grownups are expected to do, they come to work because they know they matter and because it feels good."

I'm startled when Doc roars, "YES!" and then laughs. When I whirl to look at him, his hand is out. "Toldjya!" he chuckles and Mickey is grinning and reaching for a wallet made of leather which looks soft as butter.

As Mickey pulls out a single dollar, he explains, "When I conduct on-site 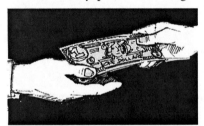 evaluations, I have to explain this stuff several times to pretty smart men and women before they begin to see what I mean. Doctor Pitz said you'd get it before our first try was even complete. We had a little wager." He hands the dollar to Doc, who snatches it playfully and holds it up like a trophy.

I smile my sweetest smile at Mickey—Is he blushing?—and I say, "Don't bet against me, Mickey."

Meanwhile, Doc pockets his winnings and continues, "Naturally this isn't as simple as identifying or labeling particular values. Often we help people change their value hierarchy or behavioral priorities in order to achieve value-behavior alignment and optimal self-directed performance."

At this point, I'm just staring at him. "Doc," I say slowly, "You may have to give that dollar back. I've known you a long time, and I'm not exactly brand new to the field, but I'm afraid I couldn't quite keep up with that one."

They both chuckle but Mickey is watching me closely. "Come on Joanne. Work through it..."

I concentrate. "If I had to guess," I started, and glanced at them, "and from the looks on your faces, I do...I'd say you mean you get people to change their minds about what's important to them and leads them to work harder and better. And if I'm right," I added, "then my prize is, you get to tell me how that means something other than brainwashing, because I'm pretty sure you're not in the brainwashing business."

Mickey laughs again, "That'd be perfect!" He adopts a robot voice: "Do not fear us…We will optimize your value-behavior alignment for maximum output…"

I'm laughing along with him, but I'm also nodding, and I look at Doc for help as I giggle, "Well yeah!"

Doc is nodding gravely, his mind already focused on this as a serious ethical question, even though I hadn't intended so deep a reading. "I wouldn't say we ask people to change their minds about what's important," he says slowly. "Rather, I suggest we point out alternative values of seemingly equal importance. These values are made more salient, or increased in priority, in order to achieve a closer harmony between personal values and work-related behavior."

Mickey leans in playfully, "Djya get *that*?" I swat at him, as Doc continues, staring into space as though the idea were taking shape on the far wall.

"When your job requires of you specific actions which are in disharmony with your personal values, your self-motivation to perform the task decreases, probably on a plottable curve. Engagement becomes less and less likely without the promise of extra compensation or the threat of negative consequences. Extrinsic motivators alone, whether promises or threats, rarely result in optimal long-term participation."

I feel as though there's a huge unspoken reality in the room, the proverbial five-hundred pound elephant. I decide to take a light tone, "So I guess sometimes you find out maybe you oughta be working someplace else, eh?"

Mickey's eyebrows go up and his face grows thoughtful. Doc continues to stare into the distance, maybe plotting his invisible self-motivation curve. I press my point, "I mean, seriously, isn't it possible that someone takes a clear-eyed look around and says, 'You know what, this place operates in a way that makes no sense to me, I need to be elsewhere,' doesn't that sometimes happen?"

Mickey glances at Doc, who doesn't seem to be in any hurry to address this, so he begins thoughtfully. "It's certainly not impossible…but it would be pretty unusual. We're not usually in situations in which things are that horribly out of whack. It's not like the vegan wakes up to find herself working at a sausage factory, you know? It tends to be smaller things, like how communication happens, or how responsibilities are organized."

I press the point, "Okay, but you have to admit, it's not unreasonable to assume there are employees out there saying, you know, 'this company's values seem to differ from mine, but times are hard and there aren't many jobs out there, so I have to suck it up.' "

Mickey is looking at me steadily, "Is that what you did at Perfect Plastics?"

I'm surprised he has taken this turn, and it makes me angry, maybe because it's too close to home. "I hadn't yet become unhappy enough to think in those terms. And they fired me before I could."

He's still looking right at me, unaware of what the flash in my eyes means, or perhaps well aware but unconcerned. "You think they would have wanted you sticking around, working unhappily, sucking it up?"

"Obviously they didn't want me around at all!"

This outburst draws Doc's full attention, and Mickey sits back, instantly apologetic. "I'm sorry Joanne. That was very rude of me, you were doing so well being one of the guys that I forgot how fresh it all is for you. I didn't mean to poke fun at it like that. I apologize. Okay?"

His dark eyes are fully upon me and worried, and my anger wilts. I nod, "I'm sorry too Mickey, I know you didn't mean anything negative. I guess I just…it's more raw than I expected, maybe, you know?"

He nods, "I do."

Doc speaks, "There's a great deal of research in this area, and it all shows that the overwhelming majority of workplace complaints, the things which make workers feel undervalued or otherwise unhappy, are almost all legitimate concerns—the sorts of things most of us would agree are problems. Even more significant—and more exciting if you're in our business—they're all things which can be remediated."

"Hey Doc?"

"Yes Joanne?"

"You mean 'fixed,' right?"

His eyes crinkle in amusement, Mickey laughs, and just like that the room is back to the warm, congenial feel it held before my little tantrum. I wonder for just a moment why I gave my sensitivity such free rein. If I'm going to be shopping for the best job, I'll need to develop thicker skin.

But the more I hear, the longer I sit with them, the clearer it becomes to me. I don't want to shop for a job. I want *this* job.

Doc speaks, "Moving back to your earlier point, Joanne, one of the challenges of our work is finding ways to bridge the gaps between employee values and employer expectations."

Mickey leaps in, "Sometimes it's as simple as asking out loud what seems like an obvious question. You might have an employee who's fretting about the lack of communication. Maybe he feels management never reaches out and that communication isn't a valued part of the culture."

"Has this worker tried reaching out himself?" I ask.

Mickey smiles and spreads his arms, sitting back, "Send her out, Doc, she's way ahead of me."

I laugh, "Hardly! But okay, here, I'm sorry to be Miss Glass-Half-Empty over here, but I guess thinking like a Safety Director means always seeing the worst-case scenario. What happens when this worker *does* gather his courage and tries to reach across this gap and is ignored...or worse, rebuked?"

Mickey is still sitting back. He shrugs, "Company's gonna die."

Now it's my turn to lift my eyebrows. Doc quickly takes over, "Mickey can be a bit cold hearted, but it's certainly worth noting—"

Mickey overrides him, "C'mon Doc, you know I'm right, all things being equal, a company that ignores workers' attempts to communicate with management is a company that's got cancer."

Doc looks at Mickey for longer than seems comfortable. I'm glad it isn't me in the laser beams, but it's disconcerting that once again the warm, relaxed feeling has left the room. After a moment, Doc says softly, "We're in the fortunate position of often being able to step in and cure that cancer. Not all cases are terminal."

He returns his gaze to me and seems to brighten a bit, "I'm not saying Mickey's wrong," he continues, "Without question, no company could defend a statement such as 'Communication from employees is a bad idea and all such efforts along these lines should be discouraged.' Which is not," he adds, "to say that lots of companies don't unwittingly send this exact message."

Mickey re-enters, "That's right, and that's why lines of communication are always one of the first things we look at when assessing a company's culture."

"I don't know, guys," I say, a rueful smile on my face, "It sounds like you're describing this wonderful world of what ought to be true, and I'm not disagreeing with you for a second, and maybe I *am* still a little raw" I say, glancing at Mickey, "But I think we all know plenty of managers who would take the position of 'Hey, sorry they don't feel all warm and fuzzy and loved, but this is not a romance it's a *job,* and they don't have to love it, they have to show up and *do* it.' "

"Well, listen," Mickey begins, "I'm not gonna say those guys aren't out there, but I will say that th—"

"And girls."

He blinks, "Sorry?"

"It's not just guys," I say, thinking of Kathy Miller, the Ice Queen. "It's girls too."

He nods, "Fair point. Those guys and girls are out there, but here's what I always try to remember: If we're looking for these sorts of gaps, there's exactly one reason behind our search."

"What's that?" I ask, curious.

He leans forward and speaks slowly and emphatically, "Someone called us." He gives that a moment to sink in and then continues, "They called *us*. They know *something* is wrong. Productivity is down or retention is down, profits are down, something is wrong and needs to be fixed. You know?"

This simple fact hits home. I'd been sitting here imagining all sorts of resistance from the Kathy Miller types who never want to hear bad news…but the clients of Make-A-Difference have bad news and are willing to confront it. If they can learn the source of their bad news, then that's *good* news.

I look up and both men are watching me expectantly. I rake my mind quickly for questions and find an obvious one: "I mentioned earlier about the way my brain works because of my safety background. I'm wondering whether you've thought about whether my background in safety will be an asset or a liability?"

They look at each other and then chuckle. I feel as though I'm on a topic from an earlier conversation which is suddenly relevant again. Mickey speaks first, "Joanne, you established nationally-prominent improvements in workplace safety, and I think you know better than anyone how difficult it can be to remake a company's safety culture."

Doc takes over, "Safety ought to be closely aligned with self-determinism. It's certainly in our best interests to be safe, to get home each night in one piece. Yet history shows us again and again, safety is an area which has great resistance to change. Even though the cost-benefit analyses are childishly obvious, companies again and again make the mistake of believing regulations can substitute for culture.

"You helped create a new improved culture at Perfect Plastics, Joanne, and that means you ought to be a splendid fit for Make-A-Difference. You've successfully empowered your staff across historical and cultural boundaries."

Empowered? There's a word I don't care for. It smacks of all the psychobabble Doc and I worked for so many years to put into its rightful place—in the dustbin of doubletalk. "You know I'm not crazy about that word, Doc."

"I know," he chuckles. "But it's still the best word we've got. We're not talking about management empowering people to do more with fewer resources. We're talking about people *feeling* empowered."

Mickey speaks up, "I know exactly what you mean, Joanne, it sounds like all nuts and granola. But look—it really only means you can say 'yes' to three questions. If you feel empowered on any one issue, it means you can say 'Yes' to—Can I do it? Will it Work? and Is it Worth It?

"Let's say your team has been told to rearrange the equipment on a factory floor. Can you do it? If 'yes' it means you have the technical know-how and the manpower. Will it work? If you can say 'Yes' it means you understand the total operations of the floor and you can say with confidence what will and won't be effective.

"Is it worth it? If you can say 'Yes' to this last question, you don't just understand operations in a mechanical sense—you understand more deeply that some arrangements have more utility than others, and it means you know both the current arrangement and the proposed arrangement in great enough detail that you can say 'yes', the new one will be better for the company. In other words, you believe the expected benefits from the change are worth the extra effort to make the change.

"Now let's think about that for just a second. You're a regular floor worker. But if you can say 'Yes' to those three questions you understand your equipment, your people, and how they all fit into the overall system, and you see clearly why a particular change is good. You feel empowered."

LEADERSHIP LESSON 2

People feel empowered when they answer "yes" to three questions: Can you do it? Will it work? Is it worth it?

Doc leans forward, his eyes gleaming, "Can you imagine an entire company of employees with that kind of understanding, that amount of buy-in? Those employees will want to work hard, because they'll understand exactly where they fit in, and they'll know they're part of something larger than themselves, and they'll want to be successful at doing their part."

Mickey is now leaning in, too. They're both excited, and I have to admit, it's contagious. "Plenty of consultants can give you some acronym for improving communication, or doing quality control. We do more. We teach companies how to develop a culture in which employees feel empowered to do their very best for the company. They are self-motivated on the job."

"Three C's" says Doc. "That's what we want every company to have." He holds up his fingers and ticks them off—"Competence. Choice. Community."

Mickey is nodding, "Every worker feels competent, and is given the education and training to stay that way. Every worker is present by choice—

their personal *active* choice. And a community spirit, a sense of belonging to something important, is omnipresent. They all work interdependently to make a difference."

Doc nods, "Make a difference. We all do. And that's what we're about."

His phone rings with a loud electronic chirp, and all three of us jump and then laugh. "That's our two o'clock conference call."

Mickey jerks a thumb at the phone, "Want me to stall em a minute?"

Doc nods, "Yes, please."

Mickey holds out a hand to me. "Good to meet you, Joanne. Glad you're with us." Again I feel the warm power in that hand before it's gone. I watch him answer the phone, jovial and confident, and after a moment I realize Doc is speaking to me.

"—until Thursday, does that work for you?"

I shake my head, clearing it, "I'm sorry Doc, a lot going on up here, gimme the first half of that again?"

Doc smiles, "I know, it's a lot to take in. And I don't expect you to learn everything all at once. I was saying I'd like for you to travel with Mickey to our next site evaluation. He's flying out on Sunday to be with a client for three days and then back on Thursday, how does that sound?"

Almost a whole week out of town. My mind begins instantly sifting through all of the domestic logistics Keith will have to take on or get help with—soccer practices, Spanish tutoring, groceries…I realize Doc is waiting for my answer and I'm suddenly ashamed to have kept him from his call. I can figure this out on my own time. "Yes, Doc, absolutely. That sounds exciting."

He smiles, "Good." He leans across for a quick embrace and then says, "I'm afraid I have to join them now."

"Oh yes, sure." I begin gathering my things.

Moving toward Mickey, Doc says, "We'll have a car sent to your house on Sunday, all right?"

Sending a car! I smile, "That sounds wonderful."

He nods and then without another word he turns to Mickey who puts their call on speaker. As I move to the door I glance back to see them deep in conversation, finding gaps, bridging them—Making a difference!

THAT NIGHT IN OUR LIVING ROOM, I'm sipping a glass of wine as Keith pores over a gardening catalogue. The azaleas and the rhododendrons out front are his pride and joy, and he's forever seeking new ways to make them more lush, more vibrantly colorful than they were last year. At the moment, his attention to the catalogue is willfully focused. He's working damned hard to avoid looking at me.

After an uncomfortable silence, I say, "You don't seem very happy about this."

He still doesn't look up, "I'm happy..."

I snort and take another sip, "This is happy? What does *un*happy look like, do you set the house on fire?"

He's still looking at his fine print as he murmurs, "Well, if I do, you be sure to call nine-one-one on your way out of town, okay?"

I cover the distance between us in two strides and pull the catalogue from his hands, tossing it aside. He looks up at me, not totally surprised. He knows about my temper. Perhaps that's what he's doing; trying to get a rise out of me so if we *do* fight he'll be able to say later *I* was the one who lost her temper.

Not fair. Not fair. He's not like that. Get a grip Jo.

I sit down next to him. "You're allowed to not be happy. You're allowed to resent it if the job makes your life harder. You're allowed to yell and I hereby give you permission to throw any two objects in the kitchen." At this, his mouth twitches into almost-a-smile even though he is still like a little-boy looking away.

"What you're not allowed to do," I continue, "Is ignore me, ignore this. You're not allowed to sit stony faced and say you're happy when you're not. We can survive a lot of things baby but the day either of us starts lying to the other, that's bad. That's, like, maybe unsurviveably bad. You know?"

He's not speaking but this time I wait. I can wait as long as he needs me to. After a long silence he says, "I guess I'm scared."

This surprises me. Scared? Keith? Big ex-surfer dude Keith, broad-shouldered big-chested Keith, Keith who can pick up *both* our kids, one under each arm, like squealing sacks of potatoes? "Baby, there's noth—"

"Please don't," he lifts a hand, and looks at me, and my goodness, he's telling the truth, I can see it in his eyes. He is scared.

"Baby," I try again, softly, "You weren't scared when I was fresh out of work, but you're scared now that I might be back in?"

He gives a small laugh, "I know. But, like, you were so upset, so sad, I had an easy job, you know? Be big. Be strong. Tell everyone it's fine. Believe it.

"But now," he continues, "and I know, it's crazy, but now you don't need that anymore. And so now I can slow down and think about how different everything might be. You might travel a lot. You might have to work long nights at home.

"All of the little routines we had gotten so used to, everything that made our life feel easy and safe is going to change. And you know, I'm sure it'll be fine, I'm sure it'll be wonderful, I want to be happy, I *will* be happy…but right this second it's just…a little spooky."

I look at him, smiling. I adore this man. How many husbands could say what he just said? How many of them would trust their wives enough to say, "I'm scared."

I go and wrap my arms around him, "I'll protect you my angel."

He holds my arms tight, "Promise?"

I kiss his temple, "I promise."

I feel him smile, inches from my lips. He whispers, "Then I'm happy."

CHAPTER 4

"The illiterate of the 21st century will not be those who cannot read and write, but those who cannot learn, unlearn, and relearn."
—Alvin Toffler

MY SLEEP IS SO LIGHT the small "click!" my alarm clock makes just before filling the air with harsh beeping is all I need to awaken; my fingers find the "off" button before the first beep is even complete. Keith barely stirs.

I lie in bed for a moment longer, centering myself. Today. Today is here. Today I start. Today, today, today is the first day of the rest…oh good heavens shut up Joanne okay *up*.

I swing my legs around to the floor and rise as smoothly as I can, moving about the darkened room with ease. I smile softly at how familiar this feels. How many times have I moved through this darkness, nursing Matthew or Jessica, tending to a bad dream or a fever…but now, this is all me. I'm on my own.

My hands find all of the little arrangements I made the night before. Here are the clothes I will wear for this morning's flight. Here is the makeup bag, ready to pack as soon as I fix my face after my shower. Here is my carry-on suitcase, ready to receive my makeup bag. Here is my leather portfolio. Here is my book. Here is my purse.

I like how ready I feel, and the way this feeling flows into the utter mystery of what I'll actually be *doing*. I've got my first half hour schemed out to the micrometer and after that, it's as vast and unknown as the sea. Quite the contrast.

Move downstairs, still in darkness, idly considering the just-past weekend, and the two lenses with which I can view it. Seen through one lens, it looks like a perfectly ordinary family weekend. Normal chores, Jessica's weekend for bathrooms, Matthew's for vacuuming, mine (as always) to go behind both of them saying, "Nope, try again"…the three of us giggling and taking bets for the first time Keith would track garden-dirt onto the just-cleaned floors (Most of us picked very early times, but Matthew won with the wildly optimistic wager of 11:45 a.m.)

Grocery shopping, laundry, all with an eye toward making sure everyone would have what they needed to weather my absence over the next few days… and underlying all preparations of this sort, an unvoiced tension—the kind of tension which feeds on itself, growing, because no one wants to mention it. Wondering if Keith is upset because he's being so quiet, resulting in me working harder to make him laugh, or at least talk, resulting in what felt like even less talk…but then what if I'm imagining things…and so on.

It was hard for me to gauge. Was he really even upset, or just preoccupied? Was he doing his best to make the necessary adjustments, and thinking hard about those? Did he need space? Or was he just pouting? I wavered between concern and being amused at myself that we could know each other for so long, and yet when we encounter a brand new circumstance, we revert pretty quickly to the communication skills of the average high-school couple.

As I pour my coffee, my thoughts of Keith are interrupted by a quick thank-you to the universe for hot coffee that's waiting for you when you wake up. I have no idea how we survived in the days before programmable coffee makers. I sip the hot, welcome liquid as my thoughts return to Keith and his mood.

Complicating my assessment is the fact he's been saying all the right things… they're just a little bit late, or a little bit less enthusiastic than I'd like. A slightly-distracted-sounding, "That's great baby" when I tell him I'm excited…or "You'll do great" when I tell him I'm nervous. The right response, but not the full-throated, optimistic endorsement I'm hoping for.

I smile again. The poor guy can't win. I *know* he's nervous and confused about his own feelings, yet he's able to summon more or less the correct statements when called upon…and here I am, wanting to beat him up because he's not convincing enough. "It'll be better," I tell myself. "We'll find a new rhythm for this, we'll learn what the adjustments are and we'll be like old pros at this stuff in a few months, and our worry will be a vague, amusing memory."

I occupy myself by making lunches for the kids. This simple task, performed thousands of times, has a meditative quality which eases me. Lay out the bread. Put the sandwiches together assembly-line style, bag up some Cheetos, four Chips Ahoy apiece. Pop the brown paper bags open with a flick of the wrist, pack the foods, a few extra napkins, and then I stand with the magnet pad from the fridge and write each of them a little note.

To Matthew I write, "Just because I'm out of town doesn't mean I can't see what you are doing, do NOT blow things up with your chemistry set or I will call the authorities and have you shipped to the subcontinent to be the personal boy-slave to a cruel and heartless King. Or maybe make you clean the garage. Either way, a fate worse than death, so BEHAVE YOURSELF. Love, Mom."

To Jessica I write, "Take care of your Dad while I'm gone. Make sure to water him three times a day and also make sure he gets plenty of sun, and if you see aphids on him, you should spray him with the hose. If you claim I told you to do this, I will deny it and then follow you on every date you have for the rest of your life asking if you need a sweater. Ignore this warning at your own peril. Love, Mom."

I kiss the notes and tuck them into the bags, pour myself another cup of coffee and step back upstairs, cradling the warm ceramic in my cupped palms.

As I move down the hall, I nudge the kids' doors open just enough to look in on them. Matthew is sprawled as always, as though he were a marionette whose strings were all cut at once…and in contrast, across the hall, Jessica is curled up into such a tight lump she's barely discernible among her mounds of covers.

Seeing my babies asleep like this sends a sharp, shooting pang through me. Leaving them suddenly feels like the worst thing in the world…but then I remember how excited they've been for me, how eager to hear the details of where I'm going and what it will be like. To them, Atlanta and Kansas City are as exotic as the Amazon. Keith could have taken a page out of their book.

There he is, snoring lightly on our bed as I move past. If he's worried, it doesn't show right now—he's out like a light. I pick up the traveling clothes I had laid out so carefully last night, and I step into the bathroom, careful to shut the door soundlessly before turning on any lights or water. Moving quickly, aware of having taken longer than I meant to, I shower and put on simple makeup and slip into the dress I had chosen. I inspect myself in the mirror. Not too shabby.

I'm just zipping my makeup bag into my carry-on when I hear the soft double-toot of a car waiting for me out front. I peek through the blinds—sure enough, there's a sedan down there, exhaust puffing gently out.

I quickly lean over to kiss Keith. "I gotta go baby," I whisper. "I'll call you when we're checked into the hotel, okay?"

He rolls over and squints at me, trying to put it all together. "You got everything you need?" he manages.

I smile, "Yeah, unless they change the rules about husbands in suitcases."

He grunts an effort at a laugh and I lean down to kiss him again. "Go back to sleep," I say softly.

"Mmm kay" he manages. I stand up. A tearful farewell scene it certainly is not. Which is a good thing, I suppose. The two soft honks of the horn sound again, and I pick up my bag, pat my purse, and make my way down the stairs and out into the cool morning darkness.

THE TRIP TO THE AIRPORT is smooth and quiet. The driver is obviously a professional and keeps to himself, handling the large sedan with expert smoothness. As I glance out the window, I'm a little surprised there's already so much traffic on the roads. My normal commute (*you don't have a normal commute anymore, Joanne*) would still be two hours away, and goodness knows there's plenty of traffic by then…but I suppose even this early, plenty of people have places to go.

It feels good to be one of them.

It also feels good to sail past all the satellite parking, the econo-lot with its dreary plastic shelter and its every-fifteen minutes shuttle bus always smelling faintly of disinfectant. My driver pulls right up to the terminal, and I suddenly realize I'm not sure what happens next. I lean forward with my purse and I say, "Do I—," but the driver anticipates me.

"It's all taken care of, ma'am," he assures me.

"Oh!" I say, startled that he so easily interpreted my action, but relieved nonetheless. I begin to open my purse anyway, saying, "Well, let me—"

"Gratuity has already been included," he finishes smoothly.

I'm left with nothing to do. "Well," I murmur. "Umm…Thank you."

He smiles into the rearview mirror, "Have a good flight, ma'am."

I nod, "Thank you," I repeat, as I grab my bag and open the door, stepping out to the curb. I suppose I never stop assessing potential for improvement, because I note my driver did not step around to open my door for me. Not quite in the Donald Trump Club yet…still, I could get used to this. *My driver.* I grin at myself for having this thought.

"There's a nice smile for such an early hour," calls a cheery voice, and I look up to see Mickey, in a different but equally devastating suit; I would swear I actually see his eyes twinkling in the early morning light. I've only seen the man twice, but both times he seems to have stepped straight from the pages of a men's fashion magazine.

I'm angling toward our airline's check-in counter, but he angles to cut me off, shaking his head. "Not that line, Joanne, over here." I follow him to an almost-abandoned area of the counter marked "Diamond Club." The treatment we receive would make it easy to believe that somehow Mickey *owns* the airline.

Sadly, there's no "Diamond Club" for the security check point. We put ourselves through the rituals of removing our shoes, laptops into industrial grey bins, the monotonous repetitions of the barked orders from the TSA officers. I wonder, as I do whenever I encounter them, about the nature of their jobs. Such overwhelmingly dull repetition, every day the same cranky passengers who don't understand why they can't keep their shampoo or who demand to speak to a manager, as though any local manager is going to rewrite federal statutes…and yet these government employees are the last true barrier between outside threats and my personal safety.

As I always do, I make eye contact with the officers at each end and I say, "Thank you *very* much." I've grown accustomed to the welcome look of pleased surprise I see when they hear this.

In just a few minutes we've reclaimed and re-packed our bags. At the end of the line, slipping our shoes back on, Mickey again cocks his head in a direction away from the crowd. "We'll wait in there." I follow his eyes and again see the "Diamond Club" logo; this time on the door of what I imagine is a private lounge.

As we walk, I look back at the TSA workers. "Now there's a challenge for self-determinism," I say to Mickey, "Those folks have zero latitude in their duties, and I guarantee there was no effort for inclusion when the regs they have to follow were being drafted."

"Yeah, government jobs are always a particular challenge, they're so regulated…but I did write up a project proposal for working with the TSA. We're still waiting to hear back from the subcommittee that has oversight. I should show it to you sometime."

I try not to keep the incredulity off of my face. Bad enough he's handsome and charming and competent and so easy in his skin, he's also already figured out how to improve air travel. Maybe Health Care is next. I wouldn't be surprised to hear him say, "You know, I was having lunch with the President and the First Lady, and *they* think…"

Next thing I know, I'm behind one of those doors I've always wondered about, and in a room which I have to admit, *is* nicer than the terminal outside. As I help myself to another cup of coffee, a much nicer blend than what I had at the house, Mickey makes sure our flight is in order, complete with first-class seats at the front of the plane. He checks me over his shoulder. "You doing okay?" he asks.

I smile at him, "If a girl's gotta get up at the crack of dawn, it's nice to at least do it in style!"

In the lounge, there are no loudspeakers. An attendant comes to us and speaks quietly to Mickey, "Sir, we're ready for you at the gate." We walk almost without pause down the jet way, the flight attendant gesturing toward the cushiony seats which await.

I settle in, stretching luxuriously. "Ahhhhh," I murmur contentedly. "Leg room!" I glance over at Mickey, who is busily stowing his bag under the seat in front of him. After flight attendant announcements, we're taxiing and then hurtling down the runway and into the air, ears popping, and we're off.

Once we've leveled off, I turn to Mickey, "So!" I say, my tone chipper and all business—the eager apprentice, excited about today's lesson. "What can you tell me about where we're going? What should I expect?"

He reaches down and rummages in his bag and then sits up, holding a neat folder, full of tabbed dividers. The front is labeled "Joanne." He looks a little sheepish. "Sorry about all the paper, we try to keep things digital but I didn't know whether you'd be checking your e-mail at four in the morning, so we have to brief the old fashioned way this morning."

I take the folder from him, my eyebrows going up at the sheer density of the thing. "We like to be thorough," he says apologetically.

As I turn to the first section, he gives me the basics. "We're heading to Stone Mountain Flooring, a company just outside of Atlanta. They brand themselves 'Always Underfoot' and they have a sizeable piece of the domestic and international flooring markets, with particular strength in the plastic products— linoleum-type stuff. They have about forty-five hundred employees, but almost half of them are in some area of sales. The workforce we're dealing with is just a few more than twenty-five hundred."

"They're having troubles?" I ask as I page through the document. It's so detailed—charts, graphs, survey results, in-house documents, outside assessments…I realize Mickey is in mid-answer.

"…started using one of our competitors about seven years ago, and worked with them steadily until three months ago. The stated mission has been the creation of an improvement in quality culture, but the improvements were significantly less than had been envisioned."

"Quality Culture?" I smile.

"Yes?"

"Oh, I don't know," I shrug, "I mean, presumably this means everyone caring about doing things properly and making things well, right?"

"Yes…?" Mickey looks half-patient, half curious.

"I guess sometimes I wish folks in the consulting industry would call a spade a spade. 'Quality Culture' sounds like some slick brand name, like it was a term invented for a brochure, you know?"

"Well," he says, shifting in his seat. "You know, now *you're* one of those folks in the consulting industry. At least for the next thirty days. What would you call it?"

I'm slightly startled by both the pronouncement and the question…and was that also a warning, lurking in that thirty-day line? I gaze into space for a minute, collecting my thoughts. It's possible more is riding on my answer than a casual conversation about nomenclature.

"I think," I begin slowly, "the problem that results in these catch-phrases is we want something which can serve as an emblem for the fairly complex work that lies beneath it. It's very hard to distill long-term processes of quality reform into a single phrase, yet we *do* need to call it *something*, is that fair?"

Mickey nods, listening intently.

I continue, "I guess my objection is that it sounds so slick. As though the language itself is standing between the audience and the process. If you go home and your husband says, 'What'd you do today, honey?' and you say, 'We did quality culture!' I don't think your husband knows any more about what you did today than before he asked, wouldn't you agree?"

"Yes…"

"Well then," I say, relieved to have gotten to this point. "That's the thing. You'd like a name that actually describes, rather than a name that obscures. I'm saying, in a perfect world," I add hastily.

Mickey's gaze is direct. "So again, the question: What would you call it?"

I think for a moment. "I'd go for something more down to earth. 'Everyone On the Same Page' maybe, or even 'Making It Better.' With, you know, 'it' meaning not just the product itself, but the processes, the work environment, the communication. You know?"

Mickey is nodding and smiling slightly. "Not bad. I don't know though, "culture" is a pretty entrenched noun in our business. I don't see it going anywhere."

"No, I know. It was just a kind of stray thought. When I'm Queen of the World, I'll take care of that one." I flash a grin at him and then ask, "So what did our competitor try?"

I'm a little surprised by the inadvertent audacity with which I've used the word "our" but Mickey doesn't seem to have registered it, leafing through the file. Hey, *he's* the one who said I was one of them, "at least for the next thirty days," right? Might as well talk the talk.

Mickey is answering me, "Appendix B summarizes a series of mid-level management reports which form the history of that exact question, the issue of what's already been tried. They basically tried to implement leaner manufacturing through a *kaizen* process."

"Kye-zen?" I ask, trying carefully for the phonetics.

"Japanese," Mickey explains. "Big deal process implemented by Toyota a number of years ago, spread to the west *Kai* meaning change and *zen* meaning good. An improvement…although it's come to mean ongoing improvement, a never-ending process of seeking and implementing improvement."

"A culture of improvement," I say dryly.

He laughs, "See? It's not so easy to get away from, is it? But yes, that's it exactly. And by the way, be careful not to say Kigh-*zahn*. That means change for the worse."

"When we fly to Japan I'll be sure to brush up. So our guys tried kaizen and it took them seven *years* to notice it wasn't working? And they're *not* the federal government??"

Mickey laughs again, "Nope, just a medium-sized company."

"With morons for managers," I add quietly.

Mickey's eyes get a little wide, "Sorry?"

I'm dismissive, certain that Mickey sees what I mean. "Oh, you know. Drive around on a flat tire for seven years and somehow that's okay." A quick check of his face tells me that maybe he *doesn't* see what I mean.

I feel exasperation bubbling up as I continue, "I mean, you know, what does that even look like, 'hey, do you think the tire is flat?' 'it sure does *feel* flat' 'well yeah but we've got a Consultant, *yay*, and *he* says it's not as flat as it used to be, let's keep driving!' I mean, for the love of Pete people, didjya maybe think of *getting out of the car and looking??*"

Mickey says quietly, "Faith is a powerful thing."

I snort, "Yeah, so is stupidity."

Mickey takes a deep breath and I can tell he's working carefully to frame something. I hear dim alarm bells ringing, the ones that mean Watch Out, Joanne, Your Big Mouth Just Did It Again.

After a quick moment Mickey says, "In my experience, people who ask for help tend to be people who actually want help. Is it helpful for us to point out to them they should have asked sooner? Is it helpful for us to call them stupid?"

Ohhhhhhhh crap. I try to lighten it, "Come on, Mickey, you know I wouldn't call them stupid, like, out loud or anything, We're on an airplane a hundred miles from the place, you know? I was just saying it to *you*."

His answer is quiet, "You need to not say it at all, not even to yourself—especially because you don't even believe it."

I'm surprised, "What do you mean?"

He continues to speak carefully, almost as though speaking to a slow child, and I'm trying not to feel like one. He says, "Do you believe we have something to offer this company? Do you believe we can help them?"

My head shakes a fraction, not in negation, but in confusion. The question makes no sense. "Well, of course, I mean, sure, we—"

He cuts me off, his explanation rolling smoothly forward. "Do you imagine our solutions are quick and easy, fix it all in a single visit, or do you imagine we'll need a little time?"

Surely he's not comparing what we're going to do with what our competitors did. "Sure, Mickey, but it won't be seven *years*, we won't—"

He leans a hair closer, "So we can help them, it will take time, it won't be easy, and they called us anyway. And somehow they're stupid in the bargain? I don't think so, Joanne, and neither do you. We want to teach and exemplify compassion, and you know Doc always says, compassion is empathy plus action. They've been going in the wrong direction for too long and they're trying to change, and if they were stupid, you and I wouldn't have jobs, you know?"

I hear him. And I also hear, or imagine I hear, the reminder that all employment is fragile. I nod. "If they were here, I'd apologize. I just hate to see waste, Mickey. Time. Effort. Materials. Any of it. It makes me mad. But I'll watch myself."

He smiles and pats my arm, "When you're in the business of stopping to fix things, you need to be okay with finding stuff to fix because you get a 'two-fer'—your firm gets a gig *and* you get to leave something better than you found it. That's win-win, but it doesn't happen if there's nothing needing our attention, you know?

"Now," he continues before I can apologize further, "You get to have the fun of reading the rest of that report and I get to close my eyes for a minute. Four thirty in the morning comes a lot sooner and hits a lot harder when you get to be my age." And with this he faces front and his eyes close.

I almost offer a bit of flattery, protesting his claim of age, but I bite my tongue in the nick of time. He wants to rest. And it might come out wrong anyway. Flirty. No. Better to study this report, learn the details inside out. So far on this flight I've managed to make fun of our firm's vocabulary and called a valuable client stupid. I'm not exactly acting like someone with only thirty days to prove herself.

Shaking my head in frustration with myself, I immerse myself in the file.

THE NEXT COUPLE OF HOURS move swiftly. An uneventful landing in Atlanta, no checked bags to claim, quickly through the truly gigantic airport, another car waiting for us in the ground-transportation area, the two of us into the roomy backseat of the sedan.

I've flagged several pages of the report, with questions for Mickey about the ways certain decisions were reached. The report contains internal assessments performed by our competitor and I look at these with special closeness.

"You know," I say, paging through one of them, "I've got a lot to learn but something about this feels like wheel-spinning. This employee survey, it asks a ton of questions, but I get the idea none of them were the right one."

I'm surprised to see him smiling at me. "Very good," he says.

"It is?" My surprise must show on my face, because he laughs.

"Yep. You nailed it. But that's what we start fixing today."

WE ARRIVE AT the company complex, a fairly typical layout of manufacturing plant in one corner of the property and administrative offices in another. Mickey outlines the plan: "We'll meet a committee of mid-level managers, outline our basic philosophy, and then conduct some interviews. We'll be talking to wage workers first, to get a sense of overall morale and how things work, and then we'll talk to the Plant Manager."

Mickey warns me the meeting with the committee will feel a lot like a sales-pitch, enabling them to relax in the belief they're in good hands, that we *do* have a process, that there *is* a plan.

Indeed, that's exactly what happens—Mickey presents the Make-A-Difference approach with warmth, humor, and sympathy for the fact that everyone in the room wants the same thing—to make Stone Mountain Flooring a place where workers know their role and are happy to perform it—a place from which only the very finest products are allowed to move on to market. The listening group of managers seem pleased, even relieved, to find themselves in Mickey's hands. I smile; glad to know he seems to have this effect on everyone.

We then move along to the plant itself, where we gather in a small meeting room with a randomly-selected group of five wage workers. The conversation is very preliminary, nothing more than an effort to get a feel for the status quo.

Mickey begins by asking what's normally done to ensure high quality. Variations on the same answer come as a dutiful murmur from all five mouths at the same time: "Kaizens." and "We do kaizens" and nods of agreement.

Mickey asks for a bit more of an explanation and there's a sense of a collective shrug. A worker named Ed says, "We do one kaizen per quarter. That's, you know, that's the schedule, that's what they decided would work."

"And does it?" Mickey asks.

Again, a few shrugs, and Ed says, "I guess so. I mean, we get er done."

"Why?"

The question seems to bring them up short. They glance at one another, and another worker, Liz, adds, "Cause that's what the bosses want!" There's laughter and nodding, and glances to check for Mickey's reaction. He's smiling too, but I can tell we're not done with this topic.

Liz continues, "Also, don't forget—we do our four kaizens a year like we're supposed to, we all get a half-day paid leave." More nods.

"Can you see any improvement? What sorts of things have you gotten done?"

Ed answers, "Last quarter, we got bigger trash bins for the floor, that way we don't have to shut down the line and empty em as often. And before that…what was it?" he asks, turning to Liz.

"The pallets," she replies to murmurs of agreement.

Ed turns back to Mickey. "Right. We got stronger pallets down in receiving. They take a bigger load, and they don't break as often."

"And are these things working?" I ask, and Mickey glances at me for a half second before returning his attention to the group. I can't tell whether he's irked with me for speaking, but I feel like a fifth wheel, and it's a good question.

Ed looks at me, "The new trash bins really do hold more trash. And the new pallets really are better. We're doing a kaizen a quarter, one K per Q, is how they talk about it. Now if you're asking me whether the bosses are *happy* with this stuff, hey, you know—ask them."

"I wouldn't mind hearing the answer to that myself!" pipes up another worker and they all laugh.

Again, Mickey laughs along with them, but he's still working the edges of what's not being said. "I guess I'm asking, quality wise, are you seeing any changes?"

I'm starting to think the only thing these people know how to do is shrug. Liz says, "I have a girlfriend who works in the mailroom and she says she heard about some big report showing a spike in customer complaints…"

"Yeah," says a young burly man, "but we don't *know* that, we're not seeing a lot of product coming back as defective or anything, you know?"

Murmurs of agreement. They simply don't seem to know very much about the state of things. It's almost as if they've been abandoned on some island down here, terribly far from the company at which they actually work.

One of the women says she's very confused about why her suggestions go unanswered. "I don't expect everyone to say 'oh, she's a genius' ("good thing, too!" calls one smart aleck) "…but," she continues, glaring back at her mouthy colleague, "it would sure feel nice if they at least *answered*, you know, anything is better than a black hole, right?"

After a few more similar questions, Mickey gives me a nod. We're done for this session. Then, almost as an afterthought, he says, "Lemme ask you something. Suppose, Ed, you see Liz doing something you know isn't safe. Do you point it out to her?"

"Not if he knows what's good for him!" Liz calls out to raucous laughter.

Ed is grinning and nodding with her, then he answers, "She's right, it's no joke. I mean, Liz is a decent worker…" ("Thanks a lot!" she calls out to more laughter) "…but you know, you don't wanna be calling out your line mate on stuff. If it turns into some kind of fight, you *both* get in trouble. No point in that, right?"

More murmurs of agreement. Mickey nods significantly at me, and we thank all of them for their time. They file out, and I start to ask Mickey for his impressions of all this (I certainly have plenty of my own) but he simple says, "There's a lot to talk about, let's do it later," and it's a good thing, too, because into the room comes Patricia, the plant manager.

Initial pleasantries are exchanged, and then Mickey gets to his questions. He starts with a big one, "Can you tell me how it is that Stone Mountain Flooring arrived at the goal of four kaizens per year?"

Patricia cocks her head and says, "Is that how you say it? I've been saying kigh-ZAHNs." I'm quite certain Mickey can feel how hard I'm working not to smile. I hope he can trust it's all on the inside. Patricia continues, "It was explained to us as a best practice, already implemented by several other companies."

Mickey nods as though this is a totally satisfactory answer. He follows up with, "Did you happen to hear where this idea of four-per-year as best practice might have originated?"

She shakes her head, "I never heard. Why, have you heard differently?"

Mickey answers her almost distractedly, "No, I haven't heard anything." Again the corners of my mouth twitch because I know the unspoken, full sentence is "No, I've never heard anything about any fixed number of kaizens per year being anyone's notion of a good idea." But I can see Mickey knows that sometimes saying less is better.

Patricia continues, "I asked that because it doesn't seem to be working for us, at least especially well. We haven't seen a reduction in our complaints or in our overhead."

It seems to me the obvious question is whether they've tried to steer the *kaizen* process specifically in those directions, but Mickey seems content to move on. "I'm wondering if you can tell me a little bit about how management goes about the process of gathering ideas from employees?"

Patricia nods, and then continues to nod while speaking; she obviously believes she's answering his question when she says, "That's something which falls under the supervisor's duties, he or she is responsible for all of that."

"Mmm…" Mickey says, as though mulling this answer, "Do you get the sense your supervisors are being diligent about that?"

Patricia smiles a tough-girl smile, "I hope they are. It's part of their job, you know? If it's part of their job, they'd better be doing it, right?"

Mickey smiles, "Absolutely. Let me ask you this; is there any kind of formalized process for acquiring this kind of feedback?"

Her brow furrows, "I'm not sure I understand, when you say 'formal'…"

I can't take it anymore, maybe Mickey likes playing good cop with this lady, but we'll be here all day if someone doesn't give it to her in child-sized portions. Fine, I'll cut her food for her: "What we're asking is, do you make use of any surveys or tools of that sort to check what your workers think about quality issues and their own involvement in improving things?"

Mickey keeps his eyes on Patricia, so I can't tell whether he's okay with my stepping in or whether I'll catch hell later.

Patricia's face relaxes, "Ohhh, I see, no, we don't do much of that. We did for awhile, but you know what we found?"

Mickey answers quietly, "Mixed signals."

Patricia points at him as if at a prize pupil. "Yes, exactly. First of all the survey itself, the fact that it was happening, raised all kinds of false hopes, like everyone thinking they'd get to vote on new vending machines or whatever. But on top of that, we didn't really know what to do with all the answers once we got them. There'd be this pile of data, but it seemed to be conflicting, contradictory. And we didn't really have the expertise to analyze it.

"And I'll tell you," she says, drawing herself up a bit more proudly. "I'm not one of those managers who says, 'Let's do a survey' just to do a survey, you know? Some folks I know think that, you know, 'look how good our communication is, we did a survey!' But it's fake communication, because the answers never really mean anything, nothing ever really happens."

I speak again, "So you decided to just leave em alone."

"Absolutely," she nods energetically. "Spend that time working, you know? Getting the job done, that's what we're really here for anyway, right?"

Mickey says, "Without a doubt."

I can't quite believe what I'm hearing, "Hang on, I'm not clear about something, are you saying your preference, your *choice*—"

Mickey cuts me off, and although his voice doesn't sound any louder, it has an edge that would carve diamonds like butter. "It's okay Joanne, I'm clear about what Patricia is saying; I think we need to move on."

Patricia seems oblivious to what's just happened, but I feel about two-feet tall. Apparently my mouth has gotten me in trouble again. Apparently I've crossed some line I didn't see. Mickey is probably going to give me some version of "The customer is always right" as soon as he can talk to me in private. But how can the customer always be right when the customer is so clearly, obviously *wrong*?

I try to maintain a calm and professional demeanor, but I feel my head giving little shakes and my jaw is so tight I'm worried I might destroy a filling.

Maybe I'm not cut out for this.

CHAPTER 5

"Tell them and they'll forget.
Demonstrate and they'll remember.
Involve them and they'll understand."
—Confucius

T HE NEXT FEW HOURS are a whirlwind of travel and even though I
expect a stern talking to at any moment, it keeps not happening. We get
back into the waiting car (Is it really the same car? Did it really never leave?)
and off we go, returning to the Atlanta airport.

Along the way, Mickey is on his cell phone almost non-stop, confirming arrangements for our visit in Kansas City and speaking briefly to Doc. At one point I get the impression he's been asked about my performance, because Mickey says, "She's gonna be fine," with a quick glance at me.

We've got over an hour before our flight, so after we clear the TSA checkpoint we spend a bit more time in the Diamond Club. Again I prepare myself for a reprimand…but Mickey keeps to himself, typing information into his laptop. He excuses himself quite thoroughly, apologizing for being such poor company, "…but I always make my best entries when the memories are all fresh, you know?"

After I assure him it's okay he adds, "You know, they have a wireless signal in here and Make-A-Difference has all its blank forms on our FTP server, why don't you download a site assessment form and take a crack at it?"

I'm happy to have something to do and even happier it's work related. If I can generate a useful site report, perhaps it'll help my case—the case my impatient mouth keeps trying to torpedo at every opportunity. I download the form and start to examine it. There are lots of procedural or specialized questions I'm not sure about ("Please enter an approximate percentile for a value alignment in each of the following areas," whaaaaat??) so I make note to ask Mickey about these later.

In the meantime, I focus on basic descriptions. I return again and again to the sense of isolation among the wage workers, the feeling that they were out on the factory floor with only the vaguest sense of why they were there. No one expressed a meaningful purpose for their work.

"We're here to make flooring, so make flooring and shut up!" seems a perfectly reasonable summation of their position. That and *kaizens*. "We make our kaizens!" "Four kaizens a year!" Why? To avoid trouble and to earn a whopping half day of pay (and oh, my, an entire *half day*, such extravagance for helping the company grow.)

"Most popular answer: We don't know!" I type. "Why kaizens? We don't know. Do they work? We don't know. How do you communicate with management? We don't know. Does management hope you'll communicate with them? We don't think so. Has quality improved? We don't know."

In my summary regarding the wage workers I type, "They don't know why they do the things they do, they don't know if the things they do are helping, they don't know for sure whether help is needed. They avoid sharing honest feedback with one another and feel discouraged from communicating with management. They feel isolated from their processes and the purpose of their own livelihoods."

In the section which seems set aside for the meeting with Patricia, I find myself typing remarkably similar things. "Doesn't have clear rationale for the one-kaizen-per-quarter practice. Doesn't know whether supervisors are collecting input from workers. No mechanism for checking. No formal procedures for assessing worker perceptions. Unclear regarding efficacy of quality practices."

The more I write, the more sorry I feel for these people. It's one thing to be lost at sea, but it's worse to have no idea there's any such thing as dry land.

When Mickey touches my arm, I'm startled; I've been so deep in my own thoughts, I've lost any sense of my surroundings, including time. Our flight is boarding.

WHEN WE'RE ONCE AGAIN comfortably airborne and winging toward Kansas City, I decide to take the bull by the horns. "I wanted to apologize for back there," I say quietly to Mickey. "My mouth sometimes pops open a little faster than my brain can stop it. I think maybe I was in a leadership position alongside a bunch of factory-floor roughnecks for so many years that I've got some pretty stone-aged ideas about tact and diplomacy. I'll do better, I promise."

Mickey wears a gentle smile, but he seems to take a lot of time weighing his response. I suppose I had been hoping for a quick, "Oh, I understand Joanne, no worries, you're doing great!" Apparently things are going to be a little more involved than that.

He begins slowly, carefully: "I appreciate you saying that. I was actually weighing how to broach this subject because, you know—our relationship on this trip is a little bit weird, isn't it? I think it's simple to think of me as running the show, but if you end up joining us permanently it won't be as though I'm your supervisor or anything. I had sort of tentatively arrived at something like the way cops work, two detectives might be peers, but one is always identified as Lead Investigator on any given case, you know?"

I nod, "Works for me. And Mickey?" The urgency in my tone gets his attention, and I'm glad, because I need this point to be heard. "Don't soft talk me, okay? I'm here to learn and part of that is always going to involve criticism, it's a *good* thing, even if the comments themselves might sting a little, you know? I know you don't hate me or anything, all right?"

He chuckles, "Good. I appreciate that…and for the record, over here in consultant-land we never say 'criticism,' since most people think any criticism is bad criticism. We prefer 'corrective feedback.' " He grins, and then pauses, re-summoning his thoughts.

"Here's the thing," he begins, "I'm hearing you apologize for speaking out of turn, or for your tone, or maybe for both, and those things aren't unimportant. We need one voice at a time and we need them to be respectful voices…but what I've been wrestling with, the reason I've waited until now to speak about it, is that I'm thinking these things you're apologizing for, they're only symptoms. They're not the real problem."

I'm nodding, but I'm concerned. I understand the concept, but I'm not clear about what he might think my "problem" is. He gets there pretty damned fast: "I'm trying to figure out how we, you and I and Doc if need be, can move you away from responding to other people's mistakes with anger."

I've been nodding along, encouraging him to speak whatever hard truth has been lurking, but now the nodding stops. Anger? Me? I'm startled by this claim, but I give it its due and hold it up as a kind of filter over my behavior as I replay the last few hours. Yes, okay, I can see how he might arrive at this conclusion. Harsh tone. Impatience. But he's overshot the mark a bit, and I need to reassure him. "I can see how I might have come off that way, but I think what you're perceiving as—"

He holds up a hand, stopping me, "You asked for my feedback, and I know this goes a little deeper, but I think it's going to prove terribly important. Answer me as honestly as you can, please, true or false: Patricia made you angry?"

Okay, there it is, and again, I get why he's saying this, but I feel the strong urge to be very clear about why I think he's mistaken.

"Anyone who shows disregard for the basic duties of his or her position is a disappointment for sure. When that disregard has a measurable impact on the lives of other people, I tend to see it as hovering somewhere between disrespect and arrogance, and yes, I don't care for it when an arrogant and disrespectful person demonstrates not only a lack of any interest in reflection, but a lack of any interest in considering whether such a thing as 'reflection' might even exist in the world."

Mickey is watching me closely, but that's fine—I'm comfortable of my ground here. "And you think that's Patricia?"

I snort and do a Patricia imitation: "I don't know what my workers think, that's someone else's job. I don't know if that job is happening, which, you know, also means I don't *care* if that job is happening. The things we tried for making life better around here don't seem to be working, but there's no way to know. There's no point asking the workers what they think—they might work themselves into a spirit of false optimism, thinking that we actually care.

"I mean, come on," I continue, "I'm sure she's a perfectly swell human being and she would never torture kittens or burn down the library or whatever, but seriously, she's not much more than ballast."

Mickey is nodding. He says, "What if I told you I agree with ninety percent of what you're saying, and you're still one hundred percent wrong?"

Wrong? Why is he picking a fight? There's not a single mistake in anything I've said, but I struggle for a light tone, "I'd say one of us is confused about how percentages work."

He grins, and nods, "Fair enough, but here: I think your point-by-point assessment of where Patricia needs to improve is bang on-the-money accurate, you know? But you're still wrong to get worked up as though these things are her fault."

My brow furrows and I know I look incredulous. "They're *not* her fault, did I somehow not see the gun being held to her head, and the big gangster saying 'don't move and don't you dare care about your people?' I mean, come on Mickey, there is such a thing as personal responsibility, self-accountability, you know?"

I know my voice has risen a little bit, and there are other passengers around us, and I remind myself to slow down and take it easy, but this is important, this matters to me.

I continue, "Look, I have plenty of forgiveness in me, I don't mind mistakes, but I'm someone who places a high value on owning what you do, taking responsibility for it, you know, and she's not doing that. She's just shrugging her shoulders and saying, 'I don't know' and 'It's not my job' and that's…I'm sorry, but that's just cowardice, you know?"

Mickey is nodding, but I can tell he's half pacifying me, and that makes me all the more frustrated. Are we seriously unable to agree on something as basic as personal responsibility? But his next question surprises me: "Do you think she wakes up in the morning and says, 'My plan for today is to avoid my responsibilities and treat my workers with disrespect?' "

I'm shaking my head, irked at the obviousness of the question. "Of course she doesn't, but that doesn't mean—"

"Or!" he says, again lifting a hand to stop me. "Or does she wake up and say, 'Today I'll do my best even though I don't really understand what's happening or what I can do to make things better.' "

I roll my eyes. "That's your thing? Poor Patricia, she's doing her best, it's not her fault, she doesn't know any better?"

He sits back a bit, "Yes. That's exactly my thing. She doesn't know any better, and that's what we're there for, to help her see where she's been missing opportunities."

He leans in and his voice is low but intense, "That's our job, Joanne. That's why we exist. There are people who don't know any better, and we *help* them know better, so they can *do* better. We help people and organizations make the leap from unconscious incompetence to conscious competence."

He sits back and says, "We can't be mad at them for needing us, that's the same as owning a gas station and being mad at someone for coming in with a low tank."

Everything he says makes sense. It's absolutely bulletproof. Yet for some reason, I can't let go of this. I feel as though there's some unacknowledged truth or hidden wrinkle in his argument, it's too simple…and then I realize what it is.

"I guess," I say slowly, "but I'm skeptical about whether these are people who really *want* to learn. I mean, Patricia didn't call us, you know? She has nothing to do with us being there, so it's not quite logical to say she came to the gas station, you know? I mean, seriously, Mickey…"

I realize I'm just short of pleading with him; it has somehow become terribly important to me that I'm not just some impatient bitch who came in off the street in a sweep of judgmental accusations. "You and I have both been around enough to know there are plenty of people who seek improvement, yes, but there are also *lots* of people who just wanna cash a check and go home.

"They're on the factory floor, they're behind management desks, they're even in the executive suites, and they just don't give a damn. And no charts of promises or catch phrases are going to make them give a damn, and if the existence of those people somehow makes *me* a mean person for noticing them, well, you know, I guess I'm guilty. Put the cuffs on me."

I slump dejectedly into my seat, feeling as though I've failed in some way I can't quite figure out yet. I know I'm right, my entire life experience tells me I'm right, but I still feel as though there's something I'm missing, either in Mickey's argument or my own.

I'm suddenly aware he's been responding for the last few seconds, and I tune in to hear: "…not just a couple of studies but *years* of data which show that pretty much everyone, given the choice between doing something well and doing it poorly, will choose to do it well, especially when no dramatic change in their lives is required. Improvement free of sacrifice is a pretty easy sell."

I'm still feeling gloomy. "I dunno Mickey. It oughta be true, I'll give you that, but people oughta wear safety belts, you know? The newspapers are full of people who could have done something better and with no sacrifice—but they don't."

"They didn't have us to teach them."

I turn my head to see his confident smile. "I wanna believe you Mickey. I just…it's hard to ignore what looks like a whole pile of evidence to the contrary."

He nods. "I'll make a deal with you," he says.

"Mmm?"

He leans in a fraction, "You keep your eyes and your ears wide open at tomorrow's site. At the end of the day, if you still believe everything you said here, I'll draft my letter of resignation on the spot and you can sign it as a witness."

I wave a hand at him. Meaninglessly high stakes. "I won't be able to say it even if I do still believe it; how will you be able to afford all your nice suits?"

He cracks a smile and then says, "Fair enough. How about dinner then? The expense-account credit card stays in my wallet, and it's either you or me footing the bill. Is it a bet?" He extends his hand.

I smile wearily, tired of arguing, tired of even thinking. I shake his hand quickly and say, "It's a bet." Then I close my eyes for a quick nap. My last thought before drifting off is of how small my hand felt in his.

MICKEY NUDGES ME AWAKE just before we land and I can't seem to shake off the grogginess. Days that start at 4:30 and include two different flights, a high-energy site visit and a confusing argument don't leave much energy for anything else. We trudge from our gate, find our ground transport and travel in near silence to the hotel. Mickey checks us in, and I wonder briefly what the desk girl might think of us until I see him coming back to me, holding out my key card, which I take blindly.

"You wanna grab a bite?" he asks.

I shake my head with a small smile. Part of me knows it's probably not smart to decline the invitation; Day One of my probation hasn't gone so well and it wouldn't hurt to sit in a nice restaurant and listen to Mickey tell stories and smile

charmingly at him. It wouldn't even have to be an act…but I can't; I'm wiped out.

"Sorry," I say. "I'm gonna need some practice with these long days. Right now I'm feeling too old and tired to do anything but fall into bed."

He nods and grins, "Tired maybe, but never old. I'll meet you down here in the morning, okay, let's say eight o'clock?"

I'm grateful for how easy he's made it. "Thanks, Mickey. "

I move toward the elevators, his last compliment about my not being old ringing pleasantly in my ears, so much so that when I reach the shiny doors I glance back to see if he's still there…but he's long gone. Probably for the best.

Into the elevator, push the button for eleven, sag against the back wall as it carries me, whisper silent, to my floor and the doors ping open. I glance around for a second, figure which way my room lies, make only one mistake and then find it, tucked at the end of a hall. I go in and I can actually feel myself wishing I had the energy to be impressed. Our family vacations haven't been built around five-star budgets, so I'm unaccustomed to such first-class accommodations.

Like the car and the driver and the Diamond Club and the seats on the plane, this too feels decadently nice, almost like a trick…but I'm literally empty. If there were a chandelier made of diamonds I probably wouldn't even look at it except to sigh that it was making the room too bright. I need sleep—starting about two hours ago, but I'll settle for right now.

I KICK OFF MY SHOES and I'm contemplating the fall into the bed the way a cliff diver contemplates the water below, and somehow the notion of bed and sleep brings an image of home and I realize with a guilty start I haven't even checked in once today. That never happens.

I slide into one of the soft chairs by the window, and pull out my cell phone, thumbing the button for Home. Keith picks up on the second ring, "Joanne??"

"Hey baby.

"Are you okay? What's happening?"

I'm confused. What does he mean? "I'm fine, what do you mean?"

"I've been going a little crazy here, you said you'd call!"

I feel a tiny flame of irritation kindle, but I suppress it. "Well, I'm calling."

"No, I mean—" and he pauses and I know exactly what he looks like in this moment, I've seen it a hundred times; he's taking a deep breath and closing his eyes for a second and letting go of something he's decided isn't worth a fight. Yet this habit, this good and strong sign of compassion, which ought to make me smile with admiration and love, fans that little flame of irritation. As though *I've* done anything *he* would be correct to fight about.

He continues, "It's okay. You're right. You're calling now, So?"

Part of me is still looking for the fight he thought he might pick. If I were smarter, I might realize I had been geared up for dire combat with Mickey, and he had ju-jitsued me neatly to the side, leaving me with all this unused adrenaline, but there's no outlet here.

No outlet and no good reason, either. Still, I can't quite muster wifely, motherly cheerfulness. I can't do a five-minute presentation on my day. Ask me a question, I'll answer it. Don't make me dance. I give back exactly what I've gotten, "So?

The confusion in his voice makes me feel terrible. I'm being snippy to him for no good reason, and he's taking it like the champ *I* ought to be. "So, you know, how *was* it, how was your flight, how was the company you visited, how do you like this guy, you know—how was it?"

I sigh. They're all reasonable questions, they're the questions I'd ask, and I can feel him trying so hard to give me the enthusiasm and support he knows he should have given me all weekend. He's trying to fix it. My trouble is the weekend was when I needed it, and right now I need to sleep. "It was…okay."

His ears are sharp, "You don't sound so good, Jo."

Some part of me is welling up, desperate to say, "I'm not good I had a bad first day and I'm confused about this job and I'm not sure it's for me but what else can we do, and I miss my family and I'm hungry and I'm exhausted!" and then burst into tears…

…but instead I grab instinctively for the 'Mom's Fine' lever, and I pull, saying simply, "I'll be all right, I'm just totally worn out. We did Atlanta, and that was pretty tiring, then we flew to Kansas City and I'm in the hotel room now about to die, you know?"

There's a pause and then he says, "I guess so."

A silence of several seconds yawns between us and I realize he's lost interest in trying to drag details out of me. I can't blame him, but it still feels childish to me, like he's pouting.

I've been the mommy for fifteen years, could someone maybe take care of *me* for a minute while I'm out here paying our bills? What the hell am I even thinking, so tired, too tired to even be properly nice to the man I love, need rest, what are we even talking about, oh yeah, my turn, ask the mommy question: "How're things there." Not even enough energy to give voice to the question mark that oughta be there.

"Okay."

Ah. Giving me a dose of my own medicine, punishing me, *scolding* me even, Here lady, see how you like it, fine, guess I need to follow up, "Is that a good okay or a bad okay?"

"Well…we had a bit of bad news from Jessica's algebra teacher."

I'm instantly more alert. "What do you mean, what kind of bad news, this is Ms. Watson, right?"

"Watson, yes, and apparently Jessica has flunked her last two tests and it's suddenly an open question whether she's going to be able to pass the semester or not."

Gosh! I knew she had been struggling, but nothing quite this bad. "What does it mean, 'apparently,' is there some question of what the final grade is going to be or—"

"Good heavens, Joanne, slow down, I'm telling you, okay? I mean, I'm sorry to snap, but I'd love it if for the five minutes you decide to give us we could actually *talk* instead of you barking questions at me. I said 'apparently' because I haven't actually seen the tests myself, but we got a note home from Ms. Watson and she says the last two tests are F's and so, you know, we need to address that."

I'm blinking from Keith's mini-eruption and somewhat on autopilot. "Okay, well, damn, okay, so, we need to set up a meeting, a conference with Ms. Watson, her number is on the fridge with the kids' schedules, on the telephone side, right where—"

"It's done, we're meeting Friday morning at nine, are you going to be able to be there?"

"I don't know," pops out without thinking.

Brief silence. "Okay," comes Keith's calm voice. "Well, you know, when you find out just lemme know, the meeting has to happen whether you can be there or not, but obviously we'd rather you were there…"

"We?" Suddenly "we" means Keith and Ms. Watson instead of Keith and me. I'm confused about work and now my kid's in trouble and my husband doesn't mean me when he says "we" anymore. Fix it Jo.

"Yeah, absolutely, I'll—I'm sure Doc can let me free for that, and Keith, listen—I'm sorry I'm so tired, I know I snapped, it's just been a…really hard day, I didn't do so well and I'm so tired I can't think and I probably shouldn't have even called in this mood but I wanted to—"

"Shouldn't have called?" Keith's voice is incredulous. "Are you serious, baby I woulda called the cops if you hadn't, you promised to call when you landed in *Atlanta,* you know? I mean I've been watching the news going 'Okay, well, no plane crashes, I guess she's okay,' I've never been so relieved to see your number on caller ID, you know?"

Oh no. He's right. I forgot to call, I said I would…I just caught up in the day. Still, this Jewish Mother act about plane crashes is pretty lame. "You can always go online and check flight status, you know," pops out.

Keith's voice drops five degrees. "Yeah, well they're weird about those things, they tend to want a flight number or a flight time or some kind of, you know, valid information, none of which you left with us, but yeah, absolutely, from now on I'll expect updates about my wife from the internet instead of from her own mouth, she's very busy, you know."

My eyes fill up, not the least because I have a sick feeling he's right to be mad. "That's not fair," I quaver.

I hear another big sigh, "You're right, it probably isn't. Look, we're both tired. I'm sorry I snapped, I bet you are too, let's say mutual complete take-backs and let's both get a good night's sleep and try again when we're not both stressed, maybe tomorrow morning, before breakfast? Whaddaya say?"

I take a deep breath of my own. He's right. "Okay."

"Joanne?"

Yeah?"

"I really am sorry. I do love you. You know?"

Another deep breath. Not so bad. He's feeling sweet enough to remember our little 'you know' ritual. I speak softly, "I do. And I love you too. You know?"

"I do."

I smile in the shadows of the room. I do. Just like our wedding day. "Okay baby. Good night."

"Night, Jo."

I spend ninety seconds in a blur of confused regret thinking dully that I haven't done much right today, peeling off clothes before I fall into the bed.

If I dream, I won't remember it in the morning.

THE NEXT MORNING, I'm short of time but I shoot Keith a quick text message: "Sorry I was a bitch last night, the light of day makes everything better, wish I was seeing it with you." I send it and just a few moments later a reply comes—a smiley face with simply "me 2, luv u so."

It's amazing what a few text characters can do for one's outlook.

In our car a short time later, Mickey is busy explaining the mission. Today's firm, Precision Parts, manufactures key parts which are used in private jet air-conditioning systems. I assume this is a small, niche-based operation...but I'm startled to hear that while it is niche based, it's nothing like small, employing over twelve hundred people at the site we're visiting.

"Make-A-Difference has been working with them for almost two years," Mickey tells me. "They brought us in because production quality had been declining over the prior year, lots of returns, lots of complaints, business was falling off...and they were positioned to win a very nice contract from a large client, but the management team in place was concerned that if things didn't change right away, they'd lose the business as quickly as they had gained it...

"They knew if they managed to lose a client of that size, their first major client ever, they'd take a public-relations hit that would never fully go away. They needed help and they needed it fast."

"And did you help?"

Mickey smiles, "We're almost there. Let's do our visit, and then you tell me."

Well…it becomes immediately clear Mickey knew he was playing with a stacked deck when he made his dinner wager. Precision Parts is, quite simply, one of the happiest, most smoothly-run businesses I've ever seen. I have to smile at the way the overall feel of the place seems to resonate strongly with their name: Every aspect of the business feels precisely machined to work in perfect harmony with all the other parts.

Structurally, the day isn't that different from the time we spent at Stone Mountain Flooring. We meet with a management committee, then with wage workers, and then we conclude with speaking to the plant manager. But that's where any similarity stops.

It's no surprise the first meeting, with the management subcommittee, feels different—after all, Make-A-Difference has established a presence here. There's a history among these people, and everyone is clearly happy with the new direction. There's an easy rapport and the kind of verbal shorthand which develops between long-time collaborators who trust one another.

Mickey inspires a certain respect right out of the box for any presentation— confident, handsome, passionate, charming—but among these folks there's another layer visible, the sense of knowing he's welcome and he belongs. It's very pleasant to witness, but again, not wholly startling.

"Startling" announces itself in our meetings with the workers. Again, they all seem to know Mickey, plenty of handshaking and small talk before the meetings actually begin…and then what a difference. Where Stone Mountain had been all awkward silences and nervous laughter, this was a deeply informed and obviously-valued interchange.

Every worker we spoke to knew the status of various quality improvements— how long since implementation, reasons for the efforts, expected outcomes, actual outcomes. At one point, one worker cites a particularly arcane statistic, and another says, admiringly, "Geez, is there anything about that deal you *don't* know?" and the first responds, "There'd better not be, it was my idea!"

Again and again, I see evidence of this sense of ownership, of empowerment and mutual caring. They can all, to a person, cite the number of complaints they've had this quarter (one) versus this time last year (seventeen), and the one complaint is clearly a sore spot. Somewhere, somehow, a small percentage of one type of part is leaving the line with a particular threading that's misaligned for the part it's meant to fit.

"I'll tell you," says one older worker, "It's driving me insane. We've been over that line with everything but an x-ray machine. But we've got two extra guys spot-checking that one part, and if any more kick out this week, we're coming in this weekend, and will break the whole line down to components if we have to, and then we'll re-assemble and recalibrate the whole mess."

"You'll come in on a weekend because of one complaint?" I ask, my eyebrows up somewhere around Canada.

The worker looks at me, his face grim. "Ma'am, any part that makes it out those doors, as far as I'm concerned, they can put my picture and phone number on it, and everyone else in here too. We're promising you it's the right part. If it's not, we have to make it right." There are murmurs of agreement.

The surprises don't stop there. We're just finishing up with the last batch of workers when the plant manager shows up for his interview. Mickey rises to move with him to his office, but he waves us back into place and the workers too, and he says, "How about you ask me your questions, and then we find out what answers these folks *expect* me to give? Half-hour bonus time for every correct answer."

There's warm laughter and the sound of chairs scraping into place, and what might have been a quiet one-on-one turns into a noisy and friendly ad-hoc perception survey. Again and again I'm impressed with the fact everyone involved is obviously on the same page. There's a familiarity with all processes and procedures, and frankly, if you had asked me to pick which one of these was the manager, the necktie would have been my only clue.

Once we've said our goodbyes, we pause outside to put on our sunglasses and Mickey grins at me. "I know you were about to ask, so I'll save you some time—tell the driver to take us to Ellwood's Barbeque. You like barbeque, Joanne?"

I smile back at him, "Well it definitely goes good with crow, so I'll try to eat plenty of both."

Mickey's laugh is so loud the driver inside the sedan turns to look, his eyes wide.

A BIG ROUND TABLE, A checked tablecloth which may never recover. Two huge platters of ribs, bones, and the remains of what began as two huge piles of shredded barbeque. A near-empty pitcher of beer. Cole slaw and hush puppies here and there. Dozens of smeared paper napkins. And two very satisfied consultants.

"Joanne," Mickey announces, working to get the last piece of meat off one of the bones. "I have to say it. You know how to lose gracefully."

I throw one of the crumpled napkins at him. "Know how to walk into a con-job, you mean. I must have already been asleep when I said yes to that bet, knowing these people were already your customers. For all I knew, you'd had all the problem employees replaced with robots months ago."

He glances up, "Zat anything like what you really think?"

I take a deep breath, close my eyes, smile, and re-open them. "I was clearly mistaken about the bad apples numbering equally with the good. I am ready to receive your wisdom on this subject. Teach me, O Yoda."

He smiles, "Very well, young Jedi. First tell me this: What differences did you notice between the two plants?"

I shake my head, smiling, "Why don't you ask me what differences I notice between summer and winter? It was, you know, *everything.* The Precision Parts' wage workers knew their own quality metrics better than Stone Mountain's *managers.*

"Precision's workers couldn't wait to tell you about the ways their ideas had been implemented; Stone Mountain's workers seemed like they would fall down from amazement if anyone ever even *heard* one of their ideas. Precision just, you know, from the moment you walked in, *felt* better."

Mickey's eyes are twinkling, "You know what we call that? That feeling you get from an especially well-run business the moment you walk in?"

"What?"

"Quality Culture."

I roll my eyes. "All right all ready, Mickey, I already said you were right and I was wrong, exactly how many ways do you need me to go belly up?"

He pretends to mull the question for a second before saying, "I'll let you know if you ever get to where it's one too many."

I stare at him, smiling slightly, long past what his little joke warrants. He begins to feel uncomfortable, "What are you looking at?" I keep smiling, saying nothing, and he looks around, chuckling nervously. I keep staring and letting my smile grow and he gets louder, "*What??*"

I finally laugh out loud at the way the big blob of sauce keeps moving around at the corner of his mouth, and then I take pity on him and mime wiping my own mouth: "You've gotta, there's a little bit, right there," and he rolls his eyes at my laughing and then dabs at himself but he misses, and my laughter grows.

He looks even more confused; I shake my head and point again, he tries again, missing again, *such* a boy, I finally have no choice but to reach across with my own napkin and fix things with an instinctive wrist flip born of having done the same move to two different kids hundreds of times.

"Thanks," he smiles, and I smile back and it's a very warm moment and did I really just reach across and touch this man's face, but he's already sipping his beer and it's probably only weird to me so don't worry about it Joanne, worry about what, *exactly*…I shake my head to clear it and I say, "Okay, so, Obi Wan, what does Make-A-Difference do to bring this change about?"

He is nodding, happy to get down to specifics. "In the case of Precision Parts, we determined the most important shift would be to move them from transactional leadership to transformational leadership."

I pretend to call for the check, saying, "Dictionary, table nine?"

He laughs, "It's not that complicated. Transactional leadership is based on the if-then, incentive-reward concept—a kind of internal economy of cause and effect. Do this, and this happens. Do this thing properly, get paid; do it improperly, get punished…

"There are ongoing transactions between the workers and managers, exchanges…and all of these exchanges are designed to help motivate compliance with the company's values. "I'll pay you well for working hard; because that will motivate you to work hard and that kind of extra effort is something we really value around here."

I nod, "That makes sense."

Mickey shakes his head, leaning in, "Except it doesn't. It has logic, sure, but it doesn't really guarantee anything except the transaction itself and sometimes not even that. Remember, nothing is ever transacted without at least two willing parties. And once it's based entirely upon extrinsic rewards or penalties, you get into some very weird calculations.

"Workers are asking, 'What's the *least* I can do and still get the bonus?' And why shouldn't they? The company is treating them, directly and overtly, as people for whom paychecks are the most valuable aspect of their work life. If you tell me I'm only here for a paycheck, I'm not likely to care much past that check, you know?"

I get it. "So how is transformational leadership different?"

Mickey takes another swallow of beer. "Transformational leadership is what happens when the workers themselves are part of creating that list of things the company values, so the company's values are a direct reflection of the values claimed by the workers themselves. At that point, everyone is working toward the same objective, and you don't have to worry about achieving 'compliance.' People don't have to be led to comply with their own values; they can be counted upon to act in service of those values.

"In the presence of transformational leadership, the wage workers are partners, self-motivated and self-accountable to fulfill their part of the mission. Why? Because they understand it, they've helped to identify it, and they know how it affects them. Their level of involvement leads to them seeing the big picture—seeing it and knowing where they fit into it."

"Like those guys being willing to come in on the weekend to re-tool the assembly line."

LEADERSHIP LESSON 3

Transactional leaders hold people accountable for compliance; Transformational leaders inspire people to be self-accountable or self-motivated.

He nods, "Exactly."

I'm trying to make sure I follow this. "So, leaders who are transformational, they're the ones who tend to—"

He is shaking his head, cutting me off, "No, no, see, here's the thing. In a culture of transformational leadership, *every* worker is a leader—by example, by investment of self, by dedication to all the ways in which they personally can make the business more welcoming and more successful. The entire organization becomes an interdependent system of all employees working to achieve optimum levels of performance."

"Careful, Mickey," I warn with a smile, "You're sounding a little like Doc."

He grins back, "Different accent I think."

I'm still remembering our time with Precision Parts' workers. "You know, I had the thought in that last meeting, that except for the necktie it was tough to know who the manager was."

Mickey pointed, "There. Yes. Perfect."

"But how does it happen? I mean, how does it begin?"

Mickey's face is frank, sharing a tough truth, "It's not easy. But the first and most important step is to create a publicly-acknowledged community made up of *all* employees—and this community will work to draft some working understanding of the community's values, and the community will work together to resolve its differences."

"This sounds a little like company-as-town-hall-meeting," I muse. "The town-hall-meeting model says, 'Hey, citizens, guess who's the government, *you* are. The representatives you elect and send to Washington are just that, representatives of *your* wishes, but *you're* the government. If you just sit around waiting for the government to give you something, you're really just sitting around waiting on yourself.' "

Mickey is nodding enthusiastically, "Very good Joanne. That's exactly right. When everyone feels like an owner, they are self-motivated to move forward, to care, actively, about their community. Whereas when workers are isolated, like at Stone Mountain, they're not working to succeed. They're only working to not fail. It reminds me of a kind of parable I heard a long time ago about transactional versus transformational leaders."

He leans forward, and continues, "Imagine you're walking through the forest. It's beautiful. It's an entire ecosystem, right, a world of its own. So many beautiful plants, ferns and vines and flowers and trees and stones and lichens and moss and it's *all* the forest, you see? Everything belongs. And when you notice this and appreciate it, you start to feel as though maybe you're a part of the forest too. You belong.

"Some managers, though, they can only manage through fear. They're like people who run up to you when you're enjoying this forest and shout, 'MAKE SURE YOU DON'T GET CAUGHT IN THE RAIN!!' And, you know, you hadn't even thought about rain…but now suddenly you're thinking about it. You're worried about it. You're no longer a part of the forest, it's separate from you, it's threatening and you're just looking for shelter, all because a transactional manager got you thinking about the threat of something bad happening.

"Meanwhile, in another part of the forest, transformational leaders are enjoying the forest together…and someone will say, "By the way, we have some umbrellas if anyone ever decides they need one…but it's up to you. After all, it's only rain. It's just something that happens in the forest, it's no big deal."

I'm smiling at this idea. "Sooo…the ideal transformational leader, if it started to rain, would volunteer to walk alongside you with his or her umbrella open enough for both of you."

Mickey spreads his hands as though encompassing such notions, "Exactly."

I try to think through the elements of the issue. "We're saying that any company which already values inclusion and community would have a nice head start."

Mickey's clearing himself a small space for a note pad and he says, "I'm glad you mentioned values again, they're the big thing."

"What do you mean?"

"Well," he says, patting his pockets for a pen and finding one, "You want to make sure you achieve alignment between the values of the company and the values of the employees who work there."

This has been bothering me about the topic of values. "But Mickey, look, what do you do when a company, you know, doesn't really *have* any values? Not all companies are saints, you know?"

He shakes his head, "No but even those companies in the very worst shape still have some values. For instance, I never saw a company that didn't want to make money. They would list "profit" as a value. But you're right that ideally we're not trying to make saints out of polluting greed-heads. You're correct that not every company is *interested* in transformational leadership."

"But you think they should be?" I ask.

Mickey spreads his arms wide, "You saw how today was. Why would anyone want to work anywhere that *didn't* feel like that? And the fact is, virtually every company *can* feel like that one, if they commit themselves to it."

"I don't know Mickey," I say slowly. "I mean, I do agree with you in principle, but when you start talking about some statement of values, I can't help picturing a year of some task force or subcommittee chasing its own tail trying to come up with some one-sheet of values with which no one will be able to argue against. They're all so vague and generic, you know? We value commitment, teamwork, customer service, blah blah blah."

Mickey shrugs, "Well, both teamwork and customer service actually aren't bad as values. You just need to break em down into observable behaviors which, taken in the aggregate, will *result* in teamwork.

"But Step One is to avoid the nightmare scenario you just described, the declaration of values by administration only. The path to success lies in letting this proclamation of values be co-created by the very people who are expected to live by them—the wage workers.

"And then," he continues, "An ongoing review process assesses whether the actual behaviors performed by the workers are lining up with the mutually-agreed-upon values. I'm not talking about, you know, just gripe sessions or failure lists; I'm talking about taking the time to express appreciation, to praise. And not quarterly, nor annually—why not weekly? Why not daily, in some miniature, fifteen-minute version?"

I think back to my own safety meetings, which were held daily. "That works," I murmur, almost to myself.

Mickey continues, "When you only do it every three months, it's too easy for it to turn into a discussion of failures or some checklist about whether certain objectives or outcome-goals were met, and if not then *why* not, and then setting the next set of objectives, and so on. That version is reactive to outcomes; you want a process that's proactive about how to improve things.

The thing is, you can't have an ongoing, proactive process if you're only meeting every three months. If those process reviews occur more frequently and everyone gets a say, a regular say that doesn't have to wait so long between opportunities, the long-term outcomes take care of themselves."

I think about our two different companies. "It's the difference between 'do four kaizens a year' and 'let's stay in touch about how everything is working.' "

Mickey bows his head slightly toward me. "That's right. Look here." He turns his notepad so I can see what he's been scribbling. "Here's a basic checklist. To be self-motivated at work, people need the following things."

He points to the first word, "Heard." He says, "People need to feel management listens and appreciates their input.

"Next on the list is 'Contribute.' Everyone needs to feel they are performing worthwhile tasks competently." I can certainly relate to this one—I would love to have felt more competent today.

Mickey is moving onward. He points at the next word, "Belong" and says, "Everyone wants to trust and appreciate the people they work with, and to feel the same trust and appreciation coming back toward them."

Now he points at "Learn/Grow" and says, "People generally want to feel themselves always getting better at doing worthwhile work." Again, I feel absolute agreement, just thinking about my own circumstances.

Next he points at "Choice" and says, "We all enjoy some sense of autonomy and personal control…"

"Recognition" leads him to say, "We all want to feel our contributions are known and appreciated."

Lastly comes the word "Empowered" and when he points, he chuckles, "I know this word isn't one of your favorites, Joanne, but it's critical. Everyone needs to feel they can accomplish their daily assignments, and that these duties will contribute in a measurable way to the system—the larger community."

Mickey sits back and leaves his pad in the center of the table for me to study. He then adds, "You remember the three C-words from when we met with Doc? Choice, Competence, and Community? Well, one or more of those words lives at the heart of every one of the principles I just laid out."

I'm looking carefully at this page, and I begin to realize the restaurant seems to have grown quiet. I look around—we're the only ones still here! All of the waiters and bus boys are eyeing us with something very close to resentment.

"There's a group of employees who value getting home on time," I whisper to Mickey. "I've enjoyed the lesson, but I think we have to ring the bell and end the school day."

LEADERSHIP LESSON 4

Employees feel included and self-motivated when they believe they: 1) are heard, 2) contribute, 3) belong, 4) achieve, 5) choose, 6) are appreciated, and 7) feel empowered.

I stand and reach into my purse for my credit card. I wave it slowly at him. "Next time you bet me, I demand full disclosure of all inside information." He laughs and I go to the register to pay.

WE'RE AT OUR HOTEL in just a few minutes more, and I feel almost the opposite of last night. I feel wide awake, energized. I look at my watch, it's almost eleven. Keith might be asleep… but too bad, I'm calling.

He picks up on the first ring, "Hey baby!" If he was sleeping, he's doing a great job hiding it.

I know he can hear the smile in my voice. "I worried it might be too late, but I just had to tell you, baby, I had the *best day* and I think I might actually be starting to get what this job is about, and I think I can learn to be good at it!"

Keith takes a long pause and then says, "I'm sorry, Joanne? Joanne *Cruse?*"

I laugh. I don't blame him for faking skepticism. I couldn't be more different from the woman he spoke to last night if I tried. I tell him everything that's happened over both days, and he asks lots of questions, and it feels the way it's supposed to feel, like I'm talking with my best friend into the night.

Or, I realize when I look at my clock, into the morning. We've been talking almost two hours. I remind him of our flight's arrival time tomorrow ("you mean today," he laughs) and that he needn't pick me up, that a car will be waiting.

"Tell that driver there's an extra buck in it for him if he hurries," Keith says in a horrible Humphrey Bogart impression. I tell him I can't wait, and then we say good night.

What a difference a day makes.

CHAPTER 6

"A prescription without diagnosis is malpractice."
—Socrates

I T'S MONDAY OF THE following week and I'm right back out again, traveling with Mickey to someplace called Missoula Ironworks.

I had barely walked in my front door from the Kansas City trip on Friday when my cell phone chirped. It was Mickey telling me we'd be heading out again at the beginning of the week to work on Missoula Ironwork's 'Performance Management,' whatever that means.

I'd also learned on Friday night of the same week we'd be attending a talk being given at the University by Dr. Pitz to a group of cancer survivors. This wouldn't technically count as work, but Mickey felt Doc would appreciate our presence, and I'm sure he's right.

I'd also been sure Keith would be less than thrilled about my getting home and then turning around and heading right back out again the very next business day. I'd been right, he hadn't been thrilled…but it had helped I'd only be gone the first two days of the week, and it had also helped I broke the news after serving my pork chops with the secret coating and the super-secret sauce.

We fly out at dawn Monday, so we can be at the ironworks when the workday begins. It's 8:30 and John Doyle, the plant's HR manager, greets us in the lobby of the admin building. As we walk, he explains the day's agenda: First, we'll meet with some key managers for about an hour. Next we'll meet with a group of supervisors, followed by teams of hourly employees. At day's end, we'll review our observations with the entire management team.

John finishes laying this out for us at just about the exact moment we arrive at the conference room, where Stan, the plant manager waits next to his VP of Operations, Tim.

Stan opens things up, "We're glad you could make it out here, folks. We're seeing some trends we don't like, and it's starting to feel as though maybe a little outside help wouldn't be a bad idea."

He begins pointing to several graphs on a chart: "Total tons of steel, down. Customer complaints, up. Injuries, up. We've already exceeded last year's injury count and we've still got more than a full quarter of the financial calendar left. We've got an incentive program in place, but it doesn't seem to be doing much for us."

Mickey lifts a hand in polite interruption, "Can you tell us more about that? How does the program work?"

Stan responds, "Each month, every employee can earn up to $400 by achieving results in three areas. If they don't get hurt, they get $200. If they work on a quality team for at least a one-hour meeting, they get another $100. And if there are no teamwork issues, they get the final $100. So they can earn a bonus of $400 a month."

"And their average base pay is…?"

John fields this one, "About $26 per hour, averaging $4000 per month."

Mickey's eyebrows climb a fraction, "So the financial bonus is significant."

Stan nods in agreement, "Yes, it is, but it's not getting us the results we want."

Mickey's jotting a note, and asks, "Outside of this incentive/reward program, how do you manage employee performance?"

Tim answers, "We complete annual evaluations on all employees."

Mickey nods as though he expected this, probing further, "Do you have any reward or recognition programs?"

Stan sounds confused and a little bit irked. "I've already covered that. Our incentive system provides plenty of rewards and recognition."

If Mickey notices his tone, you can't tell. He simply makes another note and says, "Okay."

There's a bit more chat about how things work here. When Mickey seems comfortable with the basic status quo he says, "That's terrific, Stan, thanks very much. I think we can go ahead and meet with your supervisors now."

I'm not sure whether anyone but me has noticed the subtle way in which Mickey seems to have taken the reins…or perhaps they notice and they're relieved. In any event, the managers quickly say their good-byes with reminders of the end-of-day meeting, and a moment later eleven supervisors make their way in.

After a round of introductions, Mickey asks, point blank, "What is it like to work here?"

After almost one full minute of silence Paul Schultz speaks up. He's the most senior in the room, with 33 years of working at Missoula Ironworks. "I guess we're not quite sure what you're asking. Working here is like working pretty much anywhere, I think—we provide a product, we want to provide it safely, and we want our employees satisfied."

I ask, "So how's that going?" Heads turn to look at me, and I simply wait for an answer. Of course I already *have* an answer, from our previous meeting, but I want to know what *they* know…or what they think they know.

Paul answers me in straightforward fashion. "We're in the black, our injury rate isn't too crazy, and our customers seem satisfied. We all still have jobs," he adds, looking around smiling and getting smiles in return.

Mickey asks, "What kind of performance metrics do you each see, and how often?"

The smiles fade. "What do you mean?" asks one.

"Well, what do you each do that gets measured?"

Another supervisor named Brian speaks, "I've only been here about five months, but it seems pretty much like any other decent plant, you know? You check product quality, make sure things are turning out right; we look after each other on the floor. Quality and safety, you know—hand-in-hand."

Mickey takes a brief moment to frame his response, clearly aware some portion of his question isn't getting through to them. "You're right, that sounds pretty much like how things work all over the world…but how do you know how well each of those areas are working?"

Another uncomfortable silence, and again it's Paul who rushes in to fill the void, "We'd know it if there was a problem. I'd get a call from my boss. And believe me," he adds, looking around again, "When you get that phone call, it doesn't end with anyone being confused."

Mickey joins in the chuckles and then asks, "How often do you meet with your boss?"

Paul replies, "Pretty often, whenever we need to."

Mickey asks, "Exactly how many times have you met with your direct supervisor in the last three months?"

A brief pause in which Paul seems to be considering, then, "We have met about…four times."

Mickey then asks, "Could you describe what these meetings look like?"

Paul cocks his head, adopting a confused appearance. It's very clear to me these folks have decided they don't like being interrogated. It feels a little bit like we're a couple of detectives interviewing smirking gang members who know when to say "yes sir" and "no sir" without ever really saying much of anything.

"What they look like?" Paul asks. "They look like a few guys sitting around a table."

More laughter and Mickey joins in, willing to take his time. "No, I meant, what's the structure of the meeting, does your boss do all the talking, is there a checklist or any kind of agenda or…?"

"Ohhhh!" Paul's face smiles with 'enlightenment.' "Yeah okay, well, three of these were the monthly staff meeting, you know what those are like I guess, and the only other time was when my manager called me into his office to discuss an employee issue, a discipline thing. Two of my workers were fighting in the parking lot and he got on my case for tolerating bad teamwork."

Mickey says, "Talk to me a little more about those staff meetings, you know, how long and what's covered, *etcetera*?"

Paul shrugs, "I dunno, about 30 to 40 minutes long. Another supervisor interrupts jokingly, "But they feel way longer." Laughter, and Paul continues, "We cover stuff like who got hurt, how many tons of steel we have to move out next month, maintenance schedules. You know. Regular stuff."

Mickey asks, "Does everyone else in the room go to the same kind of meeting?" Everyone nods, but again there's the sense of unnatural quiet, of seeming resistance and Mickey bending over backwards to keep them talking.

If it bothers Mickey, I sure can't tell. He moves right along, glancing at his notes. "And how do you all talk with your employees? Do you have monthly staff meetings with them as well?"

Paul shakes his head, "No, if there's a need to tell the employees something, we just call for an impromptu meeting."

"Same for all of you?"

Again, all heads nod. Then, Paul seems to feel the need to justify his last comment. "The thing is, you know, this isn't some huge company. There are only about 600 people here. If something needs to get communicated, it just happens. You know?"

I lean in, "May I ask you folks, how do you evaluate the ongoing work of your employees? Are there any feedback mechanisms in place, anything to motivate them?"

Dave, a supervisor from the components area of manufacturing, seems baffled by the question. "We do annual evals just like every other place in the world, is that...?" He trails off with an inquisitive expression.

I ask, "How engaged are the employees in that process?"

Dave's confusion seems to deepen, "Engaged? Whaddaya mean?"

"How do the employees participate in the evaluation process?"

Dave's incredulity at my apparent naiveté is almost palpable. "They 'participate' by listening as we go over the eval form and then they sign off on it."

I ask, "Do they have any choice to not sign it if they don't agree with it?"

Dave is now spreading his arms and looking around as though seeking help with this crazy woman who's wandered into his workplace. "Not sign?? What are you talking about? On what planet does that happen?"

I retort, "The planet where the eval session is the first they're hearing of any errors."

Mickey shoots me a warning look and Paul jumps back in. "Ma'am, when someone does something wrong, makes a mistake, we talk to them immediately and let them know on the spot. And then we report the incident in a note we place in a file so we can capture it in the end-of-the-year evaluation. That session will never be the first time they hear of it."

Dave is smirking at me as though I've been put in my place. I'm struggling to keep my face neutral and professional. Mickey steps in smoothly, "So that explains how you deal with mistakes, tell me about how good performance is rewarded."

"That's the incentive program," shrugs Paul. "They get their $400 a month for doing right and not screwing up."

The meeting lasts a bit longer but not much else is learned. Mickey has to pull every piece of information out of them with pliers. I can't tell whether they're resisting us in particular or whether it's simply a Montana thing—maybe no one around here says much unless it's compelled from them.

AT THE END OF THE HOUR, the plant manager, Stan, picks us up at the conference room and walks us down the hallway, out into the parking lot and across to the manufacturing building. There's a ready-room where we put on safety glasses and hard hats emblazoned with the word "VISITOR," and we're then led across the manufacturing floor to the other side of the building. I look around quickly, fascinated by my brief glimpses of the work in progress. Stan opens a blue metal door leading into a conference room.

It's like entering another world. Where the prior conference room had been all business, this one feels like a Frat house. The room is a mess, with newspapers and mostly-empty food containers all over. There's chalkboard with writings from multiple meetings, including a scrawled "BOBCATS RULE!!"

As the employees drift in the room one by one, I notice their long-sleeved blue work shirts with the company logo on the left side of their chest and their first names on the right. Stan introduces us and lets them know we are studying what it's like to work here. Then he says, "I'll leave you to  it!" and lets himself out. Is it my imagination, or does the room relax significantly when the door clicks shut behind him?

Mickey begins by telling them who we are and what our mission with Make-A-Difference is, and ending with, "Our purpose is to help Missoula Ironworks learn what it will take to become a higher performing steel plant."

Some of the workers begin to chuckle. It's clear to me they've been here before, with other consultants. One of them asks, "Okay, so lemme make sure I heard you, you're here to ask us what our plant needs to improve?"

Mickey grins, "In a way." He holds up his clipboard. "I have a set of seven questions I'd like to ask you. Please let me know how you feel about each on a scale of one to five, with one being poor and five being excellent. Just raise your hand for a 1, 2, 3, 4, or 5 to each question, and then we'll talk about it." He looks around and sees what I see: They're not jumping up and down with excitement, but they are listening.

Mickey begins, "Question One: Are your concerns or ideas for improving conditions here given any consideration? Remember, a one would mean never in a million years and a five would mean lots of serious conversations up and down the line."

I observe the faces of everyone in the room as they look around as if to check in with each other. They all write down a number. Mickey waits a minute more, walks over to the dry erase board and tries to wipe an area clean. When nothing happens, a large bear of a man hauls himself to his feet, lumbers to a file cabinet, picks up an unmarked spray bottle and hands it to Mickey.

Mickey thanks him and squirts what must be alcohol or some kind of solvent onto the board and the ancient ink forms dark rivulets, running down to be caught by his paper towels. "This stuff won't eat my fingers off, will it?" he asks and a couple of them smile.

When he's made a small clean area on the board he returns to his clipboard. "Okay, ideas for improvement considered, let's hear it. How many fives?"

There are none.

"How many fours?"

None.

"Threes?" One person raises his hand, and one of the employees in the back corner yells, "B.S. Sam, you complained about the vending machine and Watson listened because he had just lost a quarter!" Everyone laughs.

"How many twos?" About a third of the group raises a hand.

"How many ones?" Another third or so raise their hands. It's obvious almost a third of the folks in the room have checked out. They don't seem too interested in our questions.

Then Mickey asks, "Okay, one of you One's or Two's, tell me more, why do you think management earns such a low number?"

After a moment of no one answering, Mickey points to the big fellow who brought him the cleaner. "How about you? Why do you give em a low rating?"

The worker rolls his eyes slightly at being singled out but then speaks, "I'll tell you what my supervisor told me. He said, 'You know we call you guys 'hands' right?

We don't call you 'brains,' and there's a reason.' So, you know, I guess you could say I'm not real, um, *motivated*, you know, to go any further down that road."

Mickey pauses a beat. Even though he's got a pretty good poker face I can see this episode, recounted by the worker in an almost bored voice implying dozens more events just like it, clearly makes an impact. I imagine I can see him choose to set it aside and move on. He simply nods and says, "I certainly understand that," and then he flips a page on his clipboard.

On to Question Two: "How good to you feel about your contributions to the company?" All of the answers are elevated a notch from the answers to the first question; a couple 4's, some 3's, and a lot of 2's. It's still clear some of the 15 or so in the room were not voting. CAVE people, I thought—Citizens Against Virtually Everything. But not true among the ones actually participating. In one another and in their own efforts they seem to have found something to be for, rather than against.

The third question is more interesting. Mickey asks, "How strong is your sense of belonging?"

One employee asks, "Do you mean how much do I enjoy working with the guys around me?"

Tricia, the only woman in the room calls out, "That's me all right, just one of the guys!"

They all laugh. She's one of those deceptively attractive women with a tomboy exterior. She probably used to play football with these fellows, or with guys just like them, and now here she is at the ironworks, laughing and joking alongside them, comfortable in her skin and in the way her co-workers perceive her.

When the laughter dies down, Mickey answers the question. "Yes—the question is asking how much you feel like you belong here—one for not much, five for it's just like home."

The show of hands for this question indicates only high marks, 4's and 5's.

Interesting.

Mickey and I share a glance, and then he asks, "Why are these scores so much higher?"

Tricia jumps back in, "I answered the question like you were asking me do I think I belong with the other people in this room. I love working alongside these guys. They make the whole place survivable. If you are asking about how I enjoy working with the empty suits outside of this room, I wanna change my score to a one." Her comment is followed by a lot of head nodding.

Mickey tells her the question is open-ended for a reason, and her first instinct about the question is what he'd like to trust. Then he walks them through the final four questions: Do they feel a sense of learning and growing? Do they feel a sense of choice or personal control? Do they feel recognized? And do they feel empowered?

No one gives a score higher than 3 for any of these questions, and the few who *do* give 3's receive snickers and good-natured-abuse from the others in the room. Mickey takes the opportunity to discuss their answers a bit more fully.

Regarding learning and growing, the group reported they got such things from their activities outside of work. One of the workers stated he was now making more money selling on eBay than at his job. He had gone to community college to learn about e-marketing and it's paying off.

Another participant reported he was on the Board of Directors for a small not-for-profit charity group, and was helping in the development of its long-term strategic plan.

When it came to the discussion regarding whether they feel a sense of choice, Mickey suddenly finds himself cast in the role of lightning rod, drawing high-voltage answers from every corner of the room. A common thread is summed up in the comment, "They throw the rules and procedures in our face, always looking for something we do wrong, and then actually citing the exact number of the rule we broke."

When Mickey expresses curiosity about this, one of the workers retrieves a company manual from a drawer in the single desk in the corner. After flipping past a couple of crude and anatomically unlikely scribblings, he shows Mickey and the rest of us page after page of guidelines and rules, for everything from bathroom breaks to shoe color. Each rule is numbered and I can tell Mickey is stunned to see there are over four hundred of them.

"And they add more every year," the big fellow says. "If we do something they don't like and they *can't* find a rule covering it, they just add one."

"Yeah, heaven forbid they should ever actually, you know, just *talk* to us," grumbles another, and there's a low chorus of unhappy agreement.

The discussion of Question Six—the need to be recognized—revealed a surprising amount of personal disappointment. I expect workers with such a clear disconnect from management wouldn't particularly care about being recognized, but I'm wrong.

We hear story after story of things these workers did to make a difference for their company, all of them going utterly unrecognized. Apparently, not one of these workers had experienced even something as simple as a direct "thank you" from anyone in the management team over the last year.

I recall the story of walking in the forest, and I realize: Here we have a group of workers who have stopped walking altogether—they simply sit, huddling and shivering in the rain while their transactional leaders shriek at them about the penalty for not having the correct umbrella. No one in this room is especially self-motivated to do well at this place.

However, I think over all the questions and find reason for hope in their sense of interpersonal belonging. One employee had poured the molten steel into the wrong mold and thus made a defective product for over an hour. But before a supervisor noticed the error, his teammates took those bad parts and put the steel back into the molten buckets of steel for reheating and remolding. The team chose to skip their break that day to make up for the lost production. No one but the team knew of the mistake and it was to be forever their secret.

I realize this story really reflects two things—a sense of belonging, a sense of community among the workers involved…but also a resistance to slowing the production process in order to see what lessons an error might provide. Learning from mistakes doesn't happen here.

Mickey goes so far as to ask, "Why'd you keep it secret? Was maintaining your incentive bonuses a part of it?"

To the surprise of Mickey and me, there's a virtual chorus of "No's!" The most senior employee, Jack Baldwin states his denial the most plainly: "We work together to make things happen here without management drama. They're not gonna say anything when we do something right, they're gonna hammer us, at random, for stuff they say we did wrong even when we didn't, we usually get our bonus at the end of the month, or most of it anyway—I think we leave them alone and in exchange they leave us alone. Mostly."

Mickey wants to hear more on the topic of the incentives. He starts with the question, "You mentioned you get money for doing good work. Do you all get sufficient rewards for working here?"

Baldwin continues in his *ad hoc* spokesman role, "Yes."

Mickey asks, "How does the incentive process work?"

Jack waves a hand, as though the details are irrelevant. "We get four hundred dollars a month. There's a bunch of stuff about making enough product, and teamwork, and something about quality."

Mickey asks neutrally, "Do you have any idea of how they break it down? This many dollars for this, that many for that?"

The employees look around the room at each other for someone to answer this question. I see lots of small shrugs and headshakes. One worker says, "Listen, it really doesn't matter. We get four hundred dollars most months and once in a while it's reduced to three hundred or maybe two hundred and seventy five dollars when someone screws up. There really is nothing we can do about that. We figure, you know, we're gonna get *something* and lots of times it's four hundred bucks—but whatever it is, you know, it's good to have it right?"

Mickey double-checks, "But when it *is* less than four hundred, you never find out why?"

Tricia jumps in, "Not only do they not tell us, but we all kind of figured it was some kinda way to make us all like suspicious of each other? Like try and

find the bad guy? And you can tell em from us, that stuff won't fly down here, baby, not on *my* shift."

There's loud affirmation and a couple of high fives and I can't help but smile at the camaraderie I'm seeing, the community spirit. There's a lot wrong with what I'm seeing, but they certainly feel connected to one another.

In spite of this singular bright spot, the overall outcome of our time with these workers is very disappointing. There's no management-worker communication, no clarity, and the so-called incentive program is viewed as either an entitlement or a kind of management whip, a wedge to pit workers against each other. Not exactly a desirable work climate.

Still, we have a session to finish. Mickey shifts to the final area of inquiry: "Could you all tell me how company performance is motivated and managed?"

"Motivated, you say?" reacts one of the employees. "I don't think so." Laughs and giggles follow.

Then Mickey asks, "Well how do you get feedback about your performance?"

Mickey's questions strike a humorous chord with Russ, a heavy-set man with a long beard, glasses and a pony tail. He drawls, "If you call the annual assessment zinger 'performance feedback,' I guess you could say we all get feedback once a year."

"Zinger?"

Russ smiles wearily. "Once a year, a manager comes into this exact room to meet with us one-to-one. Holding our personnel folder in his hand like he's Moses with the tablets, you know? They hand us a one to two-page written summary of what they call our annual performance appraisal."

Mickey asks with a small smile, "And it's safe to assume you don't care for this process?"

"Bout the same as I care for a root canal."

Laughter rolls through the room, Mickey smiling with them, and then asking, "But isn't there anything good about it?"

"Sure," hoots Russ, "When it stops!"

Mickey looks around. "The rest of you are on the same page as Russ here? Has anyone *ever* gotten *anything* positive from this process?"

Tricia lashes out angrily, "They don't *bring* anything positive, how the hell are we supposed to *get* anything positive?!?"

The room falls silent, and she looks around, realizing she's spoken more loudly and angrily than she intended. She speaks again, her effort at control visible. "If they were fair, they might be good. If they said here's what you did right, here's what you need to work on, you know? But they don't do that."

"What do they do?" Mickey asks softly.

Jack answers flatly, "They come in and they say this was wrong, this was wrong, this was wrong, you screwed up this, this, this, and you know what? Number one, half of it is crap and number two, so what? We're human, you know?"

A chorus of agreement. Mickey says quietly, "I do know."

There's silence and things feel just about finished. Mickey asks, "Okay, anything else you all want to tell me, or ask me?"

There's a pause and then Tricia asks, "Why are you here?"

"To listen to what's going on and see if things could be better here at Missoula Ironworks."

Jack snorts, "Good luck. We've been hoping for that for years."

Mickey steps to him, extending a business card, "Our firm is called Make-A-Difference. Because we do. You can count on it."

The workers in the room look at each other…and then rise and, one by one, come to us to shake our hands and wish us well.

I am beginning to see how this work could become addictive.

When the last of the workers has filed out, Mickey and I meet Stan at the door. He tells us he won't be able to join us for lunch as originally planned because he was sorting out an information-systems problem. Actually, I am a bit relieved. It's been a long and troubling morning and I want to debrief with Mickey in private.

AFTER GETTING OUR FOOD, Mickey and I find a small table off by itself and sit. I look around and I murmur quietly, "My Heavens, Mickey. You know?"

"Yep," says Mickey, "This group has some real opportunities for improvement."

I watch him in amazement, chewing his food blithely, as if he'd seen nothing more troubling than a minor traffic jam. I do my best to start slowly, "I notice you worked pretty carefully to compare the impressions of the three groups, getting each to present its own views of where the company is."

"Exactly," Mickey replies, "Progress starts with listening, not speaking. A lot of consultants never learn that. They just come in yelling about what they're gonna do. I like to listen first.

"We know what the core principles of success are—so you gotta listen for 'em, see if they're already in place, or partially in place, or just AWOL. It's only at that point I can start to figure out our approach. There's no cookie cutter solution in this business. No good one, anyway."

"What were you specifically listening for this morning?"

Mickey waves his fork idly. It suddenly strikes me, he reminds me of a younger, more handsome Doc.

"Principles. Self-determinism. Self-motivation. Do the leaders and the system they've implemented lead to these conditions? If not, how much change is needed? This organization called us for help because they are not achieving certain desired results. Somewhere, they're missing the core principles. Guaranteed."

His confidence is so easy, so relaxed. I ask, "Is there some kind of special class for this? Can you just…teach them how to do this?"

He shakes his head, "You're still thinking cookie cutter. We need to figure out, how do our principles apply to *these* problems? And then we design, okay, maybe you could call it a class or a course, but it's custom-made and it's administered on-site."

I need to make sure I understand. "But our basic objective is still to help their leaders implement the prescriptions we design to get them toward self-motivation and everything, right?"

He smiles at me. " 'Self-Motivation and Everything,' that could be Make-A-Diff's motto." I blush a little and he laughs. "No, Joanne, you're totally right. And the interventions we design are going to move into every area of the business, from the factory floor right up to the boardroom. That's why the design and the implementation all take time and care."

I nod. "By the way Mickey, those questions—they seemed to pretty much cover everything from motivation to results to satisfaction and everything in between."

"Yup," says Mickey, making short work of the remainder of his lunch.

"Sooo…" I continue musingly, "You did it in seven questions. Why do so many other companies assess the same things with surveys of eighty or ninety questions?"

He grins over his plate, "I guess they get paid by the question. We'd rather get paid by the answer."

I lean back in my seat. "So what's the next step? How do we summarize all this for the managers' feedback meeting tomorrow? I assume we don't give them a piece of paper that say, 'You guys suck and your workers hate you.' "

Mickey looks at me appraisingly and I lift my hands. "Kidding! They don't suck, they're lost lambs, crying in the wilderness for someone to save them. So how do we tell them what they need?"

"Same thing I've been saying: Stick to the core principles," answers Mickey. "You know, repeat after me: Organizational performance peaks when employees are self-motivated and self-directed. Right?" I nod, smiling, and he continues, "So, we go to the foundation or source of self-motivation."

"The three C's?" I ask.

He points with his fork. "Gold star. Exactly. Each worker's sense of having Choices to build personal ownership, commitment and personal responsibility, each worker's sense of Community—a willingness to care interdependently for the overall contribution of the organization—and finally, each person's perception of Competence—the know-how to make it all happen, the confidence to contribute."

I ask, "Those workers we just interviewed seemed to have the Community part down pretty good."

Mickey gets a pained expression. "Not exactly. They've gotten tribal, and it's actually at the expense of the community. They've become their own breakaway Balkan nation down there, but true Community means the whole system. How the diverse parts of the organization work together as one system.

"It's true; the glue they feel with each other reflects community in their work unit or silo. But they don't feel connected with the many other work teams of this company, especially the management team. There is obviously a huge gap between the different work areas."

I ponder this aloud, "It's like when a family takes care of itself but doesn't want to be part of the neighborhood. Doesn't come to the block party or whatever." Mickey nods and I continue, "What did you think about the incentive-reward stuff?"

Mickey shakes his head in annoyance. "It's messed up. It's anti-

> **LEADERSHIP LESSON 5**
>
> **A community spirit extends beyond one's work team to the organizational system as a whole.**

Competence, anti-Community, and it's sure as hell anti-Choice. To them it's nothing but an entitlement interspersed with periodic bad luck."

"So that's one place where there's a serious gap between core principle and reality?"

"Absolutely. So!" He is wiping his mouth, done eating, "Tomorrow what I do is, I stick to three key areas of focus to increase perceptions of choice, competence, and community. First we have to address the absence of relevant communication with individuals and groups.

"Next we gotta move em off this incentive system; it's costing the company money but not motivating any of the desired behavior for which it was intended.

"Lastly, I will address the performance management system. They see performance management as an annual performance evaluation rather than a system of steps that can generate self-motivation.

"If this company can do good work on these three items, we'll move em a lot closer to optimized performance. Of course, this is only my thinking so far. We've got three more groups to meet. But if they're anything like the first one, then, yeah, this is the plan."

That afternoon we talk with three more groups of employees. Of the 600 employees who work here, we speak with 60 hourly employees in four groups of 15 for about 45 minutes each. While the people change meeting by meeting, the inputs do not. We hear story after story about not being heard, about feeling their ideas or suggestions do not count. A few employees say the same thing: "They see us as objects, like machines. Show up, repeat your task over and over, get it done. You are not being paid for your ideas; you're being paid to make our products."

The assessment Mickey provided over lunch has not changed. Each employee meeting just gives him more ammunition for our meeting with senior managers in the morning.

IN MY ROOM AT THE HOTEL, I plug my cell phone into its charger. I've just finished speaking to Keith and the kids, and everyone seems well. Keith sounds a little distracted, but I can't fault him for that—he's doing the work of both parents at once, and I can't seem to contemplate that fact without feeling a slight twinge of guilt.

The phone chirps again jarringly into the quiet of the room and I practically lunge for it, hoping it's Keith, hoping I can give him a little bit more moral support than in the previous call. I flip the phone open without even looking at the screen, "Hello?"

"Joanne?"

"Yes, who's this?"

"Whaddaya mean who's this, it's *Jeff!*"

"Jeff, oh my Heavens, how are you doing? It's been *forever!*"

"It's actually been ten days?"

Something isn't quite right. He sounds a little flat, distant—is he upset I didn't recognize his number from Caller I.D.? That'd be ridiculous, not like him at all. I realize I've paused in the midst of these thoughts, but he steps right in, "How are you?"

"Oh, Jeff, I'm fantastic, I've caught on with a consulting business, it's kind of a trial period but I'm learning *so* much, it's so exciting!"

"I'm glad someone's having some excitement."

Okay, something is definitely wrong. This is not like him at all. "Jeff, honey, what is it, what's wrong?"

"They're closing the plant."

I can't believe what I'm hearing. "They—what?"

"Yup," he confirms, sounding both matter-of-fact and bitter. "Not enough margin, and they acquired some down-and-out firm in Mexico. So now suddenly they've got more square footage and more labor, all at about a third of their current costs. So in twenty-nine days and counting, the machinery ships south of the border and we're all hunting for work."

I know exactly how he feels. The surprise kick in the teeth. I'm still feeling it. "Jeff, sweetie, I am so, so sorry. Is there any kind of severance?"

"Just like yours—one week of pay for every two years of service. So I get a whopping five weeks' worth. I'm updating my résumé as we speak."

"Jeff, I'm so sorry."

Jeff sounds a little embarrassed when he asks, "I don't suppose your new consultant friends need a quality expert on their team do they?"

Another stab of guilt, "I don't think so. I mean, I can ask, but…"

"No, never mind," he says hurriedly. "I shouldn't have even asked, you know, they brought in these counselors, to 'provide assistance with this difficult transition,' " The sarcasm in Jeff's voice is as thick as molasses. "And you know, these counselor, they're very upbeat, very glass-half-full, they say things like 'You know, word of mouth is perhaps the most effective marketing, although not the most efficient,' and I'm like 'what the hell am I supposed to even *do* with that nugget of wisdom??' But you know—I figured it couldn't hurt to ask."

I hate to hear him sounding so down. "Well, look, sweetie, I'll definitely put my ear to the ground and, you know, you have a *great* reputation, you're definitely going to land on your feet, you know?"

"Thanks hon. I appreciate the support, I can use all I can get right now. I'd better hang up and finish making these copies before someone kills power to the building or something."

I give a small laugh, "Good luck Jeff. Keep me posted."

"Will do." And he's gone.

As I lie back in bed, the fragility of our working lives hammers home with new force. It's almost as if *I* were the one who was just fired, I can feel it all over again—the nausea, the fear, the feeling that nothing makes sense. And I realize yes, I feel badly for my friend, but I'm also scared, for myself, for my family. I have to make this chance I've got with Make-A-Difference work.

I have to.

CHAPTER 7

*"The best kind of pride is that which compels people
to do their very best work, even if no one is watching."*
—Unknown

WAKE UP THE NEXT morning excited and ready to face what I know is going to be a very interesting day. I'm no fan of giving people bad news, but I *do* enjoy surprising people, and so this one will be a mix. We're going to surprise Missoula's management team with some bad news and *then* Mickey is going to surprise them with the good news of how it can all be fixed.

At least, that's what I'm assuming will happen.

The other exciting thing is that Mickey told me yesterday we'd have breakfast this morning, and he'd talk to me about something special he wants me to do at the meeting. Finally! Something besides listening and seeing whether I can fit both feet into my mouth at the same time.

I'm dressed and ready and down into the lobby a few minutes ahead of schedule, which leads to my least favorite thing in the world—waiting. In suspense. Questions crowding up against other questions—the largest being "What's Mickey going to ask me to do?" but right behind that one are other questions of interest.

How are the members of the management team going to respond to our assessments? How on earth are we going to be able to help these people (assuming we won't be granted hiring and firing power)?

I check my watch. One more minute. I pace back and forth in front of my rolling bag, feeling as though I'll wear a groove into the marble floor if Mickey doesn't get here soon. It's times like these I think smokers might be onto something. I check my watch again. It's time, but my watch might be fast.

The whole thing is beginning to have the vaguely reminiscent feel of a high-school Friday night—all dressed up, ready to go out, and suddenly wondering whether you're being stood up or if everyone else found out about something way cooler going on and just forgot to tell you. I glance at my watch again. Three minutes past. Ah, to hell with it, he can sue me for emotional distress if the phone bothers him that much. I punch in his cell number and wait.

When I hear the phone scraping across a hard surface and his foggy, "This is Mick—ohhhhh crap!" I know he's overslept.

"Mickey it's Joanne, we're okay, we'll just grab some food on the way, do you need me to do anything?"

"Uh, yeah, let's, um…" I can hear him fighting through the murk, and I have to smile. I know all too well this feeling of being yanked out of deepest sleep and knowing you're late but still not clearly understanding what it is you're late for. He makes a growling noise, obviously exasperated with things and then says,

"Yeah, Joanne, okay, if you could come on up to my room, I need to give you some stuff that I, I was gonna, over breakfast, not sure wh—"

"Mickey," I interrupt, smiling. "Come up to my room is all you had to say. Give yourself a minute to get oriented, I'll be right there. It's sixteen what?"

"Yeah, sixteen hang on…sixteen thirty three, good, okay, thanks Jo," and he's gone, leaving me smiling in sympathy…and some rearward portion of my brain is registering his use of the name that only my closest friends call me… and Keith…

He's sleepy, I think crisply. He'll be himself in a moment. I grab my suitcase's handle and let it fall into a rolling line behind me like an obedient pet. Onto the elevator, up to sixteen, out into the hall and then around the corner and then counting…sixteen twenty four…thirty…thirty three, here we go.

I raise my hand to knock and just as I make contact, I see that it's cracked a half inch, and my knock bumps it open a few more inches. "Mickey?" I call, holding carefully in the corridor. "It's Joanne…"

From within the room comes his voice, sounding somewhat more focused. "Hey, Joanne, come in, it's open." I push the door gingerly and peer in, just in time to see him, shirtless, rounding the corner into his bathroom. He calls out, "Sorry about all this, I just need a minute and I'll be all set, have a look on the table, there's some stuff I want you to look at for today."

I struggle to wrench my eyes away from the angled view of his right arm and side, mirrors into mirrors giving me a narrow view of him as he shaves. His skin tones, so obviously Mediterranean, and the dark hair on his chest…Keith is fair, and hairless, nothing like this vibrant, exotic…

I squeeze my eyes shut tight. Good heavens. Stop it Joanne. I shake my head slowly and point my eyes down so when they open, they're squarely upon the paperwork Mickey has left me.

It's a simple binder with a cover page marked "Modes of Communication." I turn past the cover page and see a diagram detailing five different types of communication, each with definitions and examples. I'm already considering this range of definitions when I hear Mickey, entering.

My eyes dart up quickly, cautiously, to see him expertly knotting a necktie as he says, "All three of our topics today—from feelings of inclusion and community to the evaluation process to the problems with the incentives—they all have some form of poor communication as either a causal factor or a very telling symptom. Pretty early in today's proceedings, I'm going to ask you to offer a brief introduction to the topic of communication, using this five-mode model."

I glance up sharply and I must look alarmed because he smiles and puts an arm on my shoulder (*oh my look how big his hand is on me*) and he says, "I felt like maybe it was time to give you a little bit of an audition." Then he grins and he's away again, hunting for his shoes as my shoulder glows, almost burns, with the sense of his touch.

I give myself another little mini-headshake. I have to get a hold of myself, it's insane, some teenaged-girl part of my head keeps trying to make something of this, the man overslept, he's giving me my assignment, that's all it is.

Yes, that's all says the smirking girl. *You're in his hotel room watching him get dressed and staring at his chest and his shoulders and going all gaga when his hand happens to stop for a minute on your shoulder, sure, it's an assignment, that's all it is,*

Shut up, I try on myself, but

*Sure, sure, if you don't think about it then it isn't real, you're not **really** in some strange man's room before breakfast, he's not **really** wonderful and good looking and he doesn't **really** have anything to say about whether you get the job, what kind of "audition" does he have in mind…*

SHUT UP!!! I scream at myself.

The smirking girl falls silent…but she doesn't retreat completely, just sits in the corner, watching, with that knowing look on her face.

I try for something work related, and manage to fasten on, "Do I need to have this down pat or will I be able to refer to my notes?"

He laughs from across the room. "I think if I give you a new script twenty minutes before show time, you can't be expected to memorize it. Of course you can use your notes. Just do your best. Interpersonal communication is an important topic, and I think you can give them a good strong foundation with this stuff."

I return to studying the material, feeling like a college student doing last-minute cramming for a final, and then Mickey announces he's ready and out we go. Into the elevator, down to the lobby and through the atrium where a continental breakfast buffet is laid out. Mickey smoothly palms a cheese Danish as we walk past, winking at me.

(*Diya see that?* smirking girl whispers, *diya see him wink at us?* but I ignore her)

IN THE CAR, I'm able to ask Mickey a couple of questions about the communications materials and get myself a bit more comfortable, but there's still a sense of nervousness, and it's not until we're nearly there that I realize it's not only from me. There's a tension to Mickey, a sharpness that doesn't seem fearful or anxious, but which is still different from his normal mode.

When I ask him whether I'm imagining things, he gives a small shrug and a grin. "This is game time, Joanne. This is when we find out whether we win a nice chunk of long-term business for Make-A- Diff. If you don't get at least a little bit nervous when it's game time, you need to find another game, is how I always feel about it."

I nod. I'm nervous enough for a whole season, with playoffs and championship thrown in.

AT MISSOULA IRONWORKS, it's very nice to find ourselves back in a more conventional conference room, without the graffiti or the noise right outside. Nice table, nice chairs, nice carpeting. Ice water, coffee, sodas. A clean whiteboard cleverly recessed in the wall. All the amenities. I wonder, briefly, what this says about the company too; are wage workers less deserving of pleasant spaces? Or: Do those workers care less about keeping their spaces pleasant? Or both?

I drop the question from my thoughts and focus on the meeting which is about to begin.

All seven members of the management team are present. There's John, our host who is the HR Manager; Stan, the plant manager; Tim, VP of operations; Dorothy, the Supply Chain Manager; Geoff, the IT Manager; Krishna, the Controller; and Skip, the R&D Manager. I sit in a chair in a front corner of the room while all of the managers share the oval table. Mickey walks up to the front of the room, with John by his side.

John opens the meeting very briefly, by re-introducing Mickey and Make-A-Difference for anyone who wasn't present the day before. He quickly turns the meeting over to Mickey who moves to the front of the room as John returns to his place at the table.

"Good morning everyone. I'd like to thank all of you for giving us a bit of your time this morning. As John said, my associate Joanne Cruse and I spent yesterday conducting a brief assessment of all three levels of your organization, from management to hourly employees. We did this through basic interviewing, Q and A, and although our assessment was of necessity somewhat cursory in nature, we found several points of interest.

"I hope you understand," he continues, "that cursory is not intended to mean 'careless.' I mean only that eight hours is not enough time to conduct a truly comprehensive assessment. I'm sure we both have plenty left to learn about how things work here.

"But I want to stress that the relatively surface nature of our work yesterday should not be something we try to hide behind over the next couple of hours. When two firefighters come into your house and both say, 'I smell smoke, something is burning,' you can either take it seriously, or you can take cover in the hope that maybe it *always* smells like smoke, maybe these two just aren't used to the air around here yet."

Stan speaks in a no-nonsense tone, "You're saying that in your opinion, we have a fire."

Mickey nods, "I'm saying you already thought you might have a fire, that's why you called us. I'm saying you were right. I'm also saying it's not panic time; we can save the building and the people and maybe even most of the furniture."

Stan doesn't seem to agree nor disagree. He simply says, "You have our attention, Mr. Vasquez."

Mickey gives a courtly nod. "The good news," he continues, "is that in this case, the two firefighters haven't just smelled smoke—they've also found that hey, look, guess what—your house is attached to a gold mine. All we have to do is save the house and the people and then you can start making the kind of money gold mines are known for.

"My fire and house metaphor is about to die of exhaustion, so I'll come back to the real world," he says, flashing that blinding grin. "In short, we think we've identified ways in which you can sell more products that are better and cost you less to produce, all while retaining more workers and ultimately strengthening your position as a pillar of the community. Before we go any further, is there anyone here who's *against* any of those things?"

Wry smiles and murmurs all around. They're clearly listening.

Mickey shifts gears a bit, "The first thing you need to know about our approach at Make-A-Difference is that we believe any business, regardless of particulars, lives or dies according to the happiness and the productivity of its people. Your people are your biggest asset, and our philosophy is that as managers, your role is to recognize and acknowledge this and to do whatever it takes to help your people be the best they can be on the job. We call this 'Actively-Caring-for-People Leadership' and it's proven itself any number of times."

Tim speaks up, "Forgive me Mickey, but this isn't particularly earth-shaking. A business being only as good as its people is something that's been taught for an awfully long time."

Mickey nods, "True enough, but I'm not saying your people are a causal link to good or bad business. I'm saying they *are* the business, more than any product, more than any brick-and-mortar building or meeting room. The employees are what need to be tended, and well maintained, and cared for. All of which more or less begins and ends with communication."

Geoff, the IT Manager, raises a hand, "So we have a communications issue we need to fix?"

Mickey smiles, "Well…yes, but it's not what you might be thinking. You don't need a new kind of memo or a better telephone system. You need a new way of thinking about communication."

The faces around the table are suddenly a bit confused; they're still attentive but they're beginning to appear hungry for specifics.

Of course, Mickey's timing is impeccable. "In our interviews yesterday, Joanne and I identified three specific areas in which we feel improvement would show very quick dividends. But before we address these specific areas, I'd like to ask Joanne to say a few words about the ways in which we at

Make-A-Difference think about the critical issue of communication—I think it will provide us with a useful template for the remainder of our talk today, Joanne?"

Mickey gives way, smiling warmly at me as I rise. Oh my Gosh, oh my Gosh, oh my Gosh everyone watching, my first big chance, don't blow it don't blow it…

"Good morning everyone," I begin, trying a smile on them. They wait, expectantly. They're not hostile, but this isn't the morning safety meeting at Perfect Plastics either. They're waiting to hear something they haven't heard before. I glance quickly at my single card of notes and begin.

"We've all got a pretty clear, basic understanding of what most people mean when they use the word 'communication.' We presume, quite correctly, this word is used to refer to some sort of exchange of information, from sports scores to meeting times to lifelong commitments.

"At Make-A-Difference, we've found it's useful to think a little more specifically from instance to instance about the exact *kind* of communication you're involved in—what's your purpose, and what consequences are you hoping to get out of it."

I turn to the whiteboard and pick up a marker, beginning a simple list from my notes. "In essence," I narrate, "there are five specific types of communication, each carrying its own set of expectations and assumptions. If you think you're in Type A and the person at the other end of the communication thinks it's Type C, you might have a problem. So let's identify what these types are.

"The first is *Relationship Communication*." I write the phrase in capital letters on the whiteboard and return to my listeners. "These are the simple, everyday conversations we have with people to show we care…but even these most casual forms still assume both parties are attentive to the conversation—even if it's just, 'How was your weekend?'

"Authentic relationship communication means attending to the answer you receive. Seeing someone you know in the hall and saying, 'How's it going?' as you pass by doesn't count—that's really just a multi-word 'hello,' right?

"The next is *Possibility Communication*. If the first type seems primarily to focus on the present, then this is the type which focuses on the future, whether it's what movie you might want to see tonight or what the five-year goals for your new European operation ought to be."

I'm feeling myself in the flow of things now, confident of my material, and confident of my listeners' attention.

"Next is *Action Communication*. We know that possibilities become realities in part by defining the behaviors needed to achieve them. Action Communication often involves goal setting—'if you do X it should lead to Y, and here's how we'll track whether that's really happening.' We focus easily on outcomes, but this is the type of conversation which identifies what specifically needs to occur in order to *achieve* those outcomes."

I pause a bit and risk a quick glance at Mickey, who is giving me his fullest, most supportive attention. I smack the smirking girl inside me hard before she can even open her mouth, and I continue with a small illustration Mickey might not expect me to have at hand.

"In the military, they speak of 'strategy' and 'tactics' and it can be easy to think of those as synonyms—but the differences are critical. A strategy is an outcome goal, and a tactic is a specific plan to achieve a specific thing necessary to attain the larger strategic outcome.

"For instance, you might decide the strategy for defeating the enemy is to force them to run short of fuel. The tactical support of that strategy would involve identifying fuel depots which are particularly vulnerable to air assaults, or commando raids, or whatever, okay? So, in that context, Possibility Communications are more strategic, and Action Communications are more tactical. Any questions?"

Skips hand goes up and I nod at him. "Did you serve, Miz Cruse?"

I shake my head, smiling, "I'm afraid not. It just worked out that almost every close friend I have served in some branch of the military at one time or another. Some of their vocabulary rubbed off on me. I like the whole charlie-bravo-delta alphabet, too," I grin, and Skip grins back at me.

"Moving on," I say, writing my next item on the board. "*Opportunity Communication*—These conversations define the specific locations and the specific times when the desirable actions are called for. It's pretty simple to see we're moving from generic and broad to specific and precise.

If we wanted to continue my military analogy, we know we need to make the Nazis run out of fuel, and we have targeted certain vulnerable depots—and now we've gotten word that the depot on the northern edge of Dusseldorf is going to be unguarded tonight—we know we can have success there, so we make specific plans accordingly.

"And in case I've been unclear somewhere," I say, pausing from my whiteboard notes, "I want to repeat, these definitions are worth thinking about because they help lead us to clarity. If I think I'm having an Action Communication, but the other person thinks we're only having a Possibility Communication, we're going to lose time and maybe even opportunities.

"I'm not suggesting you have to announce what you're doing—'Hello, Bob, I'd like to have an action communication with you.'—" The listeners chuckle and I continue, "But I *am* suggesting you need to be aware of what sort of communication you're attempting, and what the other person seems to think your intentions are.

"Or, if the shoe is on the other foot and the other person came to you, listen carefully and ask yourself—does this person think we're having relationship communication? Action communication? Especially if you feel the communication isn't quite working—you know that feeling you have when you and the other person are somehow *just* missing each other? Take a step back and make sure you're both on the same page about the kind of communication you're attempting."

I return to my whiteboard. "Lastly—*Follow-Up Communication.* Exactly what it sounds like, and it can follow any of the others. You can follow up on Relationship Communication—are you still having that fight with the phone company about your mother's bill? Or you can follow up on an Action Communication—is Dusseldorf now in flames?" Another appreciative chuckle. I'm feeling very good about things.

"The bottom line is simple—know what you're trying to achieve, do your best to know whether the other person is trying to achieve the same things, and

> **LEADERSHIP LESSON 6**
>
> Interpersonal communication comes in five distinct forms:
> 1) Relationship,
> 2) Possibility, 3) Action,
> 4) Opportunity, and
> 5) Follow-up.

adjust accordingly. Communication doesn't spring wholly from desire—it has to be understood and managed. Any questions?"

Stan, the plant manager, says, "I think your examples are clear and I don't think any of us would argue about there being different kinds of communication depending on what you're trying to do…but I'm still missing the particulars about *our* situation."

Mickey steps smoothly forward and I give way. "I know what you're saying Stan, and thank you Joanne," he says, turning to me with a smile and a small nod of earnest approval. "That was *very* well done." I return to my chair glowing.

Mickey returns to Stan. "We felt it would be useful to lay some foundation for some of the ways we talk about things when we're diagnosing communications issues—which are, as I said, at the heart of some big problems." On the phrase 'big problems' the faces around the table move from the pleasure of understanding a nice chat about communication to remembering our real purpose here.

Mickey moves to the white board and in three efficient swipes he clears it and announces, "This is problem number one," as he writes the word 'INCLUSION' on the board.

He now turns to face the room. "We believe successful companies—populated by the most self-motivated employees—offer a sense of inclusion, of belonging, to each and every worker. The people who work at those companies feel they have a real voice, which means they feel heard at all levels, in all kinds of communication, everything from Relationship chats to Opportunity discussions.

"We've all seen that kind of boss who thinks the workers love him because he stops for a minute to talk about their son's little league game or their wife's surgery. And it's true, this is an important aspect of leadership, to demonstrate genuine caring…but this same boss isn't very likely to ask that worker what he thinks of the merger with the Canadian firm, or where they ought to put their next retail outlet. True inclusion is about staying receptive to input from every level of employee about every facet of the operation."

Stan laughs. "Like we're really gonna listen to David the Die Stamper about where we should put our next plant!" There is laughter, but it recedes quickly when they glance Mickey's way.

Mickey is gazing levelly at Stan, "Why not?"

Stan isn't prepared for this, "Whaddaya mean?"

Mickey shrugs, "I mean: Why not? Why wouldn't you listen? Presumably David the Die Stamper has an idea. He's thought about this question and he's approached you with a particular notion he has. Maybe he knows of a piece of industrial property. Maybe his wife's brother is an alderman in a town trying to lure a big company. Maybe Dave's idea won't make sense—but there's no way his idea will be as stupid as not listening would be."

Stan flushes, "I wasn't talking about when someone comes to you with an idea, I just meant we're not gonna go down on the floor and say hey everyone, come pester us with your ideas."

Again Mickey shrugs, and this time he's smiling a little, "Why not?"

Stan's getting hot now, and he tries to summon an answer but Mickey lifts a hand. "I take your point—you can't have the whole management team down there asking every worker for personal opinions, that's not efficient." Stan sits back, slightly calmer.

Mickey continues, "But! There would be no harm, and a lot of good, in a fifteen-minute meeting explaining the question under consideration, and giving an e-mail address or even just a suggestion box. Especially when it's a big thing like a new plant location."

Tim is nodding, "Sure. Give em the feeling of having a voice."

Mickey shakes his head vehemently, "No. Don't give em the feeling of a voice. Give them a voice. *Listen.* If they think you just dump the suggestion box into the trash every Friday, it's not real communication."

"But what if their suggestions are never any good? I mean, I don't know how to make steel, I don't expect them to know how to choose the right workman's compensation policy, you know?"

Mickey is nodding, "I hear you, but you've got to hear them. I'm not saying there's some magic quota. It's not like you have to invent some way to take every tenth suggestion. Just listen. Even if nothing immediately useful comes out of it you've still begun to generate the sense of inclusion, especially if you can respond with specificity every now and then—you know, 'Hey, Kevin, I liked your idea about that location in Michigan, but there's some weird zoning stuff there that would take too long to sort out.'

"You don't have to build a plant in Michigan because Kevin suggested it, but imagine how good Kevin is going to feel, knowing he was actually taken seriously. It helps him remember this is his company; he belongs here. He becomes an ambassador for your entire team down there on the floor. Anyone has something cranky to say about management, he's right there saying 'that wasn't my experience.' "

Krishna raises a hand, "But isn't there some practical limit on how much of this sort of communication makes sense? Everyone who works here is busy, we don't have many extra hours for, you know, feel-good moments like this."

"They're not just feel-good moments," I hear myself saying clearly, and Mickey's head turns in surprise. I'm a little surprised myself, but I just can't stand how clueless they're being, it's like they *want* to not get it.

"It's like Mickey just said—you're building good will for the future and these folks might one day, Heaven forbid, have an idea that makes sense."

"Let's look at this," says Mickey, smoothly taking the reins again. "Let's pretend you were trying to reshape the work week. You've identified what you think would be significant savings if you go from six days of operation a week to five. What would be your process for working out that transition?"

Tim says, "We had something kind of like that just last year, when we were re-structuring the work day to start and end earlier. We put together a team to study it, we collected data on how it worked for other similar companies, and after a few months we made a decision."

Mickey asks quietly, "And how many of your wage employees were on that team?"

There are uncomfortable glances around the table. "Well, none, but the issues we were addressing weren't directly related to the daily work of the—"

Mickey laughs, "Not related? You're changing the basic shape of their work day, and you're doing it with zero input from them. Do you imagine they feel grateful and included, or ignored and excluded?"

Silence.

Mickey continues softly, "My mission here is not to scold you, okay? My mission is to help you see that the more included your workers feel, the more they feel this company is *their* company, the more devoted they are, and the harder they work. And again— communication is the key to this issue."

Mickey's voice grows louder, "There are several mechanisms that can be implemented over the next few months which we believe, by year's end, will result in a dramatic change in the number of employees who are able to say "agree" or "strongly agree" to the statement, 'I feel my supervisors care about my opinions.' "

LEADERSHIP LESSON 7

Authentic inclusion occurs when input for important group or organizational decisions are solicited from all participants.

John asks, "How many said 'agree' or 'strongly agree' yesterday?"

Mickey meets his eyes evenly, "Zero."

Tim seems to speak for the room when he says, "You've convinced us there is value to be found in more inclusive structures which use more thoughtful and precise forms of communication…but you said there are two other areas?"

Mickey nods, happy to move on. "The next domain of concern is your incentive scheme."

John asks, "What's the specific concern?"

Mickey lifts his hands in a small shrug, "It doesn't work."

They look at one another; there's beginning to be a shell-shocked quality to this group, and I wonder briefly whether they might check out and stop listening because the news is so bad…but again and again Mickey's voice is so energized about the potential for success that he brings them back.

At the moment he's encountering skepticism regarding his incentive comment. Krishna says, "I'm not sure how you can say it doesn't work, those people LOVE their incentive, my phone rings off the hook the second anyone's check doesn't have the full four-hundred dollars."

Mickey grins, "All you're telling us is they love *money*, that's not the same as the incentive program working."

John asks, "Why don't you tell us a little more about what you mean, Mickey?"

Mickey nods, "Sure. An incentive is meant to motivate certain behavior, right? Do this, get the reward, fail to do it, go without the reward, right?" Everyone is nodding and he continues.

"But that approach has two problems. Problem number one is we don't want to motivate people from the outside, that's carrot-and-stick thinking. We want them to be *self*-motivated, from the *in*side. We want them to do well because they feel pride of ownership, of community, 'This is Ours', right?"

More nods, less certain, but still willing to agree. Mickey continues, "But an equally important issue is that even if we liked carrot-and-stick thinking, the particular version used here wouldn't work because no one on the floor understands how it's administered. I've heard it explained twice and even *I'm* not one hundred percent sure who oversees it, or how the required participations are logged or any of that. Is there a consistent accountability system in place?"

John looks a little sheepish, "Well...for a time they had to submit all their participations but then we had to go around verifying, or at least spot-checking, and it got to be a lot of paperwork that no one really had time for..."

Krishna picks up the thread, "The way it works now is if a supervisor happens to report a specific shortcoming in one of the required areas, we adjust that worker's paycheck the appropriate amount...but in the absence of any such report, we simply add the full bonus to their salaries when we process the payroll."

Mickey is nodding, "This is more or less what I thought. And it's not hard to see why the employees have the image they have of it—it's not inspiring them to do anything extra. It's inspiring them to keep their heads down and their noses clean and if they do that, then most months they'll get the full four hundred, every now and then they'll get a bit less.

"It feels to them like an entitlement, with occasional, random bad weather mixed in, do you see? No real explanation, no real understanding, just a thing that happens. It's not even remotely connected to what they do at work, not in their own minds, not anymore. If it ever was."

The IT Manager, Geoff, speaks up, chuckling, "Man, I hope you're not suggesting we get rid of it. If it's like you say and they've gotten used to it, if they expect it, you know, then taking it away isn't going to be any good for morale."

Tim offers tentatively, "Should we perhaps have some discussion about re-designing the qualifications, make it less automatic, more something to be proud of…?"

But Mickey is shaking his head, "Our vision is for you to be totally free of extra external motivators. We want self-motivated employees, employees who do the right thing because it matters to them, because it helps their company be the best it can be."

Stan sounds belligerent, "I don't understand you then. You say it doesn't work, you say we can't redesign it, but Geoff's right, you can't just take it away. If they don't feel like they belong *before* this, then you *really* can't just—I mean, I'm not sure I understand what we're supposed to—"

"You eat it," Mickey says very clearly.

Everyone else stops whatever they're doing and stares at him. He repeats himself, "You eat it. Absorb it. You announce you're making a gift of it. One time only, in recognition of loyalty, etcetera. The incentive bonus is no longer a bonus—it's a raise. A permanent, never-have-to-wonder-about-it-again raise."

Dorothy looks horrified, "Why would we do that?"

Mickey laughs, "You're already doing it! You're spending the money anyway, give or take a few hundred dollars a year. You get nothing in return— no motivation, no good will. If anything, you get a little resentment because they don't understand why sometimes it's less and sometimes it's more, it feels arbitrary. Because it is.

> ## LEADERSHIP LESSON 8
>
> **A financial bonus based on organizational performance rather than individual behavior can become an entitlement and have no impact on what people do.**

"So. Every employee gets a one-time raise of forty-eight hundred dollars per year—four hundred per month. You get good will—and you cash it in by telling them that in place of the incentive program which never quite made sense anyway, we're going to be implementing a new communications process designed to help everyone work more closely as a team. This way you get a little buy-in cheap, from people who otherwise might be less inclined to try anything new. Do you see?"

I'm staring at Mickey in amazement. It's brilliant. Money already spent on making workers feel slightly upset and manipulated instantly becomes a vehicle of goodwill. Some of the managers still look somewhat baffled, but I can see that both Krishna and Geoff already see the logic of this approach and are enthusiastically explaining it to the others.

Tim tries to steer the meeting away from becoming too many voices at once. "It's a very intriguing thought, and it definitely seems like something we should consider. Assuming of course Make-A-Difference can indeed design this new communication process we'll be asking everyone to hop into…?"

Mickey nods. "It's what we do," he states simply.

"What's the third thing?" John asks, and the room finally quiets. John ticks off on his fingers, "Overall communication and inclusion as a means to community, okay, re-tool slash eliminate incentive program, okay, what's number three?"

Mickey is tapping his notes with his pen, as though he wishes there were an easier way to phrase this final critique. Apparently he's unable to find one, so he says plainly, "Your evaluation procedures need some attention."

This one clearly catches Tim's attention. His eyebrows are up and he says, "I'm surprised to hear you say that."

I laugh.

I don't mean to laugh. I just can't help it. It bursts out of me.

The entire room turns to look at me, and all but one of the faces are between confused and amazed. Mickey's face is a mixture of warning and disappointment. I compose myself quickly.

Stan speaks slowly, "It would be nice if Ms. Cruse would let us know what she finds so amusing."

I try to backpedal. "No, it isn't really relevant; I was just reminded of something…"

Mickey tries to override me with, "What's key here are the impressions of your employees when we ask…"

But Tim lifts a hand and says, "I'm sorry Mickey, but I would really and truly like to hear from Ms. Cruse's own lips why it is that my surprise regarding any shortcoming in our evaluation process would strike her as amusing."

That measured syntax, the ostentatiously sarcastic tone—it's calculated to come across as icy, to frighten me…but I can also hear the slight quaver in his voice. It's he who's frightened, not I.

He tries to continue, "In fact, I have to say the available data fly in the face of any claim of sub-standard results with our evaluation processes. The employees themselves approve whole heartedly, and I…"

It happens again.

The laugh comes out unbidden but this time I don't try to hide or excuse it, it's too late anyway, and I simply say, "Based on *what!*"

He's astonished, "I'm sorry?"

Mickey tries one last time, but it's too little too late, I can't help laughing right in Tim's shocked little face. This clueless little man attempts to bully people he doesn't even know. What must life be like working for him? He is suddenly everything that's wrong with every bad manager in the world, clueless, and arrogant.

I suddenly can't help but see him as why plants fail, why they move to Mexico or Canada, why my best friend Jeff and I are both out of the jobs we loved as hard as we could.

I say it again, "Based on what? You've made a fairly startling claim without any data of which I'm aware, given that your company seems not to believe in data collection, so I'm really very eager to know on what you base your claim that your employees approve of the evaluation process?"

He draws himself to whatever "full height" might be for him and says haughtily, "As I've already said, each of them signs the eval form indicating their acceptance of the findings and their approval of the process."

"You know who else liked that trick?" I ask him. "The Gestapo was fond of it. The KGB liked it too. A lot of people sign anything when they fear the alternative—what happens to employees who don't sign? Has it ever happened? It must have because even the *most* popular programs meet some dissent. The only people who get elected by one hundred percent margins year after year are in charge of places like North Korea.

"Tell me Tim; is that your vision for Missoula Ironworks?"

"I don't have to sit here and take this," Tim begins, rising to his feet.

I step closer, "That's right, *you* walk *away* from bad news, it's only your *employees* who have to sit and take it, isn't that right, Tim? What kind of leader does that make you? Are you interested in hearing any of the data Mickey and I actually collected, or is it too terrifying to hear, heaven forbid, what your employees actually *think!!*"

I have to give him credit. He's got a shrieking madwoman a few feet from him and a roomful of colleagues with whom he's already lost a great deal of face... but he's got some pride. He manages stiffly to say, "If Mr. Vasquez can provide us with a few details and in a style a bit more consistent with professionalism, I'll happily listen." He turns to Mickey. "Do you think this is possible?"

I turn to go back to my chair. I can feel all the eyes of the room on me as Mickey says, "Yes sir, of course."

As I sit tensely in my chair, wondering how I'm going to tell Keith I've been fired from my second job in as many weeks, Mickey reviews the information we gathered in the interviews. He tells them about the nickname "zingers" and the root-canal analogy and the feeling of helplessness expressed again and again by employees. The managers are quiet. They realize this is all very bad news.

Mickey then outlines the corrective steps he envisions—a paradigm shift from annual evaluations to a much more frequent interpersonal schedule until eventually the evaluations aren't occurring as separate events, but simply as a natural function of how people work together.

He asks them to imagine a company in which an evaluation isn't something that occurs on an annual basis, but as a regular part of the ongoing work process, with workers at any level of the company and at any opportune time receiving meaningful, behavior-based feedback—not just corrective advice whenever there's room for improvement but recognition for exemplary performance.

"I'm asking you to imagine a workplace in which every employee knows the company's core values, and can use them as a template for evaluating the behavior they observe—both their own and their co-worker's. A company in which every employee is the actively-caring-for-people colleague for every other employee. Each, a transformational leader."

At one point Stan asks, "But then what's the point of even *having* managers? Are you recommending we implement a plan to put ourselves out of work?"

> # LEADERSHIP
> # LESSON 9
>
> **Performance appraisals improve behavior when they occur periodically and include goal setting and behavior-based feedback customized for the individual.**

The room laughs. "Yes," I think bitterly to myself.

Mickey answers that self-management and self-discipline are optimal but managers will always be needed, to steer in times of crisis and to help guide things toward consensus when it might at first seem impossible. He adds, "No one is self-motivated all of the time. We all need people to hold us accountable sometimes."

Krishna says, "So wait a minute, if I happen to be running late for a meeting and I'm jogging in the halls, you're telling me Davie the Die Stamper can tell me I'm at risk, and ask me to slow down?"

Stan chimes in, "Dave sure does get around!" and there's a bit of laughter, but Mickey is nodding.

"Why not?" Mickey asks rhetorically. "If your company truly values safety, *really* values it beyond mere lip service, why wouldn't you want all employees, regardless of their place in the hierarchy, to speak out whenever they witness something unsafe?"

Krishna looks thoughtful. "I suppose I would," she admits.

Mickey then offers other examples of the ways in which employees can align themselves with a company's values, and insist upon behavior consistent with those values from every other employee they encounter. Transformational leadership again. It's a very large leap to imagine, but you can feel the excitement in the room as it's discussed.

After a few minutes Tim speaks up again, "I have a question for Joanne, if I may."

Mickey looks at me. He'd clearly love to deny Tim access, but there's no reasonable path to this so he gives a little sigh and says, "Be my guest."

Tim looks right at me and asks, point blank, "I'd like to know what exactly it is I did to you to deserve the treatment I experienced at your hands a few minutes ago."

For some reason, I flash back to that day long ago in Dr. Pitz's class, apologizing in front of the whole class. I stand, and move to him, my hand out, just as I had that day so long ago.

"Tim," I begin, "I owe you an apology. The fact is you haven't done anything to me, but you might as well know I recently suffered some pretty cruel treatment at the hands of a manager whom I believed should have known better. And I suppose I'm still getting over it.

"You see," I continue, "The Missoula employees Mickey and I talked to— they really actively care about each other. They want to do well, but they really do feel isolated from management, and uncared for. In their current condition, they represent a tremendous waste of a valuable resource—and the resource happens to have names, and faces, and children and parents to care for. We heard about their pain, and I suppose when I heard you insist there was no pain, something in me snapped."

I look directly at him, "I don't want you to make the mistakes the managers at my last firm made—because that firm is now gone. I don't want Missoula Ironworks to be gone. There's too much good that can be done here. But I had no right to speak to you the way I did, and I apologize to you, and to all of your co-workers who had to witness it."

Startlingly, there's a slight smile on Tim's face. "Are you saying you chewed me out because you care about our company?"

I stop and consider, "Yes sir, I suppose that's what happened."

He extends his hand, "Then I can't very well hold that against you, can I?"

I take his hand in a kind of shock. He holds it for a moment and says, "Right now, I'd like to think you're seeing me embody what I hope are a couple of core values here—honesty and the ability to accept criticism. I hope you and Mickey will both keep working with us, Joanne." He addresses the following endnote to the room: "And I sure hope I don't make you angry again!"

There's a round of relieved-sounding laughter, and I join in, and Mickey is smiling too.

But one look into his dark eyes and I know this subject is a long way from closed.

CHAPTER 8

"We make a living by what we get, but we make a life by what we give."
—Winston Churchill

ON THE FLIGHT HOME from Missoula. I try, just once, to broach the subject of my loss of temper back at the plant. Mickey stops me.

"I'm not going to say I'm not worried, Joanne. I am worried. I need to talk to Doctor Pitz about things, get his sense of what our next step should be."

I try to get some traction, laying my pride on the line. "Mickey, I know I was outta line. I know I need to get control of myself; I'm over-reacting. I want you to understand, I recognize the problem and I am absolutely willing—

"Hey." He's holding up a hand, and his expression holds a rebuke. "I need to talk to Doc. Okay?"

There's really no argument for this.

On the plane, Mickey seems very busy with his Blackberry. I feel myself assuming every message is somehow related to me, to my pattern of selfish impulsive outbursts, to my unsuitability for the mission of Make-A-Difference. I have to laugh. The same ego that assumed I had the right to speak harshly to the Missoula managers is now assuming I'm the subject of all of Mickey's electronic communications. Paranoia, thy name is Joanne.

When we part, Mickey reminds me of Sunday evening's cancer fundraiser at which Doc is to speak. I wince inwardly at the idea of another night away from my family, but I've already promised I'd be there, and the ice I'm standing on with Mickey and Doc is already perilously thin. Pledging to do something and then backing out is not an option right now.

THROUGHOUT THE WEEKEND and then on Sunday evening, it's clear being away from my family is not the concern I thought it would be. Keith is headed over to his best friend's house for poker night, and the kids are riveted in front of a movie which might be horror, or might be comedy, or might even be both.

"Where's my lucky shirt?" Keith bellows from what sounds like the inside of the master closet upstairs. Down in the kitchen, I do my best to ignore him, having made a rule for the kids long ago that civilized people don't scream from one room to the next. My silence does nothing to prevent his second attempt: "JOOOOOOOOOOOOO!!!!!!"

When I don't answer this, it's clear to him volume alone won't solve his problem. I hear him thumping to the top of the steps. "Jo!" Nope, still not close enough. An exasperated sigh absolutely designed to be heard by the entire house is followed by heavy feet upon the stairs. As he approaches the bottom, he peers around and sees me in the kitchen, "Jo!"

I look up as though surprised, and give him my sunniest smile, "Sweetheart! I didn't know you were up there! Oh!" I say, as though noticing, "Baby, you need a shirt, you can't go out like that."

He grins, acknowledging he's been outplayed, "Do you know where it is?"

I tilt my head toward the utility room, "It's hanging over the drier."

"Excellent!" He bustles past me and asks, "Tell me again how long this thing of yours is tonight?"

"I don't know," I shrug. "I don't imagine it's longer than a couple of hours."

He's found his shirt and is taking it off the hanger and slipping it on, across his broad shoulders. This is my week for watching handsome men get dressed, I suppose. "It's for cancer?" he asks as he fixes his collar.

"Mmhhm," I murmur as I move to him to lend a hand to the stubbornly resisting collar.

"And you're getting there how?"

"Mickey's coming by," I say, struggling for a casual tone, aware that even this attempt at forced lightness is its own warning light. The smirking girl in the corner of my mind simply giggles, not even bothering to speak—she's happy to let me do her work for her just now.

Keith's no idiot. He knows when I'm trying to make less out of more, and he also knows about how far he dares to push such a thing. "Mister Mickey," he muses, watching me. "Mister Mickey who takes my wife away on business trips and then decides that's not enough, he's going to squire her around town on a Sunday night…"

My collar-fix complete, I turn away, waving a hand in exasperation. "Nobody is squiring anybody. I don't even want to go. But it's like I said, I already promised I'd go, I told you about it last weekend, and you know, I can't help feeling it'd be kind of suicide to back out now…"

(talking pretty fast to explain something you just said is nothing, aren't you Jo?)

"… cause, you know, it's like I said, I screwed up a little bit this past trip, I have to do everything I can to make amends. We need me to get this job, Keith, you know?"

Keith's eyes are slightly wide at this gush of defensiveness. Smirking girl was right—too much talk.

I'm saved—or so I think—by the toot of a horn in the driveway. I glance out the window and freeze for half a second at the sight. Mickey is wearing a designer track suit and driving a Porsche Carrera Convertible with the top down.

Keith joins me at the window and looks out. "Oh my goodness..." he breathes. "He looks like some Euro trash-film producer, *that's* Mickey??"

I move quickly to get my purse. "That's Mickey. And I'm not sure the trash thing works when he shows up driving a Carrera." I'm hurrying for the door, wanting very badly for this scene to be over, but Keith isn't about to let it go that easily.

"Wait up, lemme meet this guy," and he falls into step behind me. I try to make sure my eye roll isn't visible as I feel his hand fall heavily onto my shoulder. Oh, heavens, here we go with the chest beater alpha-male crap...

Keith moves smoothly past me, big, fit, his weight on the balls of his feet, his best meeting-the-enemy smile in place. "You must be Mickey," he calls out, extending his hand. "Please, no, you don't have to shut it off, I just wanted to say hello, I'm Keith Cruse, quite a ride here!"

"Thanks," Mickey grins, taking Keith's hand and shaking quickly. I wonder about the data exchange in that half-second handshake. Grip. Aggression. Warning. Mickey releases the hand and says, "Yeah, I have to live in a 700-square-foot studio to free up the cash for payments on this baby, but she's worth it."

Keith is still smiling broadly, "Man, I always thought about something like this." This aw-shucks-who-me mode is another tactic I know well, oh so friendly, gregarious, butter wouldn't melt in his mouth. "The insurance on this thing probably costs more than my whole car!"

Mickey feigns alarm, "Insurance??? Oh no, I *knew* I forgot something!"

They both laugh heartily and I couldn't be more uncomfortable. I recognize the behavior from Keith's football playing days. The posturing, the turf claiming, all masked with jocular banter and too-hard slaps on the back.

Keith notices me standing quietly and makes an elaborate courtly bow, reaching for the door handle and opening it for me, "Your carriage, milady."

"Thanks," I say dryly, sliding into the bucket seat and catching Keith's eye just in time for him to wink at me. I suppose it's better for him to think of Mickey as a tawdry joke than for him to know how many times I've replayed the scene of Mickey shaving since I first saw it.

Keith steps back, his hand up in farewell, "Now listen here, Mickey, you have her home by midnight, and Jo, if he tries the old whoops-I-ran-out-gas you just call my cell, okay?"

More chest beating, but I stifle my distaste and play my part: "Gosh, Daddy, you're so strict!"

He's still waving, all innocence, as we back out, "Bye, kids!"

As the gorgeous little car purrs through my neighborhood, Mickey ventures so far as, "Seems like a nice guy."

The graciousness of the one who ended up with the girl in his car, I recognize this one too, and for some reason feel the need to clarify that nothing was won or lost by saying, "He's the nicest guy I've ever met. Among many other good things."

Mickey smiles and nods, genuinely pleased to hear this, and I'm a little ashamed to have felt the need to defend something not under attack. The entire moment had been more than a little high school, and I do my best to shake it off and return to the land of the grown-ups.

AS WE APPROACH THE CAMPUS, it becomes clear something very, very big is happening. Not only is every parking spot taken but I'm beginning to see cars parked on the grass in some places. "What is this thing again?" I ask.

Mickey slows, muttering, "It looks more like a Friday night than a Sunday night…" There seems to be no lack of nineteen-year-old, male pedestrians who all want to holler something about his car. As he waves at one such rowdy group, he remembers my question and explains, "It's a walk-a-thon kinda thing, they're calling it 'Relay for Life,' raising money to help cancer research."

"Why is Doc speaking?"

Mickey glances at me, surprised I don't know, "He's a cancer survivor. This whole project is one of his babies; he's been coordinating for months with the Student Government Association and the national Relay-for-Life leadership."

I'm surprised too. Doc with cancer. I'd had no idea…which, of course, had been his choice, and a choice the privacy of which I respect, but it leaves me wondering about all the things we think we know and don't.

We enter the campus proper, driving under the arch which marks the east entrance, the motto *Ut Prosim* chiseled into the stone.

"Do you even know what that means?" asks Mickey. "I drive under it at least once a week, but I keep forgetting to ask Doc about it."

"It's the University's motto," I explain. *UT Prosim*. Latin. 'That I May Serve.'"

Mickey looks at me, startled. "For real?"

I nod, "Yup."

He muses, almost to himself, "Not a bad place for an organization calling itself Make-A-Difference."

Entering the campus proves to have been an enormous mistake parking wise, but Mickey claims to know a secret. We ease past one end of the drill field and I see an enormous crowd gathered, with a small stage at

> ## LEADERSHIP LESSON 10
>
> **When the values of organizations and individuals align, relevant behavior is predisposed to be self-motivated.**

one end, but Mickey maneuvers us onto a small access road used mainly for deliveries and waste removal. With a sharp twist of his wheel, he tucks the small car into a little space between two dumpsters, where it becomes almost invisible.

"This is my favorite weekend spot," Mickey grins. "No trash pickup on the weekends; campus security can't even see it from either end."

I mock-scold him, "Quite the scofflaw, aren't we?"

He smiles and nods, "That's me. Come on, we need to hurry!"

I fall into stride beside him and my feelings are a hopeless jumble. I don't *feel* like an employee in trouble, but I know I am. I *do* feel a little bit like Mickey's date, but I know I'm not. I have no idea what we're going to see or hear tonight, but I know it's important. Deep breath, Joanne. Take it as it comes.

When we round the corner emerging from the access road, we're both stunned. "Whoa…" says Mickey.

"Yeah," I breathe.

The University drill field is a large oval of some forty acres, its name a relic of the University's former days as an all-male military school. It's encircled by stately oak trees, lined on one side by academic buildings, including the fortress-like main administration building with its turrets defending the campus, and on the other side by dormitories.

While the ROTC continues to use the area for the occasional drill or parade, it's also used by the other students for everything from political rallies and crafts fairs to fraternity soccer and tag-football tournaments.

At the moment it is entirely filled with people.

Students. Faculty. Staff. Local residents. I ask a gentleman watching whether anyone has estimated the crowd size. "I heard a couple of the campus cops say around ten thousand," he drawls.

"That's almost half the undergraduates enrolled here!" I exclaim to Mickey. "Do you have any idea how amazing this is? Even the very biggest football games don't do much better, this is *insane!* What brought so many people out?"

Mickey nods toward the stage where a tall, distinguished-looking man and a young student in a University t-shirt are both waiting close to the microphone. "Let's listen and find out," he says. We move a bit closer to one of the large oaks, a nice vantage point, and because of the crowd, I find myself standing closer to Mickey than I might otherwise permit.

It's an entirely pleasant sensation.

The young man seems determined to start and he raises his arms for quiet, but the crowd misinterprets the gesture and begins cheering in a more organized fashion. From the cheers there emerges an audible thread of "SHH-SHH-SHH-SHH!" and at first I think some smaller subset of the crowd is pleading for quiet until I hear the sound build and resolve: "SHHH-SHHH-SHHHH-SHHH-SHAAAAAAANNNE!!!" I grin, realizing the young man at the microphone is Shane Carroll, the student body President.

Carroll keeps his arms up but flares his palms in a patting-down gesture, the crowd realizes he'd prefer quiet, and the noise quickly dwindles. He smiles at the huge crowd and can't quite resist the rock-show opening: "How's everybody doing!!"

The roar of approval which greets him makes it very clear everyone is doing quite well, thank you. Carroll's smile grows and he again pats the air to urge quiet.

"I want to thank everyone for coming out here this evening; this is exactly the kind of thing that made me want to be your President." Another wave of applause, which he simply waits out before continuing.

"We're here tonight to offer our service to a very important mission and I know we're all anxious to get walking, but first I think we need to hear a few words from a very special guest, let's put our hands together for Mr. Timothy Lavery!"

Again the cheers and applause roll forth from the crowd to the small stage, as Carroll steps back, gesturing Mr. Lavery toward the front of the stage.

Lavery nods at the gracious introduction, and when the noise dies he speaks into the microphone in measured, cultured tones—a voice more suited to a black-tie fundraiser than to a rally of ten thousand young people. He's smiling slightly, as though aware of the incongruity. "Thank you, Shane. Good evening, ladies and gentlemen. My name is Tim Lavery and I am the National Chairman for Relay for life." A small cheer builds from close to the stage and moves through the crowd.

He allows it to ebb before continuing.

"I'm very pleased to be able to tell you that this is the single largest gathering in the twenty-four-year history of Relay for Life, both in terms of participation and in terms of dollars pledged. You've set the bar for the rest of the nation, proving that in yet another field of endeavor, your fine University is number one!"

With this he raises both of his hands in a victory salute and the eruption of cheers makes the earlier applause seem like a mistake. This is a *roar*, a wall of affirmation which builds and builds, swelling as Mr. Lavery smiles his benediction. The roar transforms into a deafening chant of "WE'RE NUMBER

ONE! WE'RE NUMBER ONE!" I'm only mildly surprised to hear Mickey's voice and my own joining in the cheer.

After a time Mr. Lavery steps forward again and the chant slowly quiets. "It is with great honor and heartfelt gratitude that I now turn the microphone over to one of the many people who helped make this happen tonight, our honorary leader of tonight's relay, your own distinguished professor and cancer survivor, Dr. B. F. Pitz!"

Again, a large cheer rolls through the crowd, and again we join it, Mickey lifting two fingers to his lips to create a piercing whistle. No pep rally was ever like this!

On the small stage, I can see Doc making his way to the microphone, and I smile in affection at the sight of him. Good old absent-minded Doc, groping his way to a spot from which he'll happen to speak to about ten thousand people who happen to be there because of something he just happened to help throw together. I will never cease being amazed by him.

As Doc waits for the noise to recede, Mickey makes a startled noise. "I almost forgot! Here…" He's fumbling into his pocket and pulls out two green rubber wristbands, handing me one as he stretches the other around his wrist. "Put it on," he urges.

I examine the writing: "ACTIVELY CARING FOR PEOPLE."

"What does it mean?" I ask as I pull it over my hand.

"He'll tell you," Mickey says, smiling toward the stage.

The crowd has quieted enough for Doc to speak into the microphone. The first thing he says is a very quiet "Thank you," which has the effect of quieting the crowd still further. Then, in the same quiet voice he holds one arm up so we can all see his wristband, and he asks, "Can I see who's wearing one of these tonight?"

I look around, and it's as though I'm suddenly in a forest of green-banded arms extended toward heaven. It feels good to lift my arm too, to be a part of things, even though I'm not sure what's happening.

"Very good," Doc says, "Now, please leave your arm up if you know anyone who has cancer."

The crowd is now as hushed as any church, and not a single arm drops. I'm not surprised; I can quickly list six people in my life who have battled this disease.

"Thank you," Doc says again, "Arms down, please." Ten thousand arms drop in a quiet whoosh. Doc takes a moment to survey the crowd, and I'm again struck by the supernatural silence of ten thousand individuals with a singularity of purpose. It's a force, a mighty force, and I can sense Doc calculating how best to deploy and release it.

He plucks briefly at the event t-shirt he's wearing over his other shirt. "This purple shirt I'm wearing, and all the others you see on over three hundred of tonight's participants, designate us as cancer survivors…but I'm afraid I don't quite agree with that term. We're not survivors, not yet. We're surviv*ing*. We won't be surviv*ors* until the disease has been thoroughly and utterly wiped from the earth. And this crowd…" he calls, his voice now building toward exhortation, "This crowd is exactly the group to do it!"

The crowd begins to cheer, but he has the instincts of a revival preacher, letting his voice roll over and pull them: "You are here to lead us to victory and we will walk *UNTIL THAT VICTORY **IS OURS**!!!*"

The crowd explodes with a roar the likes of which I have never heard before in my life, and I hear my own voice in it, crying, yelling, clapping, my eyes filling with tears at this magnificent display of commitment and community. I fancy we're audible two states away, and seismologists in China are suddenly checking their instruments in alarm.

The sound is a palpable thing, a powerful wave moving over and through us and pulling us toward the road which encompasses the drill field, the half-mile oval onto which Doc and the other purple shirts have begun to walk.

People line both sides of their course for a half a mile, cheering loudly and continuously, reaching out to shake hands or to slap high-fives with the smiling walkers, eager for any contact with their strength, their courage. After these three-hundred cancer survivors complete this ritual first lap, hundreds of other green-band-wearing participants stream in behind them.

Before long the drill field is half-empty, with hundreds and hundreds of walkers being cheered on by the many hundred more who remain to line the way. It reminds me of photos I've seen of the beginning of the New York Marathon.

Mickey is angling to catch Doc as he rounds the second curve of the oval. "Come on, Jo," he says, taking hold of my hand and pulling. I trot along with him, surprised but not unhappy at how normal it feels for us to be hand-in-hand—it's not the least bit romantic, it's tribal, communal.

For once the smirking girl doesn't have a thing to say.

We fall into step beside Doc and his face lights up. "I'm so pleased you're here!" he exclaims, hugging us. We spend a few minutes walking in companionable silence as a seemingly unending stream of people drift over to congratulate Doc, to wish him well, to thank him for his efforts. Eventually these episodes decrease and we're able to chat a bit.

Doc is clearly euphoric about the way the evening has turned out, but as anyone who knows him could predict, his elation flows from this real-world demonstration of the principles he teaches. "Look at this, folks. All three pillars, clear as can be, all three C's. Choice, Competence, and Community.

"Choice. Every one of these people chose to be here, volunteering to show they don't just *say* they care, they care with what they *do*, they *actively* care. They're giving of themselves freely, willingly.

"Competence. This event doesn't work if people just show up to cheer. They have to solicit the donations ahead of time, and they have to fulfill their end of the bargain by walking the minimum number of miles agreed to. When they do both of these things, the result is…well.

The minimum tonight is five miles, with as little as even a dime a mile and one pledge per walker, that's a half-dollar per walker, that's five thousand dollars. Which would be pretty impressive except I promise you, most of the people here were more competent than that. They've gotten more than one donor, more than a dime a mile, and many of them will exceed five miles. We're raising a *lot* of money tonight.

"But most impressive is the sense of community on display. From the way we've cheered one another to the way we've walked alongside one another, this event has created its own community with its own values and its own rewards. If you want to fight cancer, if you value human life, then you belong. And the mission of this community, its reason for existence, is nothing less than the saving of lives."

"The three C's," Mickey says in agreement.

"And!" Doc adds, striding along so energetically I feel as though I'm half-jogging to keep up, "There's another list we like which fits this entire event perfectly, the empowerment list, do you remember it Joanne?"

I feel both men's attention on me like an unexpected spotlight. "The three questions," I say carefully, double checking the accuracy of my memory as I speak. "If you say 'yes' to all three, you're empowered. 'Can I do it?' And obviously, 'yes,' everyone here knows they can and will walk these laps and raise this money. That's competence again.

" 'Will it work?' I suppose they must believe it will, at least eventually. If these exact dollars don't push research to a cure, they'll surely move it closer. Even though it probably won't be the game winner, it's still a necessary and valuable part of a long-term winning effort.

"And…" I struggle to remember, casting back to the original conversation and then I suddenly have it. " 'Is it worth it?' " I giggle at my childish pleasure at having succeeded in my battle with my own memory, and they both smile as I continue.

"I think when you asked who here knew someone who had been hurt by this disease that was the answer, everyone here has an image of someone they wish they could help. Of course it's worth it. Anyone who has ever felt the touch of this illness is a part of this community."

"Not everyone," Doc says quietly. "Do you see the President of the University?"

I look for President Lehman. "No…"

"Right," says Doc grimly. "Because he's not here."

Mickey is shocked, "Are you kidding? Half his student body is out here, and he's not?"

Doc shakes his head, "He was here briefly when we were getting started; he shook a few hands and posed for a couple of photos but then he left."

"Typical glad-handing two-faced low life," I mutter grimly, but Doc is staring at me, startled.

"I wasn't saying anything quite that...harsh, I don't think. My only point was that I believe he missed a chance to show some real leadership."

"Right," I say, nodding vigorously. "But he didn't miss the chance to get his picture taken shaking hands with Lavery and with Carroll, right? Because making sure he's in all the pictures is what's important to him, so that's what he stayed for. Demonstrating the qualities of an authentic leader, being part of his community, sacrificing something, those were things he couldn't quite bring himself to stay for, right?"

"Where do you imagine he went from here?" Doc asks, eyeing me with curiosity.

I shrug, "How should I know? Maybe home to watch himself on the news."

Doc shakes his head again, "No, his day is rarely over before midnight. I'm quite certain he left to attend some sort of event designed to raise money for the University. That's more than half of a President's job description these days."

I shrug again, aware of Mickey's quiet watchfulness, "So?"

Doc peers at me, "So he *is* sacrificing. Do you imagine he likes yet another baked chicken dinner in yet another hotel banquet room? Do you imagine he enjoys smiling broadly at the horrible jokes of people he neither knows nor likes?

LEADERSHIP LESSON 11

People with empathy don't judge others until they understand completely the other person's intentions and perceptions.

"Moreover, he's sacrificing for this community. He's putting himself in those unpleasant circumstances in order to generate financial support. He's making decisions based on what he thinks will best take care of us.

"It's always good to try and see things from the other person's perspective. It's possible he believed he was being careful not to steal Shane's thunder. It's likely he felt he needed to move on to the next event on his list of obligations. It's true, I wish he'd set his list up differently, I wish he had made different decisions, I think he could have made better decisions, but I don't think the ones he made were selfish or evil."

"Mmm," I say, nodding and thinking about this. The way Doc explains it, it makes a lot of sense.

When I gaze up from my contemplation of these ideas, I'm surprised to note that both Doc and Mickey are watching me with interest. Doc speaks softly. "Joanne, Mickey and I have talked about what happened in the conference room at Missoula. I think we have to talk about it."

My voice is quiet, "May I say something to begin?"

Doc smiles, "Of course."

I speak carefully, staring at the pavement passing beneath our feet as we walk, "I'm going to assume you both know and believe I sincerely regret both of the occasions when I've behaved…I was going to say 'badly' but I know more about it than that, when I've behaved angrily.

"I realized, too late, exactly the thing I said to the Missoula managers in my apology to them: Somehow, my head has gotten into a place from which I seem to see poor management skills as an adversarial, hostile force."

"Okay," Doc says, nodding and listening intently, "Why do you think that is?"

I give a rueful chuckle, "Doc, I think you know full well that for every manager willing to ask for help from Make-A-Difference, there are fifty who have turned pettiness into a personal creed. They ruin people, they ruin entire businesses, they ruin communities, and they ruin lives. To say 'they don't mean to' misses the point.

"Imagine someone who has never driven before getting into a car and accidentally starting it and killing someone. He didn't mean to, but he knew what cars are and what they do, but he started pushing buttons anyway, just to see what would happen.

"These managers are no different. They don't bother trying to learn their jobs, to improve the human dynamics of their day-to-day habits. And they hurt people and never even look back. And as the recent victim of one of these hit-and-run artists, I can't help thinking of them as the enemy. They make me angry, and I don't know what to do about that."

"But Joanne," Mickey speaks softly. "The managers you're talking about—they're *not* the ones who call us. We talked about this. The ones who call us are at least admitting they need help."

I nod, helpless in the face of this logic. "I know. Maybe I'm mad at them for waiting so long, maybe I feel they owe a debt for the damage they've done up until today."

"Joanne, look around this drill field." Doc is gesturing, "Is this a community you're proud to be a part of? Do you think your values and its values are in alignment? Do you feel you deserve to be here?"

I look around. The night is teeming with thousands of brave and generous people, young and old, wealthy and humble, all laboring together to do something they all agree is worthwhile, and without a single word of complaint or pessimism. "Gosh, I hope so," I say fervently.

"Would you say they have a common enemy?" Doc asks.

This is the first confusion I've felt tonight. "Well, yes," I say carefully, "I'd say their enemy is cancer."

"Would you say it's a formidable, powerful, frightening adversary?"

I nod. "I would," I answer, adding, "Wouldn't you?"

Doc looks at me briefly, acknowledging my gesture toward his Survivor status. "I've never known one more frightening," he says simply before continuing. "Here's the most important question, Joanne, so consider carefully before you answer: How many of them seem angry to you?"

Again I look around, but the sinking feeling in my stomach makes it clear to me I already know his answer, and on some level, I already know his point. Everywhere I look, in all directions, as far as I can see, I see smiles. I see determination. Self-motivation! I see gratitude and grit, grins and grimaces...but no anger. I bow my head, knowing my silence serves as his answer.

Doc's beginning to breathe a little harder due to the mixture of his pace and the additional burden of speaking at length, but he doesn't slow. "They have a frightening, powerful enemy, an enemy who doesn't care whether they live or die, an enemy that can kill them with greater efficiency than the Gatling gun, and they have no way of knowing for certain whether this enemy will ever be defeated in their lifetimes. But they know it as simply as they know their own names: There's no point getting angry at a disease.

"Now, our clients are *not* a disease. They don't kill anyone. They can speak and react and most importantly, they can change and grow, adapt, learn new ways of being. They *want* to learn those ways. Cancer has killed millions, but if cancer came to you and said, 'I want to stop killing people' would you be mad at cancer or thrilled at the chance to save lives?"

I feel warm tears on my cheek as I listen. "I wouldn't be mad," I admit.

Doc pulls up, his breathing labored, "I gotta stop a second," he puffs, and Mickey looks alarmed, but Doc waves him down. "Just need to catch my breath."

He looks up at me and lays it on the line, "If you work for Make-A-Difference, you're involved in a community that values you and the chance for positive change that you help to make happen. We don't scold people. We don't rage against our enemies. The best thing about our community is we *have* no enemies—only people who are about to be our friends.

"Mickey and I continue to think you have a lot to offer. But you need to decide for yourself—is this a community you want to be a part of? Can you start forgiving the people you're mad at, so you can get on with helping us deliver the cure?"

And just like that it hits me. Cancer is scary in part because it's unpredictable and it often seems to follow no rules. I take a deep, shuddering breath and I say, "Doc, I think I've been thinking of these people as if they *were* cancer, as if there was no cure other than radical surgery to remove the disease.

"But I know that's wrong." I look again around the drill field at the thousands of new friends working together in the darkness and I realize I want this badly, as badly as I've ever wanted anything, and the intensity in my voice startles even me. "Give me another chance," I say urgently.

"Please, Doc, Mickey, I—I *do* want to be a part of this new community, I do want to make a difference, the right kind of difference, please—guys—give me another chance. I won't let you down again."

I feel fresh tears, and Doc grasps me in a quick embrace. "You could never let me down, Joanne," he says quietly. "I just want you to lift yourself *up*."

I nod. "I will," I say evenly.

Doc brushes his hands together briskly, "Okay then! I have another five miles to do, but I don't think either of you were planning on an all-nighter."

Mickey smiles, "I actually have this really mean, crazy, purple-t-shirt-wearing boss who insists on having all client reports delivered on time, in spite of an insane schedule."

We all laugh, and I add, "Well, A, he's my ride, and B, I need to get home, especially after having been away most of last week."

Doc smiles, "Good then. Drive safely!" and without a look back he's resumed marching around the drill field with his new extended family of ten thousand and change.

Mickey and I watch him go, and then Mickey looks at me with a truant schoolboy's grin, "I know I said I have to work, and I do, but I'm still revved up by all of this, you feel like getting a drink somewhere? Or some coffee?"

The smirking girl sits bolt upright, eyes alert. She wants me to go with him. *I* want me to go with him. She whispers, from deep in my mind, *one drink, talk about the evening, unwind, what's the harm?*

I shake my head, hoping to clear it, to shut her up...and of course it's an answer, too. "I wish I could," I say, trying for the right mixture of regret and commitment. "But you know, I was telling the truth a minute ago, I really do need to get back. It was a little bit of a stretch, me being here at all. You know, Sunday night, is usually a family night."

He nods, "I understand. Another time, maybe." And I can tell, he *does* understand, and he respects the decision...but I flatter myself that there's a little bit of disappointment there, too.

Oh sure, smirking girl taunts me, *it's okay to tease him, just not to act on it. Maybe you should hold hands on the way back to his car and then tell yourself it's all about community!*

I shake my head again, and Mickey notices it, "You okay?"

Get a grip, Jo. Conversations with imaginary devils, it doesn't look good on a resume. "Oh sure," I say, overly sunny. "I was just sort of, you know, I guess I was…it's just amazing, you know? This whole thing. This whole…you know? "

Mickey brightens, "I know!" And he goes on at some length about what an achievement the evening is, what a lesson it is. He's still talking when we reach his car, and the subject manages to divert us both for most of the ride home.

And meanwhile, the smirking girl is shaking her head in slow mockery. *This whole thing. This whooooooole thing…*

I need to be home.

CHAPTER 9

"People are not successful because they are motivated;
They are motivated because they have been successful."
—Paul Chance

WHEN WE TURN THE CORNER on my street, I see that Keith's car isn't back in the driveway yet. I'm not sure whether to be irked or relieved, but relief wins. The last thing I need is any kind of replay of the barking contest Keith tried to start earlier tonight. Irked isn't far behind though—it's aggravating to have rushed home to be with a family that isn't here yet.

Especially when you could have been having a perfectly innocent drink, whispers the smirk.

Mickey says good night and I thank him for the ride and for the company. I watch his tail lights around the corner and then exhale a breath I hadn't known I was holding, and then turn to go in.

My key is almost in the door when headlights splash across me and I look up to see a car pulling up to our curb—not Keith's Eclipse, either, some kind of SUV I don't recognize. The driver's window slides down and I see the grinning face of Bo Merrick, one of Keith's poker buddies.

"Hey Joanne!" he calls cheerfully. "We took a poll and decided Keith was in no shape to drive, his car is still over at Dave's house, okay?"

I'd feel embarrassed if Bo weren't so all-in-a-days-work cheerful about the whole thing. This is clearly a part of Boyland which is old hat to him, and so I let him see me roll my eyes and I call out, "You're a lifesaver Bo, thank you so much. Can you let Dave know we'll pick up the Eclipse tomorrow?"

"You bet!" he calls in reply.

"You bet!" hollers Keith, walking unsteadily toward our yard, "You bet! I raise! You re-raise! All in! And my aces get cracked again! Ha!"

"You got him from here, Joanne?" Bo asks.

"That's what the courts say," I grin at him and he laughs.

"Okay then! See you soon. Take it easy, Tuna!" he calls to Keith as he's pulling away.

I'm going to meet Keith in case he needs a shoulder, but he's still navigating reasonably well under his own power. "Tuna?" I ask.

"Big fish," he says unevenly. " 's'waht you call a bad poker player, izza fish. So you can say tuna or carp or whale…even though, you know, whale's not akshly a fish…"

"I see…step here…step…," I say guiding him up onto our porch.

"Hey, I *built* these steps, right??" he says with playful aggression, stomping up them with exaggerated power. "Built to last!"

"Lemme get the door open," I say fumbling with my keys, but I hear a great exhalation, and I look to see that Keith has already plopped down into one of the four rocking chairs which are arrayed on the porch. He is staring at me, not quite vacantly, as though pondering what to say. "You okay?" I ask.

"We gotta have a talk."

I struggle with my impatience. I just want to go inside and sit down; I don't want to have a non-useful conversation with someone who won't even remember it tomorrow. "Let's go inside, we can talk there," I try, but he shakes his head, adamant and inert.

"Uh-uh. I wanna talk now."

I sigh and decide I can at least rest my weary feet. "Okay," I say, pulling one of the rockers closer and sitting. "What do you want to talk about?"

"This!" He gestures at himself as though to encompass his mood, his drunkenness, and who knows what else. "I drank too much beer and I lost sixty bucks in a two-bit poker game, and you know why?"

"No, tell me?"

"Because I wanted to have fun."

This statement is at once simple and perplexing. He seems so sad and lost, yet this is following a statement which seems on its face to make perfect sense. I shrug and respond, "Well of course you wanted to have fun, that's the whole point of your poker nights, isn't it, f—"

"Are we having a life where I can expect one fun night per month?" he snaps.

My confusion is growing. "No...?"

"Cause that's what it felt like!" he says, leaning forward, and then almost too far forward, catching himself. "Whoa..." He looks up and smiles, then frowns, then continues: "I realized when I's getting ready that I's excited, cause I's about to go have a good time, an' then I thought 'Why does this feel sooo *different*, I used to have fun almost every day!' an' then I thought yeah, but that was before this job thing happened."

Ah. Here we go. Okay.

Deep breath. I keep my voice steady for, "I think this is a big topic for another night, baby, I think we need to get you inside so that—"

"Heh. Yeah, another night, 'salways' 'nother night. You mean a night when I'm not hammered," he complains.

I try for warmth…"I'm glad you were able to go have fun baby, and yes, I think we should try for—"

"BUT I DIDN'T HAVE FUN!" he cries out, and I'm keenly aware of all the darkened houses around us. Keith sees my glance around and realizes we're still outside and lowers his voice to a stage whisper that would be comical under other circumstances, hissing angrily, "I didn't! Have! Fun! I had a terrible time and I lost too much and I drank too much and it was all because I was trying too hard to have the kind of fun we used to have all the time, and I was miserable!"

It occurs to me that everything I say seems to provide him with a handle for his next bit of aggression, and so I decide to simply wait and see whether the storm will blow itself out.

He continues, his voice smaller, like a little boy lost, "An now you're gone alla time with that *guy*, that *Mickey*, mister I-have-no-family-no-life-but-look-I-gotta-Porsche…an then! Whenever you get home the first thing outta your mouth is to say the next time you're going away, like we're you're *staff*, like you speck us to get the *jet* fueled or something…"

His voice dies down and his head slumps a little. Has he passed out? "Sweetie?" I try, very softly.

"Mmmm?" he lifts his head, pushing himself into an exaggeratedly alert position. "I'm up!"

"I know you are, baby, but you're awfully tired, should you go to bed?"

A slow nod, "Yeahhhh…tired…"

I step to him, "I know baby, here, lemme help you." I hold out my hand and he takes it. I have a flash of remembering Mickey's hand earlier, and tell myself firmly, No. This is the hand I want in mine.

I lean back, gripping tightly and letting my entire weight fall back, giggling at how little my mass budges him…but I do provide the necessary impetus to overcome the deep inertia of the rocker, and he rocks forward onto his feet; he's up so suddenly that I'm starting to fall back but his strong hand closes tightly.

"I gotcha," he mumbles.

I kiss him lightly, "Yes sir, you do."

As we move to the door, he says, "Oh yeah don' forget, school meeting tomorrow. Reich." He turns to look at me. " 'sadumb name for an American, innit?"

I nod in mock seriousness. "Yeah, because Cruse is sooooooo Anglo." He laughs quietly and I ask, "What time is the meeting?"

He holds up his index finger. "One. Uno."

We're now through the door and I have the idea that if I can keep him talking, I can keep him moving. "And he's Jessica's counselor, right?"

He nods again, "Ja. Herr Reich. Jawohl!" and he gives a bad-boy giggle.

We're at the stairs heading to our room. "Gonna be okay on these?" I ask.

He pulls his arm from around me and mounts the first step, waving any assistance away. "I can do it."

I step back, "Okay."

He stays on the first step and I wonder if his progress has stalled and then he says, in a voice that's more clear: "I don't like when happy has to feel special. Shouldn't be that way. Happy's sposeda be normal…"

I nod, "I think so too."

He squints, "You promise? 'Cause don't think I'm gonna forget just because I been drinking. You gonna make it so it's back to us being happy again?"

I try hard not to sigh, "I'm going to do my best baby."

He seems to consider, then nods, and then pushes himself up the stairs without another word.

It's awhile before I can bring myself to follow him.

THE NEXT MORNING does indeed feel like a return to simpler times. The kids are bustling about getting breakfast and backpacks; I'm finishing putting lunches into bags, making sure everyone has everything they need.

Keith has a meeting this morning with a couple who are renting the restaurant for an anniversary party, they want to discuss menus. He seems chipper and fresh, not suffering any ill effects of the night before. Gotta hand it to him, the boy has recuperative powers. He glances out the window, waiting for Bo to come give him a lift back to where he left his car last night.

The kids are, as usual, absorbed in their own affairs. Matthew is making short work of his Cap'n Crunch, and Jessica is splitting her attention between her yogurt and texting her friend Rebecca. Jessica isn't aware of our upcoming meeting with Mr. Reich—We haven't hidden it, but we haven't gone out of our way to advertise it, either. I'm sure we'll be talking to her tonight about whatever is discussed.

Keith says, "There's Bo!" and then he calls a reminder from the door. "One o'clock?"

"One o'clock," I call back to him, and he blows a kiss, waves, and is gone. The kids follow moments later, calling desultory farewells as they head off to school…and just like that, I'm alone in a quiet house, with a kitchen full of dirty dishes. The thing is, I *like* doing dishes. It's a simple task, you can see your progress growing in the gleaming pile of clean bowls and plates…and you're free to think.

This morning, my thoughts turn, predictably, to my new job—which may or may not soon be my old job—and how our household runs and how I used to contribute and what I do and don't do now to contribute. I think about all the things I know Keith must be doing when I'm away, and whether he knows I'm aware of that, and appreciate that.

Maybe I need to speak up more, let him know how much it means to me and to our family, the way he's embracing new tasks and doing so well. I need to let him know his competence is recognized and appreciated…

My thoughts continue down these paths and before I know it, I've got a rack of spotless dishes, an empty sink, and no clear sense of how to bridge this divide between my husband and my work.

It is on these questions that the chirp of my cell phone intrudes. I step to the kitchen table and rummage in my purse. It's a number I don't recognize…"Hi, this is Joanne."

The voice at the other end is a male whose voice isn't familiar, "Ms. Cruse? With Make-A-Difference?"

"Yes, this is Joanne Cruse, what can I do for you?"

"Ms. Cruse, my name is Anne Gilmore, I'm with a company called Coastal Solutions, I don't know if you got the voicemail I left at your office number…? But that's where I got your number, off the recording there?"

I have no idea what he's talking about—apparently my name and number are now a part of MAD's outgoing message. "I'm afraid I haven't had the chance to check those messages yet Ms. Gilmore, so I'm glad you called me, what can I do for you?"

"Well we're kind of in a jam. We're having our annual management meeting in Boston starting in two days, and I just got word our keynote speaker was in a traffic crash and won't be able to attend."

"Oh, how awful," I sympathize. "What can we do to help you, Ms. Gilmore?"

"Well, I've spoken to a couple of different people who speak highly of your organization. You guys are basically corporate consultants, right? You help

businesses accelerate their performance?"

I smile at the idea of businesses moving faster and faster like a speeded-up film. "Accelerate, optimize, fine-tune, whatever verb you'd like to use for 'improve,' yes, that's what we do, by addressing a range of leadership and motivational issues throughout a company's culture."

"Oh, that sounds exactly right!" she enthuses. "Listen, do you think one of your co-workers would be available to speak at our management dinner on Thursday night?"

Thursday. Whoa. I flash on Keith and my promises about happiness…but I'll worry about that later. "Can you tell me a little more about what you're envisioning?"

"Sure, I was thinking, you could fly in that morning, spend three or four hours in the afternoon getting to know a little bit about our culture, and then present something that evening at the dinner, and then you could fly out the next morning?"

I assess this description. "Soooo…you're not really looking for any kind of generic, motivational speech or overview of any topic. What you're really asking for is a kind of first-impressions site inspection with an oral report to follow."

"Yea, I guess so. Is that something you could do?" She makes no effort to disguise the hopefulness in her voice.

Is it something we could do? I have to assume that these sorts of talks aren't unusual in the consulting world…but what if the site inspection reveals trouble? Do they really want a keynote speaker's slot given over to a list of problems?

Still, I decide, thinking quickly, there must be ways to handle this that I'm not seeing clearly right this second; this must be an issue Doc and Mickey know how to handle. "Ms. Gilmore, I'll need to double check with my colleagues, but I'm pretty sure one of us can help you out. Why don't you go ahead and pencil us in, and I'll do my best to get back to you before the close of business today with a firm decision and a quote?"

Her relief is almost palpable, even over a cell phone. "Oh that is so great! I can e-mail you our address and some basic info about the company, and you've got my number on your cell now, right?"

I smile again at her enthusiasm, "I sure do Ms. Gilmore. You'll hear from someone within a few hours."

"Thank you *so* much!" The line beeps, and she's gone.

I stare at my phone, my mind reeling. Ridiculously prominent in my thinking is the idea that my name and number are on MAD's outgoing message…I can't resist, I have to call and listen. I hear Doc's comforting voice telling the caller, "This is Dr. B.F. Pitz, and you've reached the offices of Make-A-Difference. Apparently, we're so busy making a difference that we can't take your call right now, but you can either leave a message at the beep or call one of my associates…" and it goes on and yes, he's saying my name and my number.

It's stunning how powerfully good this feels, to be officially on the team in this way, and I feel a surge of hunger for this. I want this. I want to keep this. I need to find a way to make this work, even with traveling, even with Mickey, even with everything, I need this…I'm so lost in thought that it takes a second for me to realize there's been a beep.

"Hey, guys, this is Joanne, look, there's another message on here somewhere from a lady named Anne Gilmore, she needs a keynote speaker this Thursday and I told her I thought we could help her out, but I needed to talk to one of you first. I'm not one-hundred-percent sure about whether we do what she's asking for, if either of you could gimme a call and I'll fill you in, that'd be great, I'll be tied up from one to two, but free otherwise, thanks."

I flip the phone shut and the time shines up at me. I have to keep moving if I'm going to be on time at the school. Finish tidying the kitchen, shower, get dressed…as I'm debating the galactically difficult question of which shoes, my phone chirps and I see Doc's number on the screen. I answer it, "Hey Doc!"

"Hello Joanne. Am I correct you've landed your first client for our firm?"

I feel a flush of pride and try to control it. "Only because she called me, when the fish jump onto the bank for you, I'm not sure you're really landing anything."

He chuckles, "If the fish feeds your family, I don't think anyone worries about your technique. Tell me the situation."

I lay it out for him as I move around my bedroom, putting in earrings, rolling lint off my skirt. I finish with the same fear I had when speaking to Gilmore: "The only thing is, Doc, what if they're another Missoula Ironworks, you know? If they're hiring a keynote speaker, they're sure not expecting someone to come to the podium and say 'your firm is at the edge of the cliff of despair,' you know?"

"Which is why this task will be the perfect test for you."

I pause in my preparations, "Come again?"

I can hear the smile in his voice. "Frankly Joanne, the odds are overwhelming you'll find a strong company—they have sought an informative and useful keynote speaker, and upon losing their first choice, they have not taken the easy way out but instead have invited a stranger to assess them and then speak to their managers at an annual meeting.

"This is not the behavior of an organization that's frightened, nor one that's in the habit of deceiving itself about outcomes. Nevertheless, I almost hope you *do* find Missoula-sized issues when you visit."

I'm aghast, "Why?"

He continues smoothly, "Because that would be the ideal way for you to learn how best to phrase even the strictest criticism in the language of allegiance and optimism. I can't think of a better crucible in which to test your capacity for resisting negative responses when confronted with the unconscious incompetence of our clients."

I can't help smiling, "You mean it'll be a good way for me to see if I can shut up and be sweet for a change?"

He laughs, "If you like, yes."

We talk a bit more, about fees and ranges of services, and about appropriate expectations for a few hours' attention, and we end with the understanding that I'm to give it a try.

Then I call Gilmore back and tell her it's a go, and listen, smiling, to her thirty seconds of gushed enthusiasm and relief. I hang up feeling excited and energized. I've secured a client. My name is on the answering machine. I have a chance to demonstrate growth and commitment. I'm being trusted.

Now to go fix my daughter's school troubles.

I BUSTLE INTO THE MAIN OFFICE of the school and glance around for Keith when I hear him calling from somewhere in the rear of the warren of smaller offices to the back of the main area. I lean to see down the cinderblock corridor, and there he is, waving me toward them from a chair in front of a desk behind which a gentleman I assume to be Mr. Reich is sitting.

"I'm sorry, I didn't think I was late; I hope you gentlemen haven't been waiting long," I say as I walk in and hang up my coat, pulling the remaining empty chair a bit closer to the desk.

"Nah, Ronnie and I were sharing bad-beat stories. Turns out he's a poker player, too." Keith smiles at me and I smile back.

The fellow behind the desk extends his hand to me. "Ronnie Reich, call me Ronnie, please, Miz Cruse."

I take his hand and shake it. "Hi Ronnie, I'm Joanne."

I settle into my chair and there's an awkward moment in which we all regard one another, each waiting for another to go first. Ronnie realizes this is his role, and he opens a folder before him on his desk. "Keith, Joanne, I know this is not an easy visit, but I want to put you at ease by saying first of all, we're not here to castigate your daughter or to point any fingers of blame. We're here to figure out how to get Jessica back on track.

"Now," he says, handing various copies of printed forms to us, "As you can see here, and as I'm sure you both know, Jessica is extremely bright and has always been a very capable student. Her standardized test scores, right…there…" he reaches with a pencil to point out the figure he means, "show her to be at the top two percent of all high-school students nationally. And as you know, she was the top student coming out of her middle school to us.

"Since her arrival here, however, she's been…well, I'm afraid 'under-performing' would be putting it too mildly." He hands us each another sheet of paper. "These are her grades as of the end of last week for all her classes. These grades will be on her mid-term report, which will go home at the end of this week." He watches us each as we sag in our seats at what we see: F, D, D, C, C, F.

Keith is the first to speak. "The F in math, we knew about that, that's what brought us over here…but this other F, in Phys Ed? Can you tell us anything about that?"

"I didn't think it was even possible to get an 'F' in PE," I murmur.

Ronnie nods. "It's generally not a grade that happens, as long as the student participates…but Jessica hasn't been participating."

Keith and I both cock our heads. "Not participating?" I ask, "What does that mean, 'not participating,' you mean, like, she's cutting the class?"

Ronnie shakes his head, "Not exactly. I spoke to Coach Davis about this, and she said the policy is, any student can choose, on any day, not to dress out… but if they choose to not dress out, to not participate, they get a zero for that day's grade. And Jessica has had a great many of these non-participation zeroes."

"But that's crazy," Keith says, glancing at me. "Jess loves PE, she loves sports, and she's always been crazy about PE."

Ronnie smiles ruefully, "I think she might be crazier about Hank Baskins."

This name is new to me, but Keith is shaking his head, rubbing his temples. "I knew it," he's muttering.

I'm lost. "Who's Hank Baskins?" I ask, looking back and forth between the men.

Keith looks over at me and smiles. "Hank Baskins is another guy with a Porsche," he says, and I wonder if he can see the sliver of ice sliding neatly into my belly. Luckily the look on my face still reads as confusion, and Ronnie pitches in.

"Hank's a Junior on the soccer team and he's also got a free period when Jessica has PE. He likes to wander down to the gym—any of the varsity athletes are permitted to work out during free periods—and I don't think he has to twist your daughter's arm very hard to talk her into opting out of PE to spend time with him."

"Wait, slow down," I say, lifting a hand. "Okay, apparently some boy Jess is crushing on comes to visit during PE, but back up, this non-participation policy—on what planet can you go to a class but decide whether or not to participate?"

Ronnie is nodding, "It's a fair question…but if you think about it, the answer is 'All of them.' After all, you can sit quietly in the back of every single class you take, and do no work, and pass no tests, and probably end up with a zero or close to it. PE is a particularly sensitive area, because some kids feel badly if made to run a mile in front of their classmates for time—"

"Fat kids," Keith interjects.

"And," continues Ronnie smoothly, "other students prefer not to attempt such things as the rope climb—"

"Fat kids scared of heights?" Keith inquires, eyebrows mockingly high.

Ronnie spreads his hands, "We live in a time in which schools are asked to do everything they can to avoid making any particular kid feel different or inadequate. If a student prefers a single zero to being made fun of or looking foolish, we like to think this decision is best left up to the student."

I lean in, "We can address the socio-political forces at work in our schools some other time, we're here about Jessica, and she has not opted for a particular zero, she's opted for so many that she has an F in one of the few slam-dunk courses available at any school."

"I can fix that one damned quick," Keith says, leaning forward with a grim look on his face.

Ronnie starts to speak but I override him, "Yes, because historically a father telling his daughters she can't see a particular boy has an overwhelming success rate, right?"

Again Ronnie opens his mouth, but this time it's Keith who beats him to the punch, "You got a better idea?"

By now Ronnie has decided to sit back and choose his moment more carefully. I answer, "I think so. I think we need to ask her if she really wants to spend time with any boy who only wants to see her at times when it hurts her. It's not like he's been coming around the house or even calling, is it?"

"Who knows?" Keith's hands are spread, "Between cell phones and instant messages and a million other things, the boy could practically be her constant companion and we'd never know it!"

"Folks!" We both turn to look at Ronnie, having almost forgotten he was there. "Mr. Baskins deserves our attention, I'm sure…but we also know that as of this moment, that's a fairly simple problem with an obvious solution.

"I wonder if we could use our time to look at what are, to my mind, the more difficult issues. I know how an F jumps off the page, believe me…but I also imagine the D's and C's are unfamiliar sights, am I right?"

Keith and I both nod. It's certainly true. Jessica's lowest grade before this had been a B- and she had cried for almost twenty-four hours straight. "Ronnie, I know this may sound like an odd question, but does Jessica…does she *know?* About these grades?"

Keith has been looking at me while I ask, but he instantly grasps the significance of the question and looks keenly at Reich who shrugs and answers, "I can't swear she's done all the math leading to these averages…but she has surely seen the individual grades which brought us here."

Keith and I share a look. This means Jessica has been keeping her performance from us…which frankly troubles me more than the actual grades. An academic struggle is one thing; a struggle with honesty is an entirely different problem.

Ronnie seems to see the direction of our thinking and is quick to step in. "We see this a lot," he says reassuringly. "Kids get to high school, they aren't ready for the difference in the workload, they get in a little trouble, they think whoops, I'd better turn this around, but instead the problem gets worse and they feel as though they've already waited too long to ask for help, and they kind of dig themselves into a hole. So it's our job to help pull them out."

I'm nodding, "That makes sense. And for that job, we need a plan."

Keith snorts, "I've got a plan. How about 'Turn this train around missy, pronto, these grades are totally unacceptable!' Does that sound like a plan?"

I shake my head, "It sounds like a plan for making her do what *we* want her to do, but we don't want her working to pull up her grades because she's afraid of what we'll do to her. Someday she's gonna be out in the world, and she'll have to do things because *she* wants them, not because she's worried about Daddy getting mad. Right?"

Keith nods reluctantly. I know it's not how his Dad raised him, but that doesn't mean he can't recognize good sense when he hears it. I try to put myself into planning mode, and I realize that some of MAD's tools could be just right for this situation. "You know," I say musingly, "I've just started work with a consulting company that helps organizations cultivate a more self-directed and self-motivated workforce. There's a technique we use to encourage more effective, behavior-based goal setting called 'SMARTS' and it might work here."

Keith snorts, "Let's be sure we stay away from anything called FLUNKS."

I roll my eyes at him and continue, "SMARTS is just an acronym for remembering the key points of any well-considered goal. S for specific. You have to know exactly what you're going to do to achieve a certain outcome, like a course grade. Your actions must be defined in a specific, quantifiable way, and preferably within a certain time frame. Not just 'Get better test grades' but 'study your class material one hour per weekday until the midterm exam, and during this period turn in all homework assignment on time' or whatever.

"M for motivational. There has to be a reason for making the effort—positive consequences that can be envisioned. The grade itself might be one of these positives. It might also include approval from teachers, or from parents. It might be the vision of yourself as someone who can aim for something and then achieve it.

"A for attainable, meaning the goal is challenging but is perceived as achievable.

"R for relevant. It's gotta be a goal that makes sense for what the person is trying to do or be. Jessica always talks about wanting to be a Veterinarian, but she sure can't get into any veterinary-science program if she doesn't get excellent grades in high school.

"T for trackable, which means progress can be measured, tracked, enabling Jessica to continuously assess how she's doing, whether she's on track. For example, Jessica can readily count her hours spent studying for a course, as well as the number of completed homework assignments. These steps toward achieving a goal can be tracked.

"And finally the last S stands for shared. Jessica needs to share her goals with her family and her teachers. Once she's shared them, she knows she's not alone. She'll receive encouragement and support from the people who care about her. Specific. Motivational, Attainable, Relevant, Trackable, and Shared—SMARTS."

Keith's looking startled—maybe by the simple and effective notion of the acronym, but I think even more by hearing me reel it off with such confidence and understanding. Maybe he's getting a glimpse of his wife being a competent professional. Maybe it's something he never really thought about very closely before.

LEADERSHIP LESSON 12

Process goals are set for the behaviors needed to accomplish an outcome goal and are Specific, Motivational, Achievable, Relevant, Trackable, and Shared.

This attention makes me feel a little taller, a little more sure, and I say, "I think most of SMARTS goal setting is going to be our job at home, but I do want to talk about specific and attainable. We want to give Jessica specific targets and we want them to be targets she can be reasonably expected to achieve.

"Let me ask you, Ronnie," I continue. "If Jessica really got her act together, really buckled down, do we have any sense of the grades that are mathematically possible for her before the end of the semester?"

Ronnie looks very proud of himself. "I asked all of her teachers that exact question. These are the collated results of what I was told." He hands us a sheet of paper which lists A, B, B, A, A, C. Keith and I look at each other, surprised and pleased.

"This looks better than a lot of the report cards I brought home at her age," Keith observes wryly, and Ronnie laughs.

"Okay, here's what we do," I say, sketching out my idea on the back of one of the pages. "Tonight, we give Jessica a page with three columns. Column one looks like this, with her current grades, F, D, D, C, C, F. Column two will be these maxed-out possibilities, A, B, B, A, A, C."

"What goes in column three?" Keith asks.

I shake my head, "Nothing."

He looks baffled, "Whaddaya mean nothing? Why's it there for if nothing goes in it?"

"I mean, *we* don't put anything in it," I explain. "That's the column for Jessica to fill in. That's where she's going to write her own targets for each class. Assuming she wants to improve, of course."

"Oh, she'll want to improve," Keith says grimly. "We'll make damn sure of that."

"No, Keith," I protest, "It doesn't work if the targets and the process goals aren't from within herself. If they come from us, they're meaningless, they won't last!"

He snorts, "We've *seen* how she does setting her *own* goals, this is the problem, we haven't been involved enough, and that's what's gonna change."

"But Keith—"

"Folks?"

We both turn to look at Ronnie, almost startled to be reminded someone else is in the room. When he sees he has our attention, he continues, "She's going to want to improve. If I know one thing in this job, it's this: People want to do well at what they believe is important.

"We're wired that way, we generally don't try to do things we don't care about, and once we're trying, we want to succeed. If we can assume Jessica believes school is important, wanting to do well takes care of itself.

"Jessica's lucky to have two such devoted parents. It makes her day-to-day life a lot easier than some of the kids I see, but trust me—she doesn't need you to make her want to do well. All kids, all grownups—we all want to do well, to feel competent at what we believe is important.

"But it's critical to believe we have a chance of succeeding. My advice to you is help her see that chance. Help her believe it. She'll take care of the wanting."

We all look at one another and nod slowly. "You know a thing or two about self -motivation, don't you Ronnie?" I ask with a smile.

He smiles back, "Maybe a thing or two."

Before we leave, we also focus on making sure Jessica's process goals will be trackable. Yes, she'll get periodic grades on tests and homework assignments, but we want to be able to pay closer attention than that.

Ronnie produces a form which will be completed each week by each of her teachers. It will provide a specific window into each teacher's sense of Jessica's progress. Each week, Jessica and Ronnie will meet to discuss these forms. Either Keith or I will come to the first two or three of these meetings but then we'll back away.

LEADERSHIP LESSON 13

When people believe they are competent at worthwhile tasks, they are inclined to be self-motivated.

"Why not come to all of em?" Keith asks. "What's the harm?"

"She needs to gain ownership of all this, Keith. We're not gonna be one of those helicopter parents, always hovering overhead every step of her life, going into meetings with the Dean when she's in college, negotiating the contract for her first job.

"She needs to believe we're on top of this and we care, that we're on her team…but she also needs to own this process, and that can't happen if we're always around. We'll make it safe for her and then we'll ease back. By the time her grades are up, she'll know she did it, for herself."

We shake hands all around and then Keith and I make our way to the parking lot. Keith asks, "So we'll sit down tonight after dinner?"

"Yes," I nod. "We'll let her know how we see things, and we'll let her fill out her columns and go from there."

Keith is looking at me with something I realize is surprise. "I gotta say, Jo, you were really something in there. If this is the kinda stuff you do in this new job, then I can see why you like it. You're good at it. And like the guy was saying, we like to be good at important things." He kisses me goodbye, and I smile.

It's nice to be appreciated.

THE FAMILY CONFERENCE with Jessica is surprisingly smooth. We can tell she's nervous about our having called her into the front living room—the place where all serious business is discussed. She doesn't even let herself see the columns I've drawn—the second she sees the school's letterhead on the page, she bursts into tears.

"I'm sorry Mom! I'm sorry Dad! I didn't know what to say, I didn't know how to tell you, I've never had even one F in my life and now I've got two and I don't know what's happening, I try really hard, I really do, but I lost my math worksheets in the first week and then I kept trying to get an extension and then finally my grades were going to be so low it wouldn't have mattered anyway and I didn't want to tell you and then I was so nervous and freaked out, I started forgetting other stuff and I couldn't study and I don't know what to do!!"

We both hold her, and tell her it's going to be okay, and in a few moments she's calmed down enough to talk. We talk about how things are changing now that she's getting older, how much more important it is for her to take a good hard look at herself every day, to evaluate how she's doing and to ask for help the second she thinks she might need it.

As we talk it becomes clearer and clearer to me how much fear she's been walking around with, how she must have felt more and more trapped and crushed by her own initial decision to try to fix things herself. We let her know we're on her side, that she never has to face these kinds of fears alone, that she can always come to us and tell us what she's up against. We'll never refuse to help her as long as she can promise to be straight with us. She makes that promise right now, fervently.

Then I explain the column idea to her, and hand her the page and ask her to fill it out. She's as pleased and relieved as we were to see what a strong outcome she still has available, and I can tell she's also relieved by the idea of the weekly check in. Again, I feel great compassion for her. She's clearly *wanted* the chance to check in with grownups, and maybe she was simply expecting too much of herself, trying too hard too fast to be independent.

When she chooses her grades, we're both pleased to see her choose the highest possible grade for every class except English, where an A is possible and she chooses a B. When Keith challenges her on this decision, she looks slightly embarrassed, but then gives the sense of someone sticking to her guns when she says, "Dad, the guy is a total tool. Everyone in the school hates him, except for the ones who sleep right through the class.

"He makes up weird assignments and weird tests and changes his mind about what we're supposed to do about ten times a day, and yeah, mathematically, maybe I could get an A, but what if I kill myself and try to be perfect and the guy just weirds out and decides that anyone who got an A on the last test must take it again.

"He did that last week! And you know, some kids had crammed the first time, and they didn't know they had to do a re-take, and so they weren't ready and they did pretty badly. And that's the grade he counted!

"Then he said he proved they hadn't really *learned* anything, and his grades would only reflect *learning*. I would hate to kill myself for an A in there and then have him do something weird to wreck it. I think a B is a reasonable grade for me to hope for."

We nod. "You're the student, honey. They're your targets. Now you need to make a plan—you need to decide what you'll do, every day, to hit the target you set for yourself. We'll help you stick to it, and we'll help you keep track of how you're doing."

We go over all the other grades and talk briefly about the process goals and plans for achieving each one. Then we talk briefly but with some seriousness about the Haskins boy and PE. She's clearly startled we know about him, and sheepish. Then she mumbles something about never having liked that creep anyway, and I get the distinct impression young Mr. Haskins has moved on to some other girl—which is just fine with us.

When Jess walks out with her plan, her head is high and she has a spring in her step I realize I haven't seen in weeks. We've lightened her load, and that feels good. She's focused, she's motivated, and she wants to do well for herself. We haven't demanded anything of her, she's decided on her own targets, for her own reasons, and I know from experience she will set SMARTS goals to facilitate success.

Keith moves closer, warmed by our success with Jessica, and he says, "We done good, baby," and he kisses my cheek. Then he says, "Hey, the restaurant is gonna be closed for a private party Wednesday night, they don't need me, I thought maybe I'd cook something special for all of us. I'm gonna do some shopping tomorrow morning, any special requests?"

Wednesday. Dammit. With all the attention on Jessica's problem, I had forgotten to tell him. I start haltingly. "Listen Keith, we just got a call, today, *I* got a call, there's a firm out in Boston, and they're in kind of a bind, they lost a speaker and—"

His face falls, "Jeepers, Joanne, you're not going on *another* trip are you? You just got back!"

I hate knowing how disappointed he feels, and I hate even more that I'm the one causing it. "I'm sorry, baby, I meant to tell you earlier but then we got so caught up at the school and everything, and I—"

"You think my problem is that you're telling me a few hours late?" He gives an incredulous laugh. "Yeah, okay, right now is maybe three percent worse than earlier, but it's not the timing of you telling, it's that you're *going*, period!"

He's not the only one who's upset now. "How many times are we going to do this, Keith? Is it gonna be every time? Every third time, how often do you plan to make this scene before you figure out that my *job* involves *travel?*"

His eyes narrow and I realize a beat too late that my sarcasm has made things worse yet again. "Figure out? It's not hard to 'figure out' you're gone all the damned time!"

"I'm not—"

"And you promised!" He's practically yelling now, and I wince. I don't want our kids to hear this.

"Keith please, lower your voice, what are you—"

"Oh, right!" he exclaims even louder than before. "You wouldn't want people to hear that you can make a promise right to someone's face and then less than twelve hours later break it!"

I try to keep my tone low and level, hoping I can bring him down to my level of volume. "What promise are you talking about?"

"*LAST NIGHT!*" he roars. So much for hoping that calmness might be contagious. He continues, "You stood right in this room and told me you would do your best to get things back to where we weren't stressed all the time about you being gone; you said you'd do your best to help us all be happy again. Is this your *best?* Cause it's a piss poor effort if you ask me!"

Something in me snaps, "A poor effort?? I'm trying my level best to learn to do this job before they decide to fire me, which no matter how happy it might make you is not exactly a swell plan for this family!"

He laughs bitterly, "Right, of course, it's much better for us all for you to run all over the country all week every week, helping people you don't even know, while we're here missing you. You see more of *Mickey* than you do of *me*, is that your idea of your 'best'?"

"Gee, Keith, I don't know," I retort bitterly. "Let's think for a minute. Last night I had a chance to stay out and have a drink with an interesting and charming co-worker who's teaching me a new profession, but instead I said 'No, I need to come home and be with my family', and boy was *that* a rewarding decision.

"I got to come home to an empty driveway and then the husband I had chosen to come home to showed up almost too drunk to *walk*, so please, yes, let's have a lecture from you about people doing their best, I certainly got your best last night, huh?"

I know I'm going too far but I'm sick of this, I'm sick of this argument merry-go-round, the same thing again and again…but I can see the startled injury on Keith's face and I muster every ounce of control I have and I go for a calmer tone and say, "I know it's hard. I don't like it. You don't like it. We're going to have to figure out some way of making this work, but the phone rang, the client was in a jam, it was short notice, and sometimes things happen, and I'm sorry."

Keith is shaking his head, denying the reality of it, wishing it could all go away, and I just can't help him, I can't make it go away, and that crack about Mickey hurt more than I expected, so I add, "And for your information, I'll be going on this trip alone. Mickey won't be there, and it may not matter to you very much but this trip you hate may actually be my very last chance to prove I belong with this company. If I don't knock this one out of the park, I think I'll be updating my resume. Just, you know—FYI."

"Maybe that wouldn't be such a bad thing," Keith mutters.

I know he's confused and angry and embarrassed with my low blow about him being drunk, but this quiet wish for my failure punches some dark and corroded button deep inside me.

"Of course," I say coldly, "You're right, it would be wonderful if I lost this job, because our mortgage and our bills and the kids' braces and the new hot-water heater, those are all gonna be covered by three nights a week of you wearing your little chef's hat. How silly of me."

Keith head snaps up and his eyes are pained and I instantly wish I could take everything back. His face is wounded and disbelieving, and knowing I've done this, that my anger and my pride have brought me to a place where I could so badly hurt the person I love most in the world makes me suddenly nauseous. "Keith, I'm sorry, that was way out of line, please—"

But he's already moving past me, his head down, making for the front door. I try to follow him, calling after him, "I'm sorry, I was wrong, you know I didn't mean it, please!" but he doesn't slow, moving to the front door, yanking it open and striding through it, and then slamming it behind him so hard the windows rattle.

A moment later I hear his car start and it squeals out of our driveway and down the street.

When I turn, I see both of the kids staring at me wide-eyed, and I turn away so they won't see my own tears forming.

I feel more than ever like someone who is running out of chances.

CHAPTER 10

*"Whoever thinks marriage is a 50-50 proposition
doesn't know the half of it."*
–Franklin P. Jones

DON'T SLEEP VERY MUCH the rest of the night. I spend some time pretending to read, some time getting up every three minutes to look out the window for Keith's car, a dozen occasions with my cell phone in my hand, my fingers itching to punch the one button where his number is stored…but no, Jo, he didn't roar out of here because he wants phone calls, leave him be…

After a time I turn off the lights and try to force myself to sleep, which works about as well as it ever does. Three ideas are at war for my attentions—there's the Town Crier in my head, keeping tabs on my rapidly-dwindling chance for sleep, "Two o'clock, you've still got five hours! Two-fifteen, not quite five hours!"

Then there's the Worrier: "Where has he gone? Is he okay? Is he drinking and driving? Will he come home?" Last but not least is the Scolder: "Good job Joanne. Way to be fourteen. You found exactly the right words to make him feel bad. Oh that *wasn't* what you wanted?"

At some point, I must drift into something like sleep because the sudden beeping of the alarm startles and disorients me. After a moment's confusion, a wave of remembering rolls over me, and I practically lunge at the window to see if Keith's car is still gone. I stifle a sob of relief when I see it in the driveway. Perhaps he slept downstairs. He's still angry, but he's home and he's safe.

Down the stairs I go, and yep, there's a snoring mound wrapped in a quilt, and I feel a mix of affection and regret. The kids are both moving around the kitchen in confused quiet—they don't want to wake him, but they're not sure what's going on. After Keith left last night, I spoke very briefly to them about us having argued and Daddy needing some fresh air, but that was the extent of my explanations.

"Did Dad sleep there all night?" Jessica whispers. I nod.

"Was it 'cause you made him?" Matthew asks, wide-eyed and intrigued.

I give a small smile. "No, Sweetie," I whisper back. "It's because Mommy was a jackass."

"Daddy was a little bit of a jackass too," comes the sleepy baritone from the couch, and all three of us whirl. Keith grins at us over the back of the couch—I'm sure we must have looked funny all turning in unison at the sound of his voice.

Keith explains further, "We had an argument, and I decided I needed to get away for a few minutes because I was getting too angry to think. You know how sometimes you get so frustrated you can't even think about easy things? So sometimes it's better to step back for a minute and give yourself some room; and that's what I did. And then when I got home it was late and I didn't want to wake up your mom."

"Are you done arguing?" Matthew asks with the directness of all young children.

Keith looks at me for a beat and then says, "I don't think we're done talking, but I hope we're done being mad."

He looks at me, seeking confirmation, and I'm quick to agree. "That's right. I'm going to try to remember that I'm one of the grownups around here."

"Okay guys, get a move on, you're running late, scoot, scoot!" Keith rises from the couch, herding them toward their lunches, their backpacks, and out the door. I can see their relief on their faces and in their bodies—they're relieved things seem to be back to normal.

When they're out the door, Keith turns to me, and his face is serious. I hurry to say, "I wasn't just saying that stuff to keep the kids calm, I *was* a jackass last night, I was mean and I was hot tempered and I'm sorry for all of that."

He nods slowly, "I'm sorry for some of what I said too. But I wasn't just saying stuff either, Joanne. We *do* still have things we need to talk about. We need to figure out how this is going to work, and…" He pauses, seeking words, obviously frustrated. "I drove around and I calmed down some, but it's not like I saw some great answer come down from heaven, you know?

"I don't like the random vanishing act. I don't like thinking you're going to be home and then finding out you're not. I didn't marry a cop or a firefighter or a soldier or any of the people whose careers are structured that way. We said we wanted stability and a home and…I dunno, we have the home but just lately it doesn't feel very stable."

Whatever happens, I'm determined to not let myself become angry again. I know he's frustrated, I know he's scared, and deep down I think part of my frustration is that I don't know the answers to the questions he's asking.

"How about this," I say slowly. "I need to talk to Doc today anyway, to check a couple of things about the trip I'm taking tomorrow. How about if I ask him whether these trips are always so spur of the moment, and if he says yes, maybe I try for some arrangement where Mickey is the rapid-response consultant, and I take the jobs which have a little more lead time?

"Mickey's been doing it longer anyway, he's quicker on his feet, and it would make sense to keep me on the jobs where I have more time to prepare. The truth is, I'm pretty terrified about this thing tomorrow…"

Keith smiles, "That could work. It's worth a try anyway. And by the way, you're supposed to be scared. I never wanted anyone on my team who wasn't nervous on game day. You know?"

I move closer to him. "Does this mean I get to be on your team?"

He touches my face with one of his large hands. "You *are* my team."

And then I'm in his arms and the world is suddenly bright and warm again, and all the voices in my head are quiet and I know I'm in exactly the only place that matters.

A BIT LATER, I'm preparing to head over to the MAD office to make sure I'm up to speed on some basic concepts and strategies, and just as I'm putting my purse on my shoulder, my cell beeps. It's Mickey.

"Hey, you," I answer. "I was just on my way to the offices, are you over there?"

"Yeah, whatcha need?"

I laugh, "I have no idea. I'm heading out tomorrow and since we don't really know what I'm going to find or what they're going to need to hear, I just want to make sure I can get a decent idea of what a generic presentation about MAD's offerings would look and sound like."

"Yeah, I hear that," Mickey agrees. "We've got plenty of initial presentations and proposal stuff on our servers here; you can probably offload a fair amount of material onto your laptop and get a basic feel. They're not expecting any kind of multi-media presentation are they?"

"No, no," I answer quickly. "Just a talk. An after-dinner keynote speech. Your idea sounds perfect. Hey, they were going to messenger some tickets and stuff, has anything come in this morning?"

"Hang on…" I can hear him shuffling through a few things and then, "Yep. Here it is. Looks like your good to go."

I take a deep breath. Good to go. Okay. Better get moving then. "Cool, then, thanks, Mickey, I'll see you in a few."

"Joanne, wait." His voice sounds concerned, which has *me* concerned. "Listen, I don't want to freak you out or anything, but the reason I was calling is, I want you to know, they had to admit Doctor Pitz to the hospital last night."

I feel my breath stop, "What's wrong?"

Mixed in with his concern is a thread of frustration. "Aaaaa, they don't know. He was having back pain, and it kept getting worse, and he figured it was something tightening up from the walk-a-thon, you know, but it finally got so bad he went to the ER, and he figured they'd give him some codeine and remind him to stop acting like he's trying out for the track team…but then they said they needed to run a few tests. That's all we know."

"Is he still in pain? Have you talked to him?"

"Yeah, I just got off the phone with him, that's why I thought to call you. He sounded a little down to me, he gets the same non-answers over and over again from everyone, and there's a lot of sitting around, you know? He feels like he's just wasting time and you know how he hates that."

I know exactly what Mickey means. Doc was multi-tasking before anyone had coined the term. Sitting in a hospital room with nothing to do and no clear sense of what was happening was about as close to Hell as I could imagine for him. "Mickey, is he over at the Med Center?"

"Yeah, he's…" I can hear him hesitate and then he continues, "He's in their Oncology wing."

Again my breathing gives a hitch, "They think this is the cancer?"

I can almost hear Mickey's shrug, "I guess they must or they wouldn't have him there…but I think that's part of what's frustrating, too, no one is really saying anything for sure." He pauses for a moment and adds, "I'm thinking he's a little spooked."

"Well, I'm going over there," I say decisively. "I need to talk to him anyway about my trip tomorrow and about some other stuff. I can take his mind off the waiting and maybe even force a few answers."

Mickey chuckles, "Those doctors could talk to the folks at Missoula Ironworks to find out what they're in for."

I laugh and then say, "Yyyyyeaaaaahhhhh, and you shuddup. I'll be by later to get those files." We say goodbye and then I head for my car and point it for the Montgomery County Medical Center.

WHEN I FIRST ARRIVE, I have sudden misgivings about whether surprising him is a good idea—I remember my grandmother *hating* people seeing her in the hospital—but when I tap on his half-open door, his expression of delight makes it clear I've done the right thing.

"Joanne! What a treat, come in, come in. Please," he gestures at the chair by his bed.

I lean in to kiss his cheek and give him a quick once over as I settle into the chair. He seems fine; a few circles under the eyes, but I imagine I'm no better in that department. His face looks a little drawn, thin…but he's wearing a thick, terrycloth robe so it's hard to see whether he's actually lost weight or not…but overall he just seems like the same Doc I've known for most of my life.

"You doing okay? Mickey gave me the quick run-down on how you got here, but he wasn't sure how you were feeling today."

"Supremely irritated," he declares. "Exasperated. Powerless. Fundamentally wasteful."

"Wasteful?" I lift my eyebrows.

"There's so much to do!" he explodes. "My goodness, Joanne, do you have any idea how busy Make-A-Difference is, how many requests and offers are coming in every day? It's a critical time for us. When you left Perfect Plastics, we were at our wit's end trying to keep up. And the moment you join us, things move into an even higher gear. All I can think about are the calls not being answered, the e-mails, the proposals to weigh and evaluate, the data to analyze, and I can't do any of that from here!"

I don't believe I've ever seen Doc this worked up. I feel like a child discovering for the first time that her parents are only human, that they can feel pain, that even they can feel helpless. I lift a hand to reassure him. "Mickey is there and you know he's able to handle whatever comes in. Nothing is going to fall apart because you miss one day."

"Of course not," he fumes. "Nothing will fall apart, but nothing will grow, either. I'm of the opinion we need at least one more full time consultant, but I can't do anything about *that* from in here, either."

I have a sudden inspiration. Jeff! Jeff would be *perfect* for this work, and now that Perfect Plastics has folded its tents and vanished into the night, he needs an opportunity. This could be a really good fit across the board. "Doc, I may have an idea on this exact topic."

I fill him in; tell him about Jeff's expertise with Quality issues, the rapid improvements he made in Perfect Plastic's processes, and his easy skills with people. I get more and more excited as I talk, certain this is a home run—I can help my new company and my best friend from my old one, all in one bold stroke.

When I've finished, Doc is nodding and smiling. "It sounds like a splendid idea, Joanne. If he's everything you say and if he's interested in helping us, we can have him out on the road very soon. The trips are piling up almost faster than we can arrange the airfare."

I shift uncomfortably in my seat. "Yeah, um, actually, Doc, I was hoping you and I could talk about that a little bit."

He leans forward a bit, "Something's wrong?"

I sigh, and then give a brief recounting of my argument with Keith. I conclude with "The thing is, Doc, I'm not even sure who's right, or whether we're both right. I mean, my family needs us both to bring home a salary. My work with you and MAD is rewarding in every way, the kind of work I could imagine doing a long, long time.

"But on the other hand, I can definitely see where Keith is coming from. Never knowing when or if I'm going to be there, all the simple rhythms we think of as 'home life' aren't really available and I know that's got to be troubling. But I don't see any simple alternative and I don't see Keith suggesting one. All I see him doing is complaining, and I'm not indifferent to his worries, but..." I trail off, my hands up, helpless.

Doc nods, "You've got an equity problem."

I'm not following him. "You mean like assets? I mean, we've actually got a fair amount of equity in the house, but I don't think it's time for second mortgages or for—"

LEADERSHIP LESSON 14

Equity in a relationship occurs when each person perceives the participants' input/ output ratios are equivalent.

I stop because he has lifted a hand, chuckling. "No, no. The equity to which I refer is what we call relationship equity. Relationships are built upon a sense of trust and of justice, yes?"

"Yes...?" I answer carefully.

"Well then. An important component of that sense of justice is the belief there is equity of effort, equity of burden, and of course equity of benefits."

"You're saying each person has to believe the other is doing his or her share, in a way that's fair for what they get in return."

He smiles, enjoying how easily we revert to master teacher and prized pupil. "Precisely. We refer to what you called 'share' as input and output, and relationships are more stable when the input and output ratios are balanced.

"If either person believes that he is over-giving, *or* feels under-rewarded compared to their partner, distress develops. There's a sense of injustice—this person sees himself as giving more and getting less, with the other person giving less but acting entitled to more."

I shake my head slowly, "I dunno Doc. I mean, yeah, you sound like you're describing Keith's point of view pretty well, but you're talking about this like it's universal, and I have to say, I don't think I've ever given a moment's thought to anything like that. I can't tell you how many times I've put in an eight-hour day, came home, made dinner, packed lunches, helped with homework, and all while Keith was out teaching a cooking class for a measly fifty bucks because it's something he loves to do, you know?"

Doc chuckles, "I see why you think you're an exception, but you're not. Can you guess why?"

I know from all of our time together, Doc doesn't pose these questions if he doesn't believe the answer is within my reach. I think about what he's just said about rewards, and it hits me. "Is it because I happen to be the kind of person who finds it rewarding to pack a lunch or help my kid with her geometry?"

He claps lightly. "Well done. That's it exactly, you don't view these tasks as labor—quite the opposite, you view them as rewards.

"For you, they're naturally reinforcing. We call this intrinsic reinforcement. This is why so many relationships which appear imbalanced to a neutral observer are actually in perfect balance *for those two people*—because their particular personalities assess the consequences and the efforts differently than a neutral outsider might."

LEADERSHIP LESSON 15

Self-motivation occurs when the natural or intrinsic consequences of an action are reinforcing.

"Yeah but that's not our deal. Keith doesn't think we're the least little bit balanced."

Doc's face regains a serious composure, "I know, my dear. Which means this is what must be addressed. And just so I'm clear, it seems to me I'm hearing some part of you agreeing with him, or at least not sure whether you disagree, is that fair of me?"

"Yes."

He nods, his eyes up, working whatever complex equations he always seems to have at the ready. "This means you both require a bit of an adjustment to your vision of your home. You need to have a fuller and more accurate notion of your inputs, your contributions, to the home, and so does Keith.

"This will settle your own uncertainty, and it will address his sense of inequity. When he understands the added benefits your family receives from your new career, his comparison of the input/output ratios will come more closely into balance."

I give a wry smile, stepping into my familiar role of translator. "You're saying when we're both aware of my contributions, we'll both feel better about things."

"Exactly," Doc says, looking satisfied. "You've spoken again and again about the financial benefits, and those aren't irrelevant…but are there any other benefits you think your household is realizing?"

I consider the question. "Well," I begin, "In the same way I'm sometimes called away unexpectedly, I'm also unexpectedly home for most of the day, and that never happened when I was a straight nine-to-fiver. Maybe Keith and I need to find ways to exploit those days more fully. Maybe we could use them as surprise dates, or maybe some downtime to do whatever we like, like a little surprise vacation."

"Good!" Doc says enthusiastically, "What else?"

I remember suddenly, "Jessica!"

Doc looks at me quizzically, "Your daughter? What about her?"

I give him a quick run-down of Jessica's school troubles and our meeting with the counselor and the solutions we found. As I come to the story's end, I tell him "Keith made a special point of telling me how surprised and proud he was of the skill I showed in helping us all navigate those questions. And it felt good, you know?"

Doc smiles, "You demonstrated competence, and your competence was recognized and rewarded."

"And that's gotta count as my input, right? That's definitely a way my work with MAD benefited my household without involving a single dime."

Doc smiles with pleasure, "Yes indeed. And I'm sure you can think of other things too. This is a conversation you should have together, if possible. Keith's a smart fellow. Once he realizes his sense of inequity is the source of his frustration, I imagine he'll be eager to pay attention to it. This is also true in workplace relationships, it's not only domestic—mutual perceptions of equity are the cornerstone of support and growth."

I can feel myself relaxing. Yes. This is a conversation I know how to have, and we can talk about it together, work on it together, instead of feeling like we're on opposite sides of something. "Thank you, Doc," I say softly.

He beams, "Happy to help. Do you feel ready for your trip tomorrow?"

I pause a moment to shift my thinking in that direction. Am I ready? How can I even know? I have no idea what they want or what they're like…"I'm not sure," I admit. "I'm gonna stop by the office later today and Mickey's gonna help me get some general, introductory information from some of MAD's files, but it's hard to know what I'm going to say until I see what they're about, you know? And then, I'm a little worried that whatever I see will be something I hadn't prepared for."

He nods, pondering the problem, "You know, there's one domain which is almost always useful, wherever you find yourself."

"Really? You have a one-size-fits-all keynote speech somewhere?"

He laughs, "In a way, I suppose I do. It's about transformation, about continuous improvement. I know you understand the value of a transformational culture as opposed to a transactional culture, but whatever level of health a company might represent, there's always room for further growth, further improvement. Given this fact, it's never a mistake to talk about some of the underlying principles for how improvement happens."

I lean in, "This sounds perfect."

He continues, "Organizational improvement is inevitably founded upon personal improvement. Personal improvement starts with a sincere commitment to actually improve oneself, to actually change. It's an every-single-day component of self-discipline and self-motivation."

I'm nodding along, "Okay, fair enough, but what does that commitment look like? What do you *do*?"

"Exactly the correct question. Commitment to an idea is easy and ultimately vague. Commitment to actions that can *achieve* the idea—that's the key. There's a four-step process even I use, every day of my life, and I'm convinced it helps to focus and enables me to do my best.

"The first step is performed immediately upon awakening, every single day. I reaffirm my commitment to improvement and ask myself, 'How shall I work to improve today? What am I going to do differently?' In other words, I have a little chat with myself to figure out what situations might provide me with opportunities to better myself.

"For instance, perhaps someone has pointed out to me that I tend to go on and on when speaking, leaving my listeners behind." At this he glances up wryly at me, and I grin back at him.

He continues, "Perhaps under such circumstances I say to myself, 'Today when I realize my voice is the only one I've heard in the last few moments, I'm going to pause, and ask whether I'm making sense.' Every morning, I renew my pledge to improve, I find something to work on and I derive a plan for working on it.

LEADERSHIP LESSON 16

Continuous self-improvement starts with a daily behavior-based commitment, then noticing opportunities to perform the target behavior, self-congratulating occurrences of that behavior, and finally reflecting on relevant success and room for improvement.

"Step two occurs again and again throughout the day. I work very hard to keep myself attuned to the opportunities I identified during the morning, and I often pause and replay the last few minutes in my mind to see whether I missed any of those opportunities.

"Step three occurs whenever I'm successful at executing today's plan. Am I making sense?"

I nod before I even realize what I've done, and we both laugh. Doc continues, "You see? I was going on and on, but I did what I had pledged to do. I asked for your feedback, and now I'm congratulating myself for following my plan. And along the way was the practical benefit of actually being courteous to you and ensuring the communication is flowing.

"Finally, the fourth step, which comes at the end of the day. I reflect and have a little bit of a debriefing chat with myself. How did I do? Why did I miss this opportunity or that one? How could I handle things differently to not miss those opportunities next time? What should I be considering for tomorrow's plan?

"By the time I'm ready for bed, I know how, or if, I've succeeded in my intent to become a little bit better at something. And guess what?"

"What?" I ask.

He smiles, "I sleep *very* well."

We both laugh again and I test my understanding. "So for instance, I could wake up tomorrow and say, 'Today I want to work on helping my kids feel empowered to make their own choices about the ways in which they complete their chores.' Then maybe I decide to give them a little flexibility, like giving them a window of time and saying 'do your chores any time you like as long as you're done by dinner time.'

"Then I look for opportunities to praise them when they do well, and maybe give corrective and optimistic feedback if something goes wrong. Then at night I go over everything and grade myself. Is that the idea?"

Doc is clearly pleased, "First-rate, Joanne. You're still my favorite student."

He is reaching to pat my hand when he suddenly freezes and his face twists in pain. "Doc?" I lean forward, alarmed, "Are you okay? Is it your back?"

His teeth are clenched and the color has drained from his face. I know something about pain, and he's clearly in real distress. He manages to nod and I say, "I'm going to get someone!" and then I dash out into the hall.

I run to the nurse's station. "I'm a friend of Doctor Pitz, he's having some sort of episode, I don't know if it's a muscle spasm or what but he's in a lot of pain!"

The nurse nods and says, "Okay, I'll be right there," but continues going over the charts in front of her.

I don't know what she's doing with those charts; I don't know whether it's as important as my friend, and right now I don't care. The assertive woman Mickey joked about at Missoula Ironworks is suddenly here, and her voice cuts through whatever the nurse is doing. "His pain is not in some abstract future in which you're taking care of him, nurse, his pain is right now and he needs you *right now.*"

She regards me for a moment, sees how serious I am, nods and moves from behind her station, moving quickly toward Doc's room, with me following. Upon entering his room and seeing him, she turns to me and says, "I appreciate you letting me know, you're going to have to leave now."

"You'll take care of him?" I ask, no longer fearsome, just afraid.

The nurse is clearly accustomed to people's worries and she gives me a very professional smile of reassurance. "We're going to give him the best of everything, I promise."

From within the room I hear Doc's hoarse, pain-tightened voice: "Don't… Don't worry Joanne. I'm…tougher…than any backache."

I find something like a smile and blow him a kiss and tell him I'll see him soon. Then I turn and walk down the hall. I pull my sweater around me, suddenly chilled.

I walk a little faster…and then a little faster…and then suddenly I'm running, and when I push through the door to the outside my face is wet with tears. I glance up at the window for his room, thinking to send a little prayer his way.

The curtains are drawn.

CHAPTER 11

"Ranking people, teams or divisions induces conflict,
destroys morale, and prevents optimization."
–Dr. Edwards Deming

T HE FOLLOWING HOURS FLY BY in a complex stream of different
worries; worries about Doc tend to occupy the foremost part of my mind,
but they're occasionally crowded out by worries about the next day's trip to

Boston and my uncertainty about what will be asked of me and how well I'll be able to improvise.

I had stopped by MAD's office after leaving the hospital, and between bouts of fretting about Doc's condition, Mickey had helped me pull some key materials representing the essence of the work we do…but it would still be up to me how best to make use of these ideas once I was actually on-site.

There is also the hovering concern about what Keith and I might do to resolve his concerns about the role of this job in our lives. The concerns are not only his, if I want to be fair. I'm concerned, too—armed with the new understanding Doc has given me, I want to correct any equity imbalances in our marriage, whether they exist in his perception or in mine.

In the brief time we have to discuss it, I tell Keith how Doc's sudden hospitalization left me unwilling to mention any big adjustments in how MAD does business, but I promise to bring it up when I have returned from Boston. I also tell him I have a better grasp on why he's feeling unhappy, that I think the things I'm learning for my job are going to give me some of the tools I need to help us fix this, the same way I was able to use my new skills to help with Jessica's problems at school.

"But right this second it's like I'm cramming," I tell him, a pleading tone in my voice, "I feel as though some invisible professor just told me I have an eight-hour oral exam tomorrow, and I have exactly one night to prepare. Will you hate me too much if I beg you to wait just two more days for us to talk about everything?" And then I tuck my chin and look up at him, rapidly batting my eyes in my best, pitiful-puppy fashion.

He can't help laughing and he says it's fine. The sound of his laughter is a welcome balm. I'm sure everything will be fine…And then my thoughts turn to Doc and those curtains closing. Enough, I tell myself. Save your energy for the things you can actually do something about. Thus resolved, I return to the materials I've brought back from the office, and it feels as though I fly past the remaining hour in exactly that mode.

BEFORE I KNOW IT, it's the next day, and I'm clearing yet another line of metal detectors and x-ray machines and getting onto yet another airliner, this one bound for Logan airport in Boston. With a rueful smile, I realize I've traveled more in the last month than I have in my entire life…and the sum total of all of that travel is my new, intimate knowledge of the subtle and sublime differences in hotels and company conference rooms from one city to the next. Someday I'll have to try visiting these places again, with a little more time to take in a few sights.

When I'm studying my materials on the plane, my mind drifts back to the earlier trips and my apparent inability to keep my mouth shut when my temper rises. This time it's even more complex than simply shutting up because I don't have Mickey to lead things.

I remember Doc's self-prescription for self-improvement, and I give myself a few firm instructions: Today, I will notice when I begin to grow angry. I will remind myself the people with whom I'm spending time want to get better, that I can help them as long as I hold my temper. And I can hold back my temper. I can. I say this last part a few dozen times. There are two or three times I even believe it.

I ARRIVE AT THE PLANT a whole two minutes ahead of schedule and I'm met by Anne Gilmore, the company's HR Manager. As she leads me in, she reiterates some of the key points from the literature she had included with my tickets—I've read it all carefully, of course, but it's nice to hear which points she thinks are important enough to bear repeating. She's particularly proud of their repeat status as one of the top two companies in their industry among the Fortune 500, and of their steady and clearly sustainable growth.

As we walk, she hands me a neatly typed agenda for my time with them today. I read along as she runs down the list: First, I'll meet with plant Manager Josh Roberts, after which I'll spend a half-hour with something called the "Culture Committee."

Afterwards, I'm to spend 45 minutes with six first-level supervisors, followed by a meeting with eight hourly workers from the production lines. It's a nice cross-section of the entire workforce, and it will give me every opportunity to tailor my keynote address to the particular ways they do things around here.

The first thing I notice when Anne shows me into Josh Robert's office is the floor-to-ceiling bookcases behind his desk. It doesn't seem much like the office of your average Plant Manager—rather, it seems like the office of an attorney, or perhaps a college professor.

I can spot certain familiar dust jackets; there's the typical bunch from Covey, Senge, Block and others. There are also several addressing the specific issue of Quality, with many of the best sellers on lean manufacturing. There are the usual suspects dealing with Six Sigma and the Kaizen processes, but there are also books on workplace safety and even a couple of the Malcolm Gladwell bestsellers.

Looking at the range of his library, I'd have to say that ranking so high with the *Fortune* 500 is no accident.

My first impression of the man himself is equally compelling. As Anne introduces us, he comes from behind his desk eagerly, shaking my hand and obviously hoping to put me at ease. We exchange pleasantries, with mutual insistence on first names. As Anne excuses herself, we settle into the two chairs in front of his desk. Another plus—he's not going to use his desk as any sort of barrier. He wants to be out here with me.

When I ask him what he's hoping for from my visit, he smiles and shrugs. "As I'm sure Anne told you, we lost our original keynote speaker, but we've heard some pretty terrific things about your firm. I think we're a strong company, but I'm not about to kid myself into thinking we've got nothing to learn. If you spend the day with us and tell us we're perfect, well then that's great…but if you find a few things you think we could stand to work on, then hey, that's even better."

I nod, impressed by both his humility and his courage. The best are never afraid of hearing how they might get better. "It's clear from everything I've seen and heard that you're a very high-performing company—can you tell me anything about how you drive that performance?"

Josh points at me, "Self-motivation—that's one of your firm's specialties, right? Good, good, absolutely, I'd love to hear your thoughts on how we are doing in this area. I think we've got a pretty good system in place.

"One key to motivating our successful performance is ongoing, rigorous evaluation of all of our critical processes. We use balanced scorecards at every level of management, from the CEO right down to our first-level supervisors."

I'm not sure what he might mean by this. "Are these scorecards a way of tracking certain processes and objectives?"

He nods, "Exactly. We track twenty-five key business metrics, including both leading and lagging indicators of our performance in safety, quality, customer satisfaction, productivity, employee leadership and culture. We like to give ourselves the broadest possible view of how things are going, like letting your eyes sweep across the indicators on the dashboard of your car.

"And we're especially careful about making sure we don't focus too obsessively on any one indicator. It's a big-picture mechanism, and 'balance' is key."

I'm following him, and it all sounds smart and progressive, but I'm having a little trouble moving from the conceptual to the specific. "Could I ask you to help me see a little more clearly, maybe with how you track things under the heading of culture?"

"Sure," he says, reaching for his desk and retrieving a folder. "In our culture we track two lagging metrics and one leading one. The laggers are retention and employee visits to HR—and we learn of those *after* whatever has caused the problem, you know, so that's why they lag. They're indicative, but only of conditions that might or might not still be present.

"The leading metric is really a bundle; it's the percentage of positive responses we get from a periodic survey of twenty-eight separate questions about our culture and about how our employees feel about working here. And you know, most of them aren't really questions; they're statements about an ideal workplace and participants rate their level of agreement from one to five, from 'strongly agree' to 'strongly disagree.' It's all pretty standard stuff."

I nod. The survey may be standard, but that doesn't mean the implementation is. "Can you give me a sample question?" I ask him.

"Sure," he agrees. "The first one is exactly the kind of thing we want to know: 'My ideas are heard by the organization and are often implemented.' This is followed by the one-to-five scale of agreement, and a box for 'additional comments.' "

I grin, "Do you have a question for 'I feel the comment boxes on these surveys are carefully reviewed and discussed by management?' "

He laughs, "Once we actually asked that, or at least something like it. I think it was, 'I feel these surveys are taken seriously by the organization.' "

I'm surprised, "What percentage of 'agree' or 'strongly agree' did you hit with that one?"

He looks almost sheepish, "Ninety-one percent. And most of the comment boxes were full, too. People like working here. We know they work hard, and they know we listen. It's a good arrangement all around."

I'm getting more impressed by the second. "So this…balance, this dashboard, you like how it works for you?"

He nods vigorously, "Yes indeed. Six dials on the dashboard, safety, quality, customer satisfaction, productivity, employee leadership and culture. That way we don't get too focused on one at the expense of the others.

"We used to be terribly reactive. We'd have a safety issue and it would have our full attention, then we'd have some customer satisfaction problem and everything would swing over there—it was like watching a boat full of people, first everyone is on one side and the boat leans wayyyyyyy over, so naturally everyone runs like crazy to the other side, which makes it lean wayyyyyyy over the other way. Balanced and proactive is better."

I'm curious about how they did things in the past. "When you say reactive, what was it you were reacting to?"

"Oh, all kinds of things," he shrugs. "Sometimes it was the results of an internal survey; sometimes someone at the top would read an article somewhere and get a big idea.

"Sometimes we'd bring in a consultant," he smiles wryly at me as he continues, "and he or she would say, 'This is the process you should implement,' and then we'd devote all of our energies to doing whatever the consultant said, recording our results, shooting for whatever numbers she told us to shoot for, celebrating whenever we had the 'results' we thought we wanted. But it turns out those kinds of results are always temporary."

"Because they originate from external sources?" I ask.

He nods approvingly. "Bingo. Over the years, we've come to understand that sustained improvement comes from a sense of inclusion, which leads to a sense of ownership. Everyone who works here feels, correctly, that this is his or her company, and takes pride in mutual ownership and responsibility. Each employee develops his or her own behavior-based goals, and there's no employee in this entire organization who doesn't feel empowered to give supportive or corrective feedback to any other employee."

Well!" I say brightly, and begin pretending to gather my things. "Thanks for having me, I don't think there's anything I can add, so…"

He throws back his head and laughs loudly. It's startling how pleasant a sensation it is to hear a raucous laugh in such dignified surroundings. The sense that this is a good and comfortable place to work is palpable. "Tell you what, Joanne," he says, "If you get through the whole day  and you don't find even one thing you think needs our attention…then please, I beg you, stay for your speech and say exactly *that*."

I notice a large plaque behind his desk. On it are seven terms, modestly sized in the gleaming metal: Integrity, Quality, Safety, Continuous Improvement, Customer Delight, Employee Inclusion, and Community. "What are those?" I ask.

He turns to follow my gaze and smiles, "Those are the company values. I'll bet you whatever money you have on you right now that any employee on this property can list 'em for you without missing a beat. We make them central to our annual evaluation, every question is in the context of those seven values."

"This annual evaluation is different from your balanced scorecards?"

"Yes, we use a focal-point review process at the beginning of each new year, and by February we have the results which allow us to rank them accordingly."

"Rank who, the employees?"

"That's right," he nods. "They're ranked according to their individual contributions."

"Ranked in what way?"

"We assign a numeric value that allows us to categorize each employee in terms of the financial benefits of his or her performance. If you're ranked a Three, it means you've consistently exceeded our highest expectations, and you'll therefore be slotted for at least a five-percent salary increase plus stock options.

"A ranking of Two means an above-average performance and a raise of three to five percent. A One indicates average performance, but that means average for *us*, which is still above average in most places. This means a raise of as much as two percent depending on our profits for the year."

Something about this narrative is setting off alarm bells in my head. Coastal Solutions is clearly well ahead of most companies in terms of its understanding of the three C's, and I had only been half-joking with my early departure. However, it seems out of character for them to do something as important as an annual evaluation with such broad and clumsy strokes as reducing all workers to the rank of One, Two, or Three.

It doesn't feel compatible with true community and interdependence among co-workers—in fact, it's exactly the sort of thing that would make my blood boil, but I remember my promise to myself on the flight, and decide to hold my tongue. They're not at the top of the Fortune 500 for nothing. Maybe they have something to teach me.

LEADERSHIP LESSON 17

A ranking system that promotes win/lose over win/win thinking and acting does more harm than good.

I'm congratulating myself on my restraint when I notice Josh has stood, and I follow his lead, shaking the hand he offers. He says, "I think your next stop is to sit down with our Culture Committee. They can tell you a little more about how we integrate those values on the wall over there with our evaluation process."

He ushers me to the door as he says, "It's a real pleasure to have you with us today, Joanne. You're gonna come by here at the end of the day to debrief before your talk tonight, is that right?"

"I think so. I go wherever Anne tells me."

He laughs again, moving toward the door. "That's always a good policy. I'll be very interested to hear your thoughts later, Joanne. Thanks again." And with that, he shows me out, where Anne is waiting to escort me to my next stop.

IT TURNS OUT TO BE only a short walk down the hall to yet another—you guessed it—conference room. Inside are the eleven members of the Culture Committee, about which I'm both curious and impressed.

I've never heard of a company designating a specific committee solely to focus on culture issues…in fact, I'd be willing to bet a great many companies would think the term "culture" applies to the paintings in their lobby. The fact that Coastal Solutions understands the importance of this domain seems to me another likely reason they're so far in front of their competition.

The group lives up to my hopes. After our initial introductions, I ask the question foremost in my mind: "So folks, help me out. What's a culture committee? What do you do?"

There are smiles all around and the man sitting closest to me, whose name is Raymond, says, "Well, our mission statement is 'To help the organization define individual and team behaviors that reflect the values and mission of our company.' Which means, basically, we check that individuals and work teams within the organization are aligning their efforts with the company's core values…and when we learn of a potential gap between behaviors and values, we look into it. We talk to the group leader, or the shift supervisor, or whomever, and try to figure out what's happening and how to get things back into alignment."

"We're culture chiropractors," says a woman at the other end of the table, and we all laugh.

"How many of you are from management?" I ask.

Four of the eleven participants raise a hand. I learn that two of these are first-line supervisors, one a mid-level production manager, and the other is Anne

Gilmore—the HR manager who's been my guide today, and the only one who's a member of Josh Roberts' direct staff.

"Great," I answer. "And just so I'm clear, did this committee form as a result of a management plan or a worker idea, or was there a particular problem you were formed to address, or what?"

Appreciative nods around the table. A cheerful-looking woman to my left says, "Okay, for the record, you're the very first visitor we've ever had who didn't just assume we were formed to fix some huge problem."

"But it's not the case," says a burly man who represents some of the hourly employees. "I've been working here for almost twenty-one years, and this committee has been here for at least ten of those years, and I've been on it for six. As far as I know, it was formed as part of the company's commitment to pay attention to everything that affects the workforce. I've never heard of a company that listens more closely to its people, or works harder to keep them happy."

There are nods all around the table. Raymond speaks again and says, "Basically we work in concert with the Management Team to find new ways to keep everyone feeling included, to make sure all of our workers know they belong here, that this is *their* company. Any company that takes care of that is going to have better productivity, better quality, better customer satisfaction, better retention—just everything better, right down the line."

"Okay," I say, playing devil's advocate, "That's all great, but aren't you really describing the job of management? Aren't you just, you know, basically handling some of their work for them?"

"There's no 'their work' or 'our work' at this company, ma'am," says a slim young woman at the far end of the table. "Everything that happens here is everyone's responsibility." Again the table nods and murmurs agreement.

"Okay, so, that's good…" I muse, "But if the committee has been around for at least ten years, what's left to do? Isn't everything pretty much fixed?"

A graying maintenance worker chuckles, "Well, now, I been at this kinda work for a long time, Miss, and I can tell ya—we didn't always call it 'culture,' but the good feeling of any company can go south like that!" He snaps his fingers. "New technology, new products, new employees—the smallest thing can start to tip a smooth company out of balance. You need to keep an eye on things."

Raymond adds, "Even with nothing new entering the picture, it's not as though knowing what ought to be happening guarantees it will happen. This is a company of several hundred human beings, and human beings make mistakes. Even when things are going very, very well, we still end up spending a certain amount of time examining the range of human errors and misunderstandings. How could they have been prevented? Can we prevent their recurrence? And so on."

I nod, "I spent a number of years as the Director of Safety at a plastics manufacturing plant. Believe me; I know that intentions and outcomes don't necessarily match."

I see some of them click into a fractionally more attentive mode—it helps if they know a consultant has once worked in the 'real' world—and then I ask, "Can you tell me a little more about the…what should we call it, the maintenance aspect of your work? Do you do anything in particular to track whether ongoing work aligns with the stated values of your company?"

There's a low roll of laughter and the cheerful-looking girl says, "Sometimes it seems like that's *all* we do!"

Raymond explains, "We ask that each team meet on a monthly basis to define a variety of work-related behaviors they observed over past weeks that are consistent with our company's values, and behaviors that are not."

"And then you collect all of that data somehow?" I ask.

He smiles patiently, "We do more than simply collect it. We sort it, summarize it, offer comments, and then distribute it throughout the company so any employee in any department can have the opportunity to discuss these observations and learn from them. In fact, some of the teams actually schedule their meetings to coincide with these distributions. That way, their meetings focus on their own analysis and discussion of the same specific observations."

The twenty-year-man speaks up, "That way, a single mistake has the chance to educate the entire company."

The slim woman at the end adds, "And a single value-driven choice can reflect and support the things everyone is trying so hard to live and work by."

I have to admit, I'm seeing all three C's in abundance. Community, with everyone working together toward mutually-understood processes and outcomes. Choice, with everyone in the community feeling empowered to provide input for improvement. And Competence, with all employees believing they do meaningful work, while showing sincere desire to make themselves a better and more effective contributor on both personal and professional levels.

I congratulate them on their impressive mission and leave with Anne. As she walks me to my next stop, I tell her I'm frankly dazzled by what I'm seeing and hearing, and she smiles quietly. "It's a very good place to work," is all she says, opting shrewdly to let my experiences speak for themselves.

"Oh shoot!" I say, actually stopping dead in the middle of the hallway. Anne looks at me with concern, and I instantly smile and wave away whatever worries I've provoked for her. "It's nothing," I say, "I'm just a ditz. I really meant to ask those folks back there to tell me a little bit about their perceptions of the annual evaluations."

"Ohhh…" Anne says uncertainly. She turns and gestures back toward the room. "I could call everyone back, maybe, if you think…?"

I shake my head, "No, it's not that important. I know we're on a little bit of a tight schedule, I don't want to keep anyone waiting. Maybe I'll be able to ask some of these other groups."

"Is it anything I could answer for you?" she asks.

"No, I just…You know, Josh, mentioned them toward the end of our time, I just wanted to hear a little more about how effective they are at motivating people," I say, working to keep my tone light. I don't want Anne to think I'm fishing for trouble—even *I* don't know what I'm fishing for.

She nods, "Well, for what it's worth, I don't think they're much more than an accounting mechanism. They're certainly not the only feedback our people get, or even the most vital feedback."

"But it's the feedback most directly connected to their pocketbooks, right?" Ohh, careful, Jo, you sound like a girl looking for a fight, keep it light…

Anne looks thoughtful, "I suppose that's true. And I'd have to say we get our share of visits to HR from employees who aren't happy with the way things have shaken out…but on the other hand, you can't just give the maximum raise to every employee every year. Everyone here is trying, and everyone here is doing well, but there are some people who achieve extraordinary things in their departments, and you know, they deserve to be rewarded."

I nod causally, doing my best to back out of this topic, "It makes sense when you say it like that."

LUCKILY, WE'VE ARRIVED at my next stop, which is another meeting room in which I'm introduced to a team of five first-level supervisors: Bob, Sherry, Molly, Mike and Tim.

I ask them all some basic questions about how they monitor the people working under them, how they provide feedback, and what mechanisms are in place to sustain motivation? They tell me about their successful performance-management process, and I begin quickly to understand what Anne meant about the annual evaluation not being anyone's only source of feedback.

These five supervisors tell me they meet with every employee quarterly for one-on-one feedback and goal-setting sessions. They also mention their teams do monthly self-evaluations in personal-development groups.

As they explain how these meetings work, they smile as they remember some initial resistance from the employees they were evaluating. They tell me how the employees whined and complained during the sessions—"Isn't this the job of a supervisor?" was the common refrain.

However, over the last few years, these development teams have made believers of the employees, as the benefits of this regular one-on-one feedback have been quickly evident.

These self-development teams are comprised of no fewer than five and no more than eight employees. They are self-selected. Once a month the team members take three-to-five minutes to state how they think they did at work this month, specifying their personal strengths and weaknesses. Personal stories to support a particular self-evaluation are encouraged.

Then, the other team members give this employee frank and relevant behavior-based feedback, with an initial focus on positive observations. The employees take notes during these meetings and then bring those notes to the quarterly meetings with their supervisors. This helps both parties frame their conversation around the work accomplished to date and the specific plans for improvement in the coming quarter.

I learn that the summary appraisals I've been wondering about are an outcome of these prior continual development conversations, not a one-time surprise about what went right and what went wrong. This partially alleviates my concern, since I'd seen at other companies what the one-time "root canal" meetings do to morale. I'm still uncertain, however, about the impact of an overly simple and impersonal numeric rating system as a means to summarize an entire year of effort.

Then, out of nowhere it happens.

As I ask a question about how they manage their training functions, Bob—who oversees the training function for his entire building but who also supervises his own team of line workers—speaks eagerly, "It's a good time for you to be asking about this, Joanne. We've just finished implementing a new set of procedures for gowning-up in the clean room and everyone feels pretty terrific about it."

A distinct stillness comes upon the five, who glance at each other before Sherry asks, "Bob—what new procedures?"

Mike almost speaks over her, asking, "How long has this been happening?"

I'm suddenly uncomfortable; there's clearly something making all these people very tense all of a sudden. I know clean rooms are needed for manufacturing products that require a dust- and fiber-free environment, such as computer chips. The rooms look like futuristic operating rooms, and like operating rooms, the workers within them have to "gown up," putting on surgical gowns and caps, special glasses, even special shoes or disposable covers for their own shoes.

So the topic isn't strange to me, but the sudden hostility in the room is *very* strange, particularly in a workplace marked by good humor and camaraderie until now.

Bob answers coolly, with a kind of studied casualness, "Maybe a week, maybe more, what's the problem?"

Molly barks a bitter-sounding laugh, "Are you serious?"

Bob turns to look at her, and the lack of confusion on his face belies his words. He clearly understands what's upsetting these people—even if I don't—but he's playing dumb for reasons which don't yet make sense.

"Yes, Molly," says Bob, "I'm actually not in the habit of asking a question unless I'm actually in search of information. You've asked me if I'm serious and I've done you the courtesy of answering, so now I'd like the same favor please: What is the problem with our having implemented a superior procedure successfully?"

I'm feeling very awkward, like I'm the five-hundred pound elephant in the room everyone is pretending not to notice. Or maybe they're not pretending—maybe they're so upset they've actually forgotten me. Either way, I can't very well sit in the middle of this anonymously as though I'm stuck in bad traffic. "Folks, I'm sorry, I'm afraid I'm not quite following—"

Sherry holds up a hand, "Wait a second please, Joanne, we need to have this conversation."

Part of me feels as though I should meekly retire, but I'm here on a job and I don't work for Sherry. "I understand Sherry, but my problem is that in about two more hours Josh Roberts is going to be asking me what I've seen today, and I'd rather not have to say, 'Lots of good stuff and then a fight in the sandbox between five of your supervisors.' "

Sherry looks at me in surprise and I continue with my calmest voice, "I'd be happy to step outside for a few minutes if this is something you'd prefer to settle among yourselves, but I can't do the job you're paying me to do if I don't understand what's happening."

Tim speaks for the first time, "You will talk to Josh later, yeah? Well maybe you could tell him his training supervisor for this building is so busy running his own little popularity contest that he can't be bothered to keep his fellow supervisors up to speed about his special activities."

Bob rolls his eyes, but his face is flushed and I have a feeling Tim has just scored some sort of major point, and my feeling is strengthened by the grim looks of agreement I see on the faces of the others. Tim continues, "You can't just keep doing this Bob, it isn't how things are supposed to be, it goes against half our core values."

Bob still has the carefully-rehearsed look of disbelief on his face. "What do you mean 'keep doing this,' you're right, I should have told you about the new procedures last week, I forgot, I'm sorry, but the procedures are working great, everybody wins and you're acting like this is something I've done more than this one time, and I think yo—"

Sherry is suddenly ticking things off on her fingers. "The recycle process. The scheduling process. The holiday coverage process. You want I should keep listing things? Do you seriously think we just forget the other times because you want us to?"

Bob shrugs, as though these facts are irrelevant, "I'm sorry you're upset, Sherry. I wish it were different."

Tim laughs incredulously, "What the hell do you mean you wish it were different, no you don't! If you wanted it to be different, it'd *be* different. You *don't* want it to be different! You want your people to be the first ones to get the new, more comfortable eye protection and the better clean-room shoes, while all of our guys are still using the old glasses and the crappy shoe covers, and why?

"So you can score a few more points when they do their satisfaction surveys? And meanwhile, our people are grading us lower because they think we're somehow failing them. They see your guys getting all the best stuff and they think it's somehow our fault?"

Bob simply receives this flurry impassively, almost as though he's bored. Mike studies him and then asks softly, "Bob, what's going on? You didn't used to be like this, you used to be a team player, what happened?"

For the first time since that initial flush of color, Bob's face shows some

emotion. The corner of his mouth twitches and he turns to me and says, "You're going to talk to Josh later? Well maybe you could look at those words behind his desk and let him know that you've run into a dispute about 'Integrity,' that's the first one, isn't it?"

The other four are now back on their heels, startled at the venom in his voice and the fact he is apparently accusing their plant manager of a lack of integrity. I'm pretty shocked myself as he whirls on Mike, his voice growing louder, "You wanna know what happened?

"What happened was that you all got here *after* me. I've got seniority over all four of you and my division has always performed excellently, and in the last two years Mr. Josh Integrity-is-a-Core-Value Roberts has promised me again and again I'd be made a Three at my next evaluation."

He has all of our attention as he continues, "It kept not happening, and it was really confusing to me, you know? I had trusted him, I'd worked hard, I'd gotten good reports, but I still wasn't a Three. It didn't make sense. Until I saw what was on the photocopier three months ago. There was a document detailing all of the performance rankings of all our employees sitting right there on the glass, for all the world to read."

I can sense everyone in the room cringing, myself included. I don't know what was on the document yet, but I know that leaving such delicate confidential information where any employee might see it is a huge act of carelessness for precisely the reason unfolding before my eyes right now— people end up with information, but not necessarily with the story behind it. They leap to conclusions that can damage things, even completely destroy interpersonal relationships.

Bob continues, darkly relishing this opportunity to unburden himself of something that has clearly been bothering him for a long time. "Sherry, Mike— the two of you must be awfully pleased with yourselves. You're both six months less senior than I; we all scored the same on our performance reviews and on the balanced score cards, yet somehow…" He gives a massively sarcastic shrug, his face a mockery of confusion.

"You're both Threes! I've been *promised* a Three…but I've never been *given* a Three, you *must* share your secret with me!"

All four of the others are now clearly abashed. If anyone is able to walk this back a bit, we might ultimately agree that Bob hasn't handled this situation well… but no one is willing anymore to assume he's acting out of some cold and selfish plot. It's clear now he's been wounded, and his actions are the wounded thrashings of an animal in pain.

Mike lifts a hand, "Bob, this is all making a kind of sense now, and I get why you're upset. I can't speak for anyone else, but I can tell you that when I was transferred here I was coming from a more highly-paid position. Josh didn't have any more money in his budget for my salary, but company policy prohibits me taking a pay cut for a lateral transfer.

"The stock options for the Three ranking were the only way he could stay within policy. In a weird way, it was integrity that led him to do it—he had to be inventive and find a way to honor the promises the company has made to all of us."

Bob's face is a mask of unhappiness, "At the expense of honoring his promises to me? How is that integrity?? Again and again he's promised me, he's *promised* me…" and suddenly Bob is fighting tears. The room is silent. I can feel his colleagues wanting to reach out to him and not quite knowing how to do it. Maybe this is a good time for me to step in.

"Folks, could I ask you all something?" All five heads turn to me, startled—I almost believe they've forgotten I'm here.

I think quickly for a moment and decide the simplest approach is the best. "Do any of you believe you'd be having these communication issues or the moral dilemma you're facing right now if it weren't for the ranking system? If you weren't being reduced to a number, and feeling you had to compete against colleagues whose numbers were higher, for whatever reason?"

They look at each other, and slowly but with growing confidence shake their heads. Mike says, "If you feel you ought to be ranked higher than you are, and you feel you can get that by somehow shortchanging your co-workers, it's hard to imagine a world in which that doesn't happen."

Sherry adds, "Especially if you've been promised something and then it doesn't happen."

Molly concludes, "It's an invitation to a power struggle, especially if you think the highest powers have somehow abused you."

They're clearly willing to view things from Bob's point of view, and I have no doubt they'll be able to work out their differences without my help. I nod my agreement.

"I think I know what Mr. Roberts and I need to talk about."

TWENTY MINUTES LATER I'm sitting in Josh's office again.

After the meeting with the supervisors, I had told Anne I was sorry to have to change things around, but this last meeting had brought some important issues to light, and I felt it best to speak to Mr. Roberts immediately.

I didn't like forgoing my meeting with the rank-and-file employees, but my overall sense of the company was that it was vibrant and healthy; I wasn't likely to find any problems larger than the one I had just witnessed. I had told Anne I felt it was important to speak to Josh as quickly as I could, because I needed as much runway as possible for the talk it looked as though I needed to give tonight.

As I had waited to learn whether Josh would be able to clear his schedule for me, I fought several conflicting emotions; the nervousness which comes naturally from knowing you have to tell someone about a problem they didn't realize existed, coupled with a sputtering spark of resentment for whatever portion of Bob's story had been true.

Even if I allowed for some misunderstanding; even if Josh's promise was to "try" rather than to guarantee, it still smacked of exactly the kind of manipulation I hate most among upper-management types.

"Easy, Jo," I told myself. "He called you in. His company is hugely successful and he still wants to improve. Give him a chance. Stay cool."

I was still reciting my mantra against anger when Anne told me Josh would be able to see him.

And now I'm here. And he looks very concerned.

"Anne tells me you think you've found something important enough to rearrange your schedule because you thought I should hear it right away?"

"Yes sir," I nod.

He takes a breath and appears to be double checking he's receptive to whatever I'm about to say, and then he says, "I'd like very much to hear your thoughts, please."

I compose myself and then begin slowly and carefully. "Mr. Roberts, I'm wondering—"

His eyebrows go up a fraction, "I'm back to being Mr. Roberts? This must be pretty bad."

I smile, "I'm sorry, Josh. I'm afraid I've found something troubling, and speaking frankly, it's something I was worried I might find from the moment you described your annual evaluation process.

"But before I go any further, I need to ask you something a bit delicate, and I apologize in advance if this seems rude or accusatory, but I need you to help me make sense of something."

He leans forward, totally focused, "Absolutely. Whatever I can do."

I nod and take the plunge, "What can you tell me about any promises you might have made regarding rank to Bob Tyson in Fabrication Training?"

I'm watching carefully as Josh's face sags and he leans back in his chair. The question is clearly painful to him, and I actually feel a wave of sympathy for this man, so obvious is his discomfort. He nods slowly, agreeing with an indictment I haven't actually made.

"Yes, this particular issue has been bothering me for the better part of a year. I got myself into a real fix with this thing."

I feel irritation trying to surge at the way he expresses it, but I keep my voice cool and calm, "I beg your pardon, Josh, but whatever this is about, it's not just you who got into a fix, the entire division is in a fix. But it's not terminal by any stretch of the imagination. Can you tell me your understanding of things?"

He shrugs in the defeated way of a man who can see no options. "Eighteen months ago we had already decided to make Sherry a Three, and we had informed her of it. I had one more Three slot available to be awarded and I had every intention of giving it to Bob. I had even told him—this was my biggest mistake—I had told him earlier in the year I had every expectation of making him a Three."

He sighs, "But then Mike Perdue transferred in, and his new assignment's salary was low in a way that was actually against policy. That was a glitch and we've worked it out since then, but at the time, the only way I could maintain company policy and keep Mike's total compensation where it needed to be was to give him the last remaining Three slot.

"This left Bob out in the cold. I apologized to him—of course I didn't tell him why it was happening, I would never talk about one employee's ranking to another employee—but I told him we had some internal accounting issues which had to be worked out, and I had too few slots, and I was very hopeful we'd settle everything soon."

"But you haven't been able to make that happen?"

He gives another sad shrug, "No, we've been growing the company very aggressively, and even though our revenue stream is very high, it's going right back out the door in the form of new buildings, new plants, more workers...I still haven't been able to create another Three slot. But I *am* trying."

He eyes me curiously and then says, "May I ask how this came to your attention? Did Bob somehow pull you aside and complain about it, or..."

He sees me shaking my head sadly, and he falls silent. I tell him the whole story, simply and directly, and when he hears of the errant document on the photocopy machine, his face falls. I would not have thought it possible for him to look more disappointed but he manages it.

He can't stand sitting still and gets out of his chair, pacing slowly around his office. I remain quiet until he says, "Well, I've been trying very hard for the last few moments, but I have to say I can't imagine a way in which I could have handled this more poorly."

I'm impressed by his willingness to assume responsibility, but he's still missing the point. "Sir, I know you're disappointed to hear all of this, but I think it's important you understand, this episode isn't really the problem."

He looks at me in surprise and gives a small, wry smile. "It isn't? Please don't tell me you've found something worse?"

I return the smile, but I hold my ground. "I'm saying this is a symptom, like numbness in your left arm or heartburn. As uncomfortable as the symptom might be for you, the illness could actually be worse if it goes un-addressed."

"What's the illness?"

"The evaluations themselves. The use of numeric ranking as a way to evaluate your employees. Would it be safe for me to assume you don't need me to quote Dr. Deming to you?"

He nods slowly, "You know, I had that thought some time ago; I knew our annual evaluations were technically a violation of his interdependency principles. But to be honest, I thought it was such a relatively small piece of our evaluation process, with all the different teams and the cross-departmental synergy I knew we had going for us…I just thought, it's a small piece of a big picture, it's a way to keep track of who is getting what sort of raise, we could get away with it."

I shake my head, "I'm pretty sure we can never really get away with reducing our people to numbers, Josh. Even if it seems like it's working for awhile, sooner or later Person A will get upset that he's been ranked lower than Person B.

"It's my very strong opinion you need to implement a non-hierarchical system of evaluations here at Coastal Solutions, something that makes it impossible for any particular employee to be ranked 'higher' than any other. You'll avoid fostering feelings of competitiveness and instead you'll be helping to grow feelings of interdependence and true equality throughout the community you've worked so hard to create and sustain."

He stands very still for a moment, weighing what I've said, and then he says simply, "Yes."

I'm terribly pleased to see him make such a large decision on behalf of his entire company after only a brief conversation. "Good, I think you've got good people in place, you can probably design and implement something more satisfactory in a relatively…"

I trail off because he's staring at me with an expression of honest bafflement. "What is it?" I ask.

"I'm saying 'Yes' to *you*. I'm saying Yes, I want *you* to do this for us, you and your firm. When can you start?"

I feel genuinely confused, as though I'm only hearing parts of what he's saying. "I'm sorry, you're saying—me? You mean—you're saying, what, you'd like me to—"

He laughs again, seeming to return somewhat to the happy confident man I met earlier today. "You haven't done this part of the job very often, have you?"

I shake my head ruefully, "I guess not."

He moves a step closer, "You've done an outstanding job today, Joanne… and I think even more impressive than your ability to diagnose our problem is your willingness to come directly to me and speak difficult truths.

"I'm not about to hire a firm that isn't able to speak bluntly; we're strong enough to take hard truths, but we're not strong enough to wade through swamps of 'maybe' and 'perhaps' and indecision that stretches out for months and months. You were decisive and precise and I think you put your

LEADERSHIP LESSON 18

Effective leaders have the courage to ask for candid feedback and the *humility* to accept and apply suggestions for reasonable change.

finger on exactly the spot where we need help. So again, let me ask—when can you start?"

I know the actual contracts will have to be handled by Doc and Mickey, and the true work of designing the proper remedy won't be able to begin until that work is done…but at a simpler level, there's no time like the present. I grin and say "With your permission, Josh, I'd like to begin with my speech tonight."

IN THE COUPLE OF HOURS between my second talk with Josh and the evening's event, I try to call Mickey to give him the good news, but I get sent straight to his voicemail. I don't want to leave something this exciting in a message, and I know he won't be able to call me during the dinner, so I simply hang up.

Calling Doc doesn't make much sense, if they even let him answer the phone. I want to tell Keith, but I'm not sure how it will go over for me to say I've just secured a lot more trips out of town. Best to just wait.

I get cleaned up and into formal evening attire and look pretty smashing if I do say so myself, and I try desperately to combat my nerves, running through key points, making sure I'm familiar enough to weather the inevitable last second waves of nervousness.

DINNER IS WHAT I'm sure is a delicious meal of prime rib and tender grilled vegetables, but I don't taste a bite of it. I'm also fairly certain I make pleasant conversation with important figures from Coastal Solutions, but that's almost as automatic as my chewing. I couldn't quote a word of any of those interactions even with a gun to my head.

At last it's time for me to take my place at the podium.

After a few introductory remarks about my own background and the work done by MAD, I begin telling them about the many wonderful things I've seen in their company today. I use the Three C's as the organizing structure of my comments, anchoring everything I've seen in the context of Choice, Competence, and Community.

I tell them I've never even heard of any company approaching their sophistication in the areas of self-motivation and a commitment to ongoing improvement. I tell them I've seen the core values first glimpsed in Josh's office again and again throughout the day.

"If I knew nothing else about your company than what I've witnessed today, I would be confident in announcing that you are clearly superior to most Fortune 500 companies. And so it comes as no surprise to me when I learn that you're far beyond that, you're truly in the stratosphere of success. Coastal Solutions is, without question, a champion."

I wait for the applause at this comment to recede before I ask the question, "Is it safe to assume most of you know who Tiger Woods is?"

I see nods. I continue, "I think it's probably safe to say most of you know Tiger Woods may be the best golfer in the history of the game. Even those of you who don't golf, know in some abstract way he's apparently really, really good." I wait for the chuckles to roll a bit before continuing.

"What many of you may not know is that some time ago, while at the very top of the game, with no challenges from any direction, Tiger Woods decided to change the way he grips a golf club. He knew that even though his short game was brilliant, his drives frequently got him into jams he'd then have to play himself out of, and it made for exciting golf, but he knew deep down he shouldn't be putting himself into those kinds of situations. He knew it was an area in which his game could improve."

I pause to let this sink in before continuing. "Now again, to a non-golfer this may not sound very meaningful. It certainly didn't seem like much to me, the first time I heard it, but I know the golfers in the room will understand that for a golfer to change his grip is a change so fundamental it's as though aeronautical engineers were to say, 'Maybe the wings should face the other way.' "

I again wait for the laughter to subside before hammering home the next point: "It's bedrock, core, heart-of-his-technique stuff. Changing it meant big ripples in every direction...and indeed, Tiger's game suffered a bit while he worked out the kinks...but he believed the change was worth making. He was willing to endure short-term losses because he had deep faith in the overall long-term gains he was cementing into place."

I pause once more, and I can see some expectant faces; they have some sense of what they're about to hear, and it's my job to help them believe it's going to be okay.

I continue, "Ladies and gentlemen, I've just spent a wonderful day at the finest company I've ever had the pleasure to visit, and I've just finished an hour-long conversation with your splendid plant manager, Josh Roberts...and if you'll all have the courage to trust the culture which has done so well for you and your company, I think you're in for a rewarding adventure, because

> **LEADERSHIP LESSON 19**
>
> **Continuous improvement requires the courage and humility to change even when things are going well.**

we've identified an area in which Coastal Solutions needs to adjust its grip in order to stay on top."

I let my eyes sweep the room, and I see nothing but confident faces, willing to hear more. I smile broadly and I say, "And I hope it will please you to hear that when our work is finished, no one is ever going to go to bed at night with any anxiety about whether tomorrow they're going to be told they're a One."

I see flickers of recognition as they register what these words must mean, and I hear excited-sounding murmurs. Slowly, from the back, there comes the sound of clapping. The sound spreads, and builds, until it is washing toward me like a wave. Then an older gentleman in the front gets to his feet and suddenly the whole room is standing, applauding the change, committed to improving… and thanking me.

I can't imagine wanting to be anywhere else.

A few minutes after my speech is over, as the well-wishers are drifting away from Josh and me, I hear my phone chirp in my purse. It's Mickey. Good! I can't wait to tell him everything that's happened, and I answer eagerly, bubbling and babbling about the day and the evening, but he interrupts me with words that literally stagger me and leave me groping for support, a rail, a chair, anything. I find Josh's arm, and the surprise and concern on his face barely registers as I listen to Mickey's news.

I must get home right away.

CHAPTER 12

"If something comes to life in others because of you,
then you have made an approach to immortality."
–Norman Cousins

HAVE ONLY THE VAGUEST idea how I end up on the airplane headed home. All the traveling I've done lately has left me feeling as though all airports are somehow really just one giant airport, and now this surreal idea seems more true than ever. I don't know how I got there (*did Josh drive me?*). I don't remember clearing the security checks. I don't remember getting on the plane.

I don't remember where I put my bag! (a quick, panicky check overhead, *good there it is, but when did I put it there?*) I don't remember the speech or what happened today at that company whose name I don't remember, either. Something Solutions. Don't remember.

All I remember is Mickey's voice. Nothing comes before that voice, nothing comes after it, just his hoarse voice speaking two words, the two words to which my entire universe has dwindled:

"He's gone."

I don't remember details, but I do have the very strong sense of there having been few. An operation. Complications. To the extent I'm able to do anything like "thinking," I have to assume that whatever was wrong when I last saw him quickly became worse, bad enough to require surgical intervention, and I know how risky surgery can be on even a strong and healthy man of his age…

But mostly the thoughts keep swooping back toward those two words, their pull marking them as a black hole at the center of my heart, drawing everything, everything, every feeling, every idea, until even light cannot escape and time itself stands still in this singularity of loss.

He's gone.

I spend almost all of the flight with these two words ringing hollowly through the empty corridors of my mind, until it begins to feel surreal, almost like a dream. The words move through me and as they move I follow them, chase them, try to catch them; if I can just catch them they'll stop echoing, they won't haunt me. But just when I feel I'm about to catch them and silence them once and for all, I'm stopped dead by a crippling realization.

I never said *Thank You.*

The reality of this smashes home; this terribly important, simple ritual, doomed now to go forever unperformed. Guilt and shame sweep through me—I had so many chances, so many opportunities, had I been too afraid to say this simple thing? Or maybe too proud? A small and childish part of my mind goes scurrying through my memory in search of some absolution; surely I had thanked him at some point, probably *many* points, I'm making too much of this…

…But no. I'm not. Because I know, deeply and simply, that the *Thank You* I owed him was larger than any of the individual moments for which I might have thanked him in the past. I should have thanked him for everything, for everything he was and for everything he had helped me to become.

And now it was too late.

I cry very quietly for a very long time in my anonymous seat, flying through cold thin air that cares nothing for my pain.

But when the pilot announces we are beginning our final approach, some switch flips over in my head. Thoughts of home begin pushing their way into my thoughts, home and family and what family means, and how lucky I am to have mine and how much I've missed them…and then, out of seemingly nowhere, thoughts of my father crash into my mind, and the need to call him grows and grows until it feels like pure, animal panic.

THE PLANE'S WHEELS HAVE barely chirped against the tarmac before my cell phone is my hand and I'm dialing. I know I might be breaking the rules. I don't care. Let the air marshals haul me away in irons. I need to talk to my Dad; I need it as much as I've ever needed anything in my life.

I hear a distant "Hello? Joanne?" and I manage a quiet "Hi, Daddy."

Then, because we don't tend to call each other during the week, and perhaps because of something in my voice he asks, "Sweetheart? Is everything all right?" and I break down, crying quietly, determined not to make a scene in this confined space full of strangers, but crying freely nonetheless.

I tell him about Doc's passing, and he is warm and sympathetic and, I think, touched that he is the one I have reached out to at this moment. "I'm sorry to phone you and then fall apart like this," I tell him when I've pulled myself together. "I just really wanted to hear your voice, was all."

"You do that anytime you care to, little girl. I'll always answer."

I take a deep breath, knowing with certainty why I've called him. "Daddy?"

"Yes, Jo?"

"I just want to say Thank You. For everything. For being a great Dad, and for every time you ever stayed up worried because I was sick or took an extra shift to pay for the bike I wanted and for loving Mom and me so well and just... everything, everything. Thank You."

I'm crying a bit more now, but it's different from the sorrow about Doc, and it feels somehow healing and good. "Okay, little girl, okay," Dad's voice comes through, soothing. "You're welcome. You're welcome forever, you know that."

> ## LEADERSHIP LESSON 20
>
> **Resolve crucial interpersonal conflicts, apologize, and give thanks as soon as possible, because you might lose the opportunity later.**

I manage to chuckle through my tears. "Good thing you had my teenage years to train you to be ready for stuff like this, huh?"

I can hear the smile in his voice. "You know a little something about that yourself, I bet." From here things move naturally toward questions about the kids and Keith, and it's nice to be able to talk about them and to remember I'm about to be home and among them once more.

As bad as today's news has been, it's a comfort to know I'm not facing it alone.

THREE DAYS LATER I'm in the large sanctuary of the campus assembly hall, full to overflowing with more than 700 attendees at this—Doc's public memorial service.

Clad in black, I'm on way to the podium to say a few words.

Clutched in my hand is a note card with a few keywords chosen to help bring me back to center if I lose my way...but this would require remembering I have the card to begin with, and being able to read it. Just now, neither is especially likely. My mind is everywhere and nowhere, landing on tiny details ("they should repair those cracks in the plaster") and then swooping off to planets too huge to contemplate ("gone, he's gone, Doc is gone.")

When I arrive at the podium, I absently place the card on its dark-grained surface, and I gaze out at the quiet sea of faces. In the front row, Doc's surviving family—his wife Margaret and his younger sister, Susan and brother, Thomas. Suzie and Tom lost their Dad several years ago, I remember; now, they've lost their big brother, too.

Toward the rear I catch a glimpse of Keith and my kids, here to support me and pay their respects to a man who meant so much to me and to this community.

Between my family and Doc's family are hundreds of students, colleagues and others from every corner of this small community. Each of them touched in some way by Doc's goodness, his generosity. I see their patient faces and I'm suddenly overwhelmed by both my sorrow and by feelings of inadequacy—who am I to speak to the memory of this man, why should any of these people care to listen to me?

An inner voice chides me for these thoughts. I've been asked by Doc's wife, sister and brother to speak, asked specifically. They had smiled warmly as they had recalled the many occasions on which he'd spoken of me, and with what affection. It makes the sharp pain of his departure even harder to bear, but it's also very comforting to know I had mattered to him enough for this to be true.

I owe him so much…but at the moment, I owe him and this audience a properly organized set of thoughts. Instead my emotions, a mixture of grief and nervousness, are running away with things. In a flash I remember a piece of advice Doc once gave me, a kinesthetic trick for gaining control in such emotional moments. I perform the simple ritual: I wiggle the fingers of my left hand while simultaneously wiggling the toes of my right foot.

It works. The simple but odd physical action forces my mind to concentrate, to drop all other distractions. I feel control and focus returning to me.

Doc may be the only person in history who can help someone speak at his own Memorial.

I open my mouth and hear the way the small microphone amplifies and bounces my quiet words. "I'd like to say a few words about my dear friend and finest teacher, the man most of us know, simply, as Doc."

I see a few nods at this familiar nickname, and I continue, "It would be easy to stand up here and talk about Doc's intelligence, his breakthroughs, and his passion for knowledge…however, to me, none of these were the essence of this man. As excited as he might be by knowledge, it was nothing compared to the excitement he felt, and kindled in others, about the *sharing* of knowledge.

"If you set out to design the perfect teacher, I don't think you could do better than Doc. Take equal and abundant parts of wisdom and knowledge. Add a constant thirst for more, more information, more understanding, more opportunities to share wisdom with others. Layer in a large measure of humor and another of compassion, and then add a *ton* of excitement at the way knowledge can spread, from one mind to the next, if one can only find the correct means of expressing it.

"I don't think I'm the only one in this room who remembers him introducing the difference between sex *education* and sex *training*, and which one he imagined people would favor for their own daughters."

Smiles and chuckles move through the room, and I smile with them. "I see a lot of us have heard that one…and if you haven't heard it yet, I bet you will by sundown."

The chuckles grow and I press the point. "And you see, this is what I mean —one of Doc's many, many gifts was his ability to teach us something in ways that we would not only remember it, but would want to pass it along, want to share. He made understanding and teaching contagious. He made…caring… actively caring for people…contagious."

I pause here to gather myself, and this time it's easier. This time when I look out, I don't just see a hall of strangers. I see hundreds of people just like me, a community of us who cared for this man we've lost.

I smile at them. "There were times when it seemed like Doc thought of himself as a spelling teacher. I don't think he ever met an acronym he didn't like."

Again I hear chuckles into whose wake I continue, "He gave us DO IT for Define, Observe, Intervene, and Test. He taught us that SMARTS goals are Specific, Motivational, Achievable, Relevant, Trackable, and Shared."

These are some of the things I had jotted onto my card, but I find the card utterly unnecessary as the familiar lessons flow through me. "He didn't mind making the letters do extra duty, either. LEAD represented the presence of no fewer than sixteen qualities of effective leadership:

L for Language, Listen, Live, and Learn; E for Emotion, Empathy, Empowerment, and Example; A for Authenticity, Accountability, Achievement, and Actively Caring for People; and D for Data, Diversity, self-Determinism, and interDependency."

I take a moment to make sure I can continue with this most-deeply-felt part of my speech. I look up, and can feel my eyes filling, but I will not stop. I will honor my mentor.

"Doc, I know you're up there. I know you're smiling and listening and probably taking notes on something I left out…but in closing, I want to give you an acronym of my own, something I made up which I bet everyone in this room can share with me."

My voice is trembling, nearly breaking, but I push through. "L! L is for Legacy! Everyone in this room, everything you've taught us, everything we've gone on to teach others, we are your legacy, Doc!

"O! O is for Outrageous! You were an outrageous teacher, Doc!" I feel laughter bubble through the tears, and that's okay too, it's all real, it's all okay, and I speak through the laughter and the tears.

"Whether you were releasing thirty quail in the classroom and making a teamwork exercise out of catching them, or whether you were staging a mock assassination to demonstrate the meanings of courage and of bystander apathy, you were energetic and inventive and fun and always, always, Outrageous.

"V! V is for Visionary! A visionary isn't just someone with an idea, he's someone who can see something so specifically, so clearly, that he can describe it in ways which make it impossible for it not to happen. A visionary is not just a seer; he's someone who *enables* what he sees. He's a doer. Doc's visions for safety, for behavior-based reforms, saved countless lives, and he did it by seeing it so clearly that it *had* to happen."

I pause, and my voice grows more quiet, my eyes still up, still shining.

"And E, Doc. E is for Educate, a verb to which you dedicated your whole life. You educated us all. You taught us. You taught us to understand one another, to actively care for one another. You founded groups and scholarships and taught us all, all, to actively care for people, to care as hard as we can. As hard as you did."

My voice rises: "Legacy! Outrageous! Visionary! Educate!"

My arm is up, the green wristband showing clearly, and I feel, rather than see, the entire room raising its arms, displaying the same green, "Actively Caring for People"—AC4P—wristbands, and calling out the letters with me: "L! O! V! E!"

With one voice, in one movement, we all stand, arms up, and call "LOVE! LOVE! LOVE!"

I raise my voice above the others to cry, "We love you Doc! And we thank you for all you've given us!"

And with my arm up and hearing over seven-hundred people calling "LOVE," *roaring* the power of their caring, I realize something I should have known all along. The two words that had pulled at me with such dark force before, that bit with such cruel, sharp teeth, have lost all of their power, because they are clearly not true.

He's not gone.

He's here. With all of us.

THE NEXT FEW DAYS pass in a blur of various attempts at normalcy, interspersed with deep feelings of grief and loss. Make-A-Difference announces it will resume operations on the first of the month, which will give Mickey and me the time to determine how best to proceed. I feel confident we'll find a way to continue Doc's work, our work, and I know Jeff is expecting to start soon, and there's the new contract for Coastal Solutions and a million things which need our attention, but at the moment it all seems too overwhelming to think about.

People, including my own family, work to make sure I have the space I need, the quiet time, the lack of scrutiny. There are the predictable efforts by friends and family to ease my pain, offers of help, shoulders to cry on, ears willingly lent, but the most comforting gestures are the ones which let me know someone is there for me, without saying a word. There are no words to be said.

The third day after the service, I'm leafing absently through a new pile of mail. Credit cards. Balance transfers. The electric bill. Yet another invitation to join AARP, how old do these people think I—

A rich, vellum envelope, with an achingly-familiar script.

A postmark, the day after I saw him in the hospital. His last day alive.

Oh…Doc…

I fumble it open and do my best to read through tears:

Dear Joanne,

I don't suppose there's any point in mincing words. If you're reading this letter, it means I'm gone (gone where? To whatever happens next, I suppose, but more about that in a moment.)

I'm hopeful that someday you'll be able to smile at the irony that I, a scientist who insists upon objective evidence before choosing which paper towel to buy, am writing to you out of little more than a hunch.

The unfortunate truth is I have felt quite badly for quite awhile, and although various medications and meditations have helped me cope over the past few months, these last days have been very difficult indeed. However, I saw no point in spreading my misery about in the form of complaint, especially since there seemed little anyone could do.

Tomorrow morning they are going to attempt a procedure to relieve pressure on my spine, which might provide me some measure of temporary relief… but you and I are both too old for me to lie, Joanne. I'm frightened. I have what I can only term a kind of premonition, and I am more hopeful than I can say that I will be in a position to laugh at myself a few days hence.

But oddly, at this most critical moment, those hopes must be set aside in favor of practicality. I could never leave this earth without saying goodbye to you, and so I am taking the prudent (if irrational) step of writing this letter and giving it to Phil, my night nurse, with instructions to post it should anything go wrong.

So. If these words are reaching you, it means I have died, or passed away, or crossed over, or taken the next step, or whatever phrase gives us comfort. For me, comfort is a distant concept—I have been in such pain for so long that it is difficult to imagine what comfort might be, and perhaps that thought itself should comfort you, if you are experiencing grief at the sight of this shaky handwriting.

I smile to myself. Doc used to joke that I was the first graduate assistant who could actually read his "educated chicken scratch." I read on.

You'll recall, I'm sure, our spirited and lively conversations about religion and spirituality. I hope you'll remember that while I had little patience with thoughtless and narrow-minded dogma, I maintained a healthy respect for ritual, and for the faith in something larger than ourselves. Indeed, it is this belief—the belief that we are all only small parts of something much, much greater—that has driven my work over the years.

And so, while I don't know exactly where or what I am by the time you read this, I know one thing for certain: If you spend too much time mourning

my passing, I shall be very cross with you. Anthropological study has demonstrated, cross-culturally, the emotional value of ritualized observances at the time of death, and grief at the loss of something about which we care is natural and therapeutic. But keep all of this to a minimum, if you'd be so kind.

Because, dear Joanne, I would hate to imagine that thoughts of me bring tears, at any time. My life has been rich and full and exciting and rewarding, and while I must surely have missed an opportunity here and there, I don't feel I missed many. I did as much as I could, as joyously as I could, and I believe I could not set out to design a more fulfilling existence than the one I have lived.

Indeed, all previous statements about religion notwithstanding, each and every day I said a quiet 'thank you' to whomever or whatever might be listening, for the blessed life I had.

If I may play the avuncular mentor one final time, I'd like to make sure you understand something that may at times be difficult to see.

I know your life has been especially tumultuous these past few years. You've navigated difficult circumstances at your old company, found ways to work with difficult people and to make allies of them, found yourself out of work, found yourself new work. I've watched you keenly through all of this, and I've known you were often hurt and confused, and I've hoped fervently that you would reach that special point from which the crises may be seen as opportunities and the changes as growth.

Put more simply: These things have hurt you, but they have also made you stronger. Better.

A hurricane changes a beach, and alters its lines, often past all recognition…but it remains, always, a place where water meets land, where one kind of possibility meets another, beautiful and inviting and perfect. We humans are like a stretch of storm-tossed shoreline, Joanne, forever becoming.

I know you are probably confused and uncertain about your next steps, but I am not. I know, with a peaceful confidence, that you and Mickey will continue the work we have started at Make-A-Difference. I know you will continue to spread the gospel of actively caring for people to every corner of the working world.

You and the people you hire to work alongside you will teach people their own native instincts toward community are to be trusted, and need not be seen as interfering with any mercenary bottom line. Indeed, actively caring about one another is perhaps the only bottom line.

I'm very tired now, Joanne, and it's difficult for me to write these last lines, but I cannot end without saying this. If ever I were to have a granddaughter, if I were to list all the things I wish and yearn for her, for her heart and her mind and her spirit, I could not wish any differently than for her to turn out as you have. I can't imagine a finer woman, and I can't imagine being more proud of you.

I love you, girl. Get busy!

Doc

I surrender slowly to the tears, feeling them rise from some deep and ancient place within me, pulling through my chest and wracking me with sobs of loss and loneliness…and I know that Doc doesn't mind this, not these few moments.

But after a time the crying ebbs, leaving with shuddery breaths and that big-chested feeling which comes from having emptied oneself of the pain. I wipe my tears, and blow my nose, and I rise, carrying Doc's letter, his precious final gift, out onto my back porch, into the light.

I stand and gaze at the simple beauty of the day, and think how lucky I am to be here, with a home and a family I love and work to which I can humbly submit myself in the spirit of service.

I smile at the scripted pages in my hand, thinking that everything I have is somehow connected to this, to him, to all the things he wanted for me, and taught me. His gifts. His legacy. Isn't that the most essential point of a legacy—that it is immortal?

Doc lives on, in me, and in everyone he touched. And yes, he'll grudgingly allow us our few minutes of mourning, but afterwards he expects us to get busy.

He expects us all to Actively Care for People, and to Make A Difference.

I smile, and turn to go back to my life.

EPILOGUE

This is our second venture at teaching evidenced-based principles of human dynamics through a true-to-life story. In *The Courage to Actively Care* we illustrated the courage and compassion of actively caring for people (AC4P) leadership with authentic applications in business, community and family situations.

We used the same format in this storybook to manifest the psychology of self-motivation—the motivation to actively care for people. More specifically, we depicted realistic episodes in the work and family life of the lead character—Joanne Cruse—to clarify well-founded theoretical and empirical connections between self-motivation and an individual's sense of Choice, Competence, and Community. Most importantly, we explicated actual interpersonal interactions to provide practical ways for enhancing people's perception of personal Choice, Competence, and Community, and thus their self-motivation. The level of success in any human endeavor increases as a function of the participants' self-motivation to actively care for people.

We are convinced people's teaching/learning experiences are enhanced by storytelling. However, the personal episodes recounted in this realistic novel may not have been directly relevant to your life and thus we may have missed the mark for you. In other words, it's possible, even likely, another anecdote would have been more meaningful and thus more educational for you. Thus, we would love to hear your story. What events in your life support or refute the three C's of self-motivation illustrated in this principle-centered narrative of real-world events?

Have you observed or initiated techniques to increase self-motivation at work or at home, and which, if any, of our three C's do these strategies reflect? Or, perhaps you have personal evidence of feelings, solutions or circumstances unrelated to Choice, Competence, or Community that enhanced self-motivation.

To be sure, self-motivation does not always connect to AC4P. In fact, one can be self-motivated to harm other people. We elected to link self-motivation and AC4P together, hoping to gain interest and support for a worldwide AC4P Movement. Did this association work for you? Why or why not? We'd love to receive your answers to the critical questions below.

Personal growth and development is a continuous life-long journey, and much of this learning process involves the sharing of personal and interpersonal observations and interpretations. We hope to hear your personal stories related to any or all of the following questions:

1. What personal experiences have increased your self-motivation under certain circumstances?
2. What events in your life support the premise that a person's sense of Choice, Competence, and Community facilitate self-motivation?
3. What circumstances or interactions in your life suggest ways to increase one's perception of Choice, Competence, and/or Community?
4. What happenings in your life, if any, suggest that a person-state other than Choice, Competence, or Community can enhance self-motivation?
5. Do you have any evidence that feelings of Choice, Competence, or Community do not increase self-motivation?

We look forward to hearing from you regarding your take on any or all of our questions in this Epilogue. And of course, any other feedback regarding this realistic narrative and the principles and procedures we aimed to teach would be greatly appreciated.

Please mail your personal stories and feedback to:

Make-A-Difference, LLC

P.O. Box 73

Newport, VA 24128

Or, email your inputs to the authors at:

esgeller@vt.edu and organizationaleffectiveness@msn.com

For more information on AC4P leadership and culture enrichment, including relevant books and education/training materials, log on to: www. safetyperformance.com. To learn more about the AC4P Movement initiated and sustained by student leaders at Virginia Tech, log on to www.ac4p.org.

DISCUSSION QUESTIONS
FOR PERSONAL APPLICATION

CHAPTER 1

1. From the title and cover of this book, what do you expect it to be about? What, if anything, do you expect to learn from reading this storybook?

2. Have you or has someone you know well been terminated from a job? How was it done? What personal feelings accompanied this job dismissal? What factors facilitated and/or inhibited recovery from this job loss?

3. How realistic or common was the job-termination process experienced by Joanne?

4. If you lost your current job, what would you do? Where would you turn for emotional support?

5. Imagine you own a small company and your shrinking profit margin requires you to give notice to one of your hard-working employees. How would you do it? What if anything would you do to decrease the employee's distress during and after the dismissal process?

CHAPTER 2

1. Define self-determinism with an example from your personal experience.

2. Do you believe behavior can ever be completely self-determined? Why or why not?

3. Explain the common assertion "everything happens for a reason." Do you believe this assumption? Why or why not?

4. Explain Joanne's reluctance to react as negatively to Perfect Plastics as her family did. Is this realistic?

5. What are the psychological or emotional ramifications of losing one's job, beyond the financial loss?

6. Explain the distinction between "Safety is a Priority" versus "Safety is a Value." What are the implications of each of these slogans or directives?

7. A number of companies include "Safety is a Condition of Employment" in their mission statement. What are the advantages and disadvantages of this slogan?

8. Explain the relationships between "character," "personal values," and "self-determinism."

9. According to Doc, what is an "actively-caring-for-people culture"?

10. What quality of Joanne is revealed in this chapter that led Doc to believe she would be an asset to Make-A-Difference, Inc.?

CHAPTER 3

1. According to Doc and Mickey, why are many consulting firms ineffective at facilitating long-term improvement?

2. Why is it important to compare the values held by an employee with the mission statement of a company?

3. Explain the connection between "meaningful work" and "self-determinism."

4. How does Doc handle Joanne's concern about "brainwashing" people to change their values?

5. Why do Doc and Mickey believe Joanne's experience as a Safety Director is particularly relevant for their consulting business?

6. Define "empowerment" from the perspective of Make-A-Difference, Inc., and offer an example of this definition from your experience.

7. How is the Make-A-Difference definition of empowerment related to commitment, buy-in, and self-motivation?

8. Define the three C-words—Competence, Choice, and Community, and explain their relevance to self-motivation.

9. Is the communication breakdown between Joanne and Keith realistic? Why or why not?

10. Why is Keith now scared? Is this emotion realistic? Why or why not?

CHAPTER 4

1. What did Joanne do to handle the stress of leaving on her first consulting trip? Why are these behaviors important?

2. Why did Joanne point out the job of the TSA workers is a challenge for self-determinism?

3. Is Joanne's negative reaction to "Quality Culture" justified? Why or why not?

4. How does the concept of *kaizen* relate to the need for self-motivation among employees?

5. How does Mickey use compassion to handle Joanne's exasperation about company supervisors who seemingly do not care about continuous improvement?

6. What is wrong, if anything, about the policy at Stone Mountain Flooring that all employees submit four *kaizens* per year?

7. Define specific problems you discern in the work culture at Stone Mountain Flooring.

8. Why has Stone Mountain Flooring stopped using employee perception surveys?

9. Why does Mickey cut off Joanne's questioning of Patricia about obvious problems with the work culture at Stone Mountain Flooring?

10. What's the rationale behind Joanne's final statement, "Maybe I'm not cut out for this"? Have you ever had these feelings of ambivalence or lack of "personal fit" after an initial experience on a job? Why or why not?

CHAPTER 5

1. When completing the evaluation form for Stone Mountain Flooring, what is Joanne's main concern or criticism?

2. What does Mickey perceive as Joanne's problem underlying her intermittent outbursts of anger toward corporate management?

3. How does Mickey handle Joanne's negative evaluation of Patricia? Why does he give Patricia the benefit of the doubt? Is this realistic?

4. Explain the communication breakdown between Joanne and Keith. Have you ever had a similar communication conflict with a partner? Explain.

5. List the apparent cultural differences between Stone Mountain Flooring and Precision Parts.

6. What factors at Precision Parts apparently contribute to a sense of ownership, empowerment, and mutual caring among the employees interviewed?

7. How does Mickey distinguish between transactional and transformational leadership? From your experience, is this a reasonable and practical distinction? Why or why not?

8. How does Mickey handle Joanne's concern that "values" can be too generic, vague, and impractical?

9. What is wrong with having a management review process every three months? Define a more effective approach to management review.

10. Discuss specific connections between the three C-words and Mickey's checklist of seven things people need in order to be self-motivated at work: Heard, Contribute, Belong, Learn/Grow, Choice, Recognition, and Empowered.

CHAPTER 6

1. Do you see anything wrong with the incentive program at Missoula Ironworks that rewards every employee up to $400 for achieving results in these areas—safety, quality, and teamwork? If so, what?

2. How could the incentive program at Missoula Ironworks be improved?

3. Please describe a performance evaluation (or appraisal) program you have experienced. How was it similar versus different than the performance evaluations sessions conducted at Missoula Ironworks?

4. Which of the seven assessment questions did the hourly workers give their highest rating? Why?

5. Why did the hourly employees cover up their co-worker's error, and then keep the error a secret from management? Is this realistic? Why or why not?

6. Please explain how the opening quote to this chapter—"A prescription without diagnosis is malpractice" —is particularly relevant to this chapter.

7. What is a "cookie cutter" program? Have you ever experienced such a program? Please explain.

8. What is the difference between the wage worker's sense of "belongingness" and the more desirable state of "community"?

9. At this point, how would you define a performance management system that can generate self-motivation?

10. Why is Joanne scared? What experiences has she had to justify this negative emotion?

CHAPTER 7

1. Define the five modes of communication Joanne explained to the management team at Missoula Ironworks, and offer a personal example for each.

2. How does follow-up communication relate to each of the other four modes of communication?

3. When is the statement "how are you doing" more than a greeting?

4. Explain the corporate definition of "inclusion," and give personal examples of being included and excluded from a group or organizational process. Discuss your feeling states in both situations.

5. What two problems does Mickey see with the incentive program at Missoula Ironworks? Which of these is more critical, in your opinion? Why?

6. Do you agree with Mickey's advice that every employee at Missoula Ironworks should get a one-time raise of $4,800 per year, regardless of their on-the-job performance? Why or why not?

7. Why does Joanne get so angry during this meeting that she loses her "cool"?

8. Define an ideal employee evaluation (or performance appraisal) system. Is this realistic? Why or why not?

9. Why does Mickey assume managers will be needed even if a self-motivated work culture is developed?

10. In what ways was Joanne's apology exemplary? Could it have been improved? How?

CHAPTER 8

1. What events at the start of this chapter suggest Keith is an extrovert?

2. Explain the alignment between the University motto *Ut Prosim* and the Relay-for-Life event and Make-A-Difference, Inc. How might this alignment influence behavior to be self-motivated?

3. Why does Doc claim those wearing the "Cancer Survivor" shirts are not really cancer survivors? Do you agree? Why or why not?

4. How does the Relay-for-Life event epitomize the three pillars of self-motivation: choice, competence, and community?

5. Explain why it's more realistic and functional to claim competence leads to self-motivation rather than the reverse?

6. Explain why the participants at the Relay-for-Life event feel empowered.

7. Why is Doc disappointed the President of the University left early?

8. How did Joanne's reaction to Doc's critique of the University President illustrate a lack of empathy?

9. Define the basis of Joanne's profound anger toward ineffective managers. Is her anger realistic or well-founded? Please explain from personal experience.

10. How does Doc attempt to alleviate Joanne's anger, and increase her self-motivation to work for Make-A-Difference, Inc.?

CHAPTER 9

1. Why is Keith drunk and unhappy? Is his conflict with Joanne reasonable? Why or why not?

2. Describe some personal attributes of Joanne and Keith at this point of the story.

3. Why does Doc believe Joanne's opportunity to give a keynote talk for Coastal Solutions could be a valuable test of her competence?

4. Use a personal situation to explain SMARTS goal setting.

5. Distinguish between process goals (or action plans) and outcome goals (or targets) with a real-world example.

6. Ronnie Reich claims people have a basic need to feel competent. Do you believe this? Why or why not? Under what circumstances, if any, would a person not want to feel competent at doing something?

7. Explain the opening quotation from Dr. Paul Chance, "People are not successful because they are motivated; they are motivated because they have been successful" with reference to Jessica's problem and the proposed solution? What are the practical implications of this principle?

8. Why is Keith proud of Joanne's verbal behavior during their session with Ronnie Reich?

9. Discuss distinctions between independent vs. interdependent with regard to circumstances in this chapter.

10. In what ways are personal choice and ownership promoted in the proposed solutions to Jessica's problems at school.

CHAPTER 10

1. What made it difficult for Joanne to sleep well? Is the cognitive activity or self-talk she experienced when trying to fall asleep realistic? Why or why not?

2. What problem is threatening the Cruse family from the perspective of Keith? Does Joanne view this problem similarly? Is her proposal for a solution practical? Why or why not?

3. What special quality (or qualities) of the conversation between Joanne and Keith enabled them to progress toward exploring a practical solution to their problem?

4. What is frustration as illustrated by Doc's person-state in the hospital? Is this realistic? Would you be more or less frustrated in this situation? Why?

5. Distinguish between feeling under-rewarded versus feeling over-rewarded with a real-world example.

6. Define intrinsic reinforcement with a real-world example, and explain how this process makes it difficult to evaluate the perceived equity of another person's relationship situation.

7. How does Joanne plan to influence her input/output ratio as perceived by Keith?

8. Define a relationship issue in your life (past or present) with regard to equity.

9. Briefly define the Doc's four-step plan for self-discipline and for continuous self-improvement. Could this plan work for you? If not, how could it be improved?

10. Describe how this four-step plan for self-improvement could be applied to a personal problem or challenge of your own. Could this adaptation be effective for you? Why or why not?

CHAPTER 11

1. What was your initial reaction to the opening quotation from W. Edwards Deming?

2. What new skill set is Joanne learning from her experiences with Make-A-Difference that could help her deal with her conflicts on the home front?

3. What characteristics of Josh Roberts does Joanne notice that suggest he is an effective leader of a very successful company?

4. Explain the connection between courage and humility as these qualities relate to effective leadership? Provide examples of situations, fiction or real, where individuals demonstrate having versus not having courage and/or humility.

5. Define a problem, large or small, that could have been prevented with a proactive approach, but instead required reaction.

6. Offer a personal appraisal of the seven values posted in Josh's office: Integrity, Quality, Safety, Continuous Improvement, Customer Delight, Employee Inclusion, and Community. Are there other values you'd add to this list? How could a company evaluate whether their organizational performance reflects these values?

7. Define the mission of Coastal Solutions' "culture committee" in terms of their action plans and activities. Is such a committee realistic for your work setting? Why or why not?

8. From your impression of Coastal Solutions, how are the three C's of self-motivation demonstrated and sustained throughout their workforce?

9. Have you ever experienced or observed a disadvantage of a win/lose ranking system analogous to that used at Coastal Solutions? Please explain.

10. What characteristics of the culture at Coastal Solutions are inconsistent with their one-to-three ranking system?

11. Which of the company values are reflected in Joanne's final discussion with Josh Roberts and/or by the reaction of the audience to Joanne's keynote address?

12. What particular qualities of Joanne's after-dinner keynote speech are admirable? How could you apply these strategies when you have opportunities to address groups or teams?

CHAPTER 12

1. Explain the meaning and practical relevance of the opening quotation for this chapter by Norman Cousins.

2. Joanne didn't get a chance to say "thank you" to her mentor and friend. Relate this extreme regret to a personal experience. What practical lesson do Joanne's situation and your own example reveal?

3. If tomorrow you were suddenly killed in a vehicle crash, what would the mourners say at your funeral? With more time to live and contribute, what would you hope mourners would say at your distant funeral?

4. Have you ever heard of the trick Joanne used to block her emotional reactions during her eulogy at Doc's funeral? Do you think it works? Why or why not?

5. Why was Doc labeled "outrageous"? Give examples of your own behavior, if any, which could fall into this "outrageous" category. *The American Heritage Dictionary* (1985, Houghton Mifflin Company: Boston, MA) defines "outrageous" as "grossly offensive; heinous; disgraceful; shameful; having no regard for morality; violent or unrestrained in temperament or behavior." Is this the definition you thought of when you read "outrageous" in this chapter? Can you suggest a more appropriate label for Doc's behavior, and for your example of personal behavior?

6. Explain the relevance of the following quotation by D.L. Moody to the contents of this chapter, and to any other aspects of prior chapters: "I expect to pass through this world but once. If there be any kindness I can show, any good I can do, any help I can give, let me do it now; for I will not pass this way again."

7. List the lessons taught in this principle-centered narrative that are most meaningful to you. Why were these meaningful?

8. How does the title of this storybook, *The Motivation to Actively Care*, connect to the theme of self-motivation?

9. A common statement in self-help books is that people cannot motivate others, but can only motivate themselves. Do you believe this assertion? Why or why not? Please explain this allegation within the context of the suggested ways to increase self-motivation disclosed in this narrative.

10. How might this realistic narrative influence your life? In other words, what specific behaviors are you considering decreasing or increasing in frequency as a result of reading the teaching/learning adventures of Joanne Cruse?

LEADERSHIP LESSONS REVEALED IN THIS BOOK

Lesson 1: What you do when no one's watching or holding you accountable is self-determined or self-motivated.

Lesson 2: People feel empowered when they answer "yes" to three questions: Can you do it? Will it work? Is it worth it?

Lesson 3: Transactional leaders hold people accountable for compliance; Transformational leaders inspire people to be self-accountable or self-motivated.

Lesson 4: Employees feel included and self-motivated when they believe they: 1) are heard, 2) contribute, 3) belong, 4) achieve, 5) choose, 6) are appreciated, and 7) feel empowered.

Lesson 5: A community spirit extends beyond one's work team to the organizational system as a whole.

Lesson 6: Interpersonal communication comes in five distinct forms: 1) Relationship, 2) Possibility, 3) Action, 4) Opportunity, and 5) Follow-up.

Lesson 7: Authentic inclusion occurs when input for important group or organizational decisions are solicited from all participants.

Lesson 8: A financial bonus based on organizational performance rather than individual behavior can become an entitlement and have no impact on what people do.

Lesson 9: Performance appraisals improve behavior when they occur periodically and include goal setting and behavior-based feedback customized for the individual.

Lesson 10: When the values of organizations and individuals align, relevant behavior is predisposed to be self-motivated.

Lesson 11: People with empathy don't judge others until they understand completely the other person's intentions and perceptions.

Lesson 12: Process goals are set for the behaviors needed to accomplish an outcome goal and are Specific, Motivational, Achievable, Relevant, Trackable, and Shared.

Lesson 13: When people believe they are competent at worthwhile tasks, they are inclined to be self-motivated.

Lesson 14: Equity in a relationship occurs when each person perceives the participants' input/output ratios are equivalent.

Lesson 15: Self-motivation occurs when the natural or intrinsic consequences of an action are reinforcing.

Lesson 16: Continuous self-improvement starts with a daily behavior-based commitment, then noticing opportunities to perform the target behavior, self-congratulating occurrences of that behavior, and finally reflecting on relevant success and room for improvement.

Lesson 17: A ranking system that promotes win/lose over win/win thinking and acting does more harm than good.

Lesson 18: Effective leaders have the *courage* to ask for candid feedback and the *humility* to accept and apply suggestions for reasonable change.

Lesson 19: Continuous improvement requires the courage and humility to change even when things are going well.

Lesson 20: Resolve crucial interpersonal conflicts, apologize, and give thanks as soon as possible, because you might lose the opportunity later.

BIBLIOGRAPHY AND
RECOMMENDED READINGS

The AC4P lessons and applications revealed in this book are supported by the following books and research-based journal articles.

Aronson, E. (1999). The power of self-persuasion. *American Psychologist, 54,* 875-884.

Bailey, J. S., & Burch, M. B. (2006). *How to think like a behavior analyst.* Mahwah, N.J.: Lawrence Erlbaum Associates.

Bandura, A. (1997). *Self-efficacy: The exercise of control.* New York: W. H. Freeman and Company.

Bem, D. J. (1972). Self-perception theory. In L. Berkowitz (Ed.). *Advances in experimental social psychology,* Vol. 6 (pp. 1-60). New York: Academic Press.

Bennis, W. (1989). *On becoming a leader.* New York: Addison-Wesley Publishing Company.

Biglan, A. (2015). *The nurture effect: How the science of human behavior can improve our lives and our world.* Oakland, CA: New Harbinger Publications.

Bird, F. E., Jr., & Germain, G. L. (1987). *Commitment.* Loganville, GA: International Loss Control Institute, Inc.

Blanchard, K., Zigarmi, P., & Zigarmi, D. (1985). *Leadership and the one-minute manager.* New York: William Morrow and Company, Inc.

Block, P. (1993). *Stewardship.* San Francisco: Berrett-Koehler Publishers Inc.

Braksick, L. W. (2000). *Unlock behavior, unleash profits.* New York: McGraw Hill.

Brehm, J. W. (1972). *Responses to loss of freedom: A theory of psychological reactance.* New York: General Learning Press.

Brown, J., & Isaacs, D. (2005). *The world café.* San Francisco: Berrett-Koehler Publishers, Inc.

Carnegie, D. (1936). *How to win friends and influence people* (1981 Edition). New York: Galahad Books.

Cialdini, R. B. (2001). *Influence: Science and practice* (4th ed.). New York: Harper Collins College.

Collins, J. C. (2001). *Good to great.* HarperCollins Publishers, Inc.

Collins, J. C., & Porras, J. (1994). *Built to last.* New York: HarperCollins Publishers, Inc.

Connolly, M., & Rianoshek, R. (2002). *The communication catalyst.* Dearborn, MI: Dearborn Trade Publishing.

Covey, S. R. (1989). *The seven habits of highly effective people: Restoring the character ethic.* New York: Simon & Schuster, Inc.

Covey, S. R. (2004). *The eighth habit: From effectiveness to greatness.* New York: Simon & Schuster, Inc.

Daniels, A. C., & Daniels, J. E. (2005). *Measure of a leader.* Atlanta, GA: Performance Management Publications.

Deci, E.L. (1975). *Intrinsic motivation.* New York: Plenum.

Deci, E. L., & Flaste, R. (1995). *Why we do what we do: Understanding self-motivation.* New York: Penguin Books.

Deci, E. L., & Ryan, R. M. (1995). *Intrinsic motivation and self-determinism in human behavior.* New York: Plenum.

DeGeus, A. (1997). *The living company.* Cambridge, MA: Harvard Business School Press.

DePree, M. (1989). *Leadership is an art.* New York: Dell Publishing Group, Inc.

Deming, W. E. (1986). *Out of the crisis.* Cambridge, MA: Massachusetts Institute of Technology, Center for Advanced Engineering Study.

DePasquale, J. P., & Geller, E. S. (1999). Critical success factors for behavior-based safety: A study of 20 industry-wide applications. *Journal of Safety Research, 30*(4), 237-249.

Elder, J. P., Geller, E. S., Hovell, M. F., & Mayer, J. A. (1994). *Motivating health behavior.* New York: Delmar Publishers.

Festinger, L. (1957). *A theory of cognitive dissonance.* Stanford, CA: Stanford University Press.

Frankl, V. (1962). *Man's search for meaning: An introduction to logo therapy.* Boston: Beacon Press.

Geller, E. S. (1994).Ten principles for achieving a total safety culture. *Professional Safety, 39* (9), 18.

Geller, E. S. (1995). Safety coaching: Key to achieving a total safety culture. *Professional Safety, 40* (7), 16-22.

Geller, E. S. (1997). Key processes for continuous safety improvement: Behavior-based recognition and celebration. *Professional Safety, 42*(10), 40-44.

Geller, E. S. (1998). *Understanding behavior-based safety: Step-by-step methods to improve your workplace* (2nded.). Neenah, WI: J. J. Keller & Associates, Inc.

Geller, E. S. (1999). Behavior-based safety: Confusion, controversy, and clarification. *Occupational Health & Safety, 68*(1), pp. 40, 42, 44, 46, 48-49.

Geller, E. S. (2000). Behavioral safety analysis: A necessary precursor to corrective action. *Professional Safety, 45*(3), 29-32.

Geller, E. S. (2000). Ten leadership qualities for a total safety culture: Safety management is not enough. *Professional Safety, 45*(5), 38-41.

Geller, E. S. (2001). Actively caring for occupational safety: Extending the performance management paradigm. In C. M. Johnson, W.K. Redmon, & T.C. Mawhinney (Eds.). *Handbook of organizational performance: Behavior analysis and management* (pp.303-326). New York: The Haworth Press.

Geller, E. S. (2001). *Beyond safety accountability: How to increase personal responsibility.* Rockville, MD: Government Institutes.

Geller, E. S. (2001). *The psychology of safety handbook*. Boca Raton, FL: CRC Press.

Geller, E.S. (2016) (Ed.). *Applied psychology: Actively caring for people*. New York: Cambridge University Press.

Geller, E.S. (2016). Seven life lessons from humanistic behaviorism: How to bring the best out of yourself and others. *Journal of Organizational Behavior Management, 35*(1), 151-170.

Geller, E.S. (2017). *Actively caring for people in schools: How to cultivate a culture of compassion*. New York: Morgan James Publishers.

Geller, E. S., & Clarke, S. W. (1999). Safety self-management: A key behavior-based process for injury prevention. *Professional Safety, 44*(7), 29-33.

Geller, E. S., & Geller, K. S. (2017). *Actively caring for people's safety: How to cultivate a brother's/sister's keeper work culture*. Park Ridge, IL: American Society of Safety Engineers.

Geller, E.S., & Kipper, B. (2017). *Actively caring for people policing: Building positive police/citizen relations*. New York: Morgan James Publishers.

Geller, E. S., Roberts, D. S., & Gilmore, M. R. (1996). Predicting propensity to actively care for occupational safety. *Journal of Safety Research*, 27, 1-8.

Geller, E.S., & Veazie, B. (2014). Behavior-based safety versus actively caring: From other-directed compliance to self-directed commitment. *Professional Safety, 59*(10), 44-50.

Geller, E.S., & Veazie, B. (2017). *The courage to actively care: Cultivating a culture of compassion*. New York: Morgan James Publishers.

Geller, E. S., & Williams, J. A. (2001) (Eds). *Keys to behavior-based safety from Safety Performance Solutions*. Rockville, MD: Government Institutes.

Goleman, D. (1995). *Emotional intelligence*. New York: Bantam Books.

Henning, J. (1997). *The future of staff groups*. San Francisco: Berrett-Koehler Publishers, Inc.

Hersey, P., & Blanchard, K. (1982). *Management of organizational behavior* (4th ed.). Englewood Cliffs, NJ: Prentice Hall.

Holdsambeck, R.D., & Pennypacker, H.S. (2016) (Eds.). *Behavioral science: Tales of inspiration, discovery, and service*. Beverly, MA: The Cambridge Center for Behavioral Studies.

Katzenbach, J. (1995). *Real change leaders.* New York: Random House, Inc.

Kaye, B., & Jordan-Evans, S. (2002). *Love 'em or lose 'em: Getting good people to stay.* San Francisco: Berrett-Koehler Publishers, Inc.

Kirkpatrick, S. A., & Locke, E. A. (1991). Leadership: Do traits matter? *Academy of Management Executive, 5*(2), 48-60.

Kotter, J. P. (1996). *Leading change.* Boston, MA: Harvard Business School Press.

Kotter, J. P. (1999). *What leaders really do.* Boston, MA: Harvard Business School Press.

Kouzes, J. M., & Posner, B. Z. (2006). *A leader's legacy.* San Francisco : John Wiley & Sons, Inc.

Krisco, K. H. (1997). *Leadership and the art of conversation.* Rocklin, CA: Prima Publishing.

Langer, E. J. (1989). *Mindfulness.* Reading, MA: Addison-Wesley.

Langer, E. J. (1997). *The power of mindful learning.* Reading, MA: Perseus Books.

Latané, B., & Darley, J. M. (1970). *The unresponsible bystander: Why doesn't he help?* New York: Appleton-Century-Crofts.

Ludwig, T. D., & Geller, E. S. (2001). *Intervening to improve the safety of occupational driving: A behavior-change model and review of empirical evidence.* New York: The Haworth Press, Inc.

Maslow, A. H. (1943). A theory of human motivation. *Psychological Review, 50,* 370=396.

Maslow, A.H. (1970). *Motivation and personality* (2nd ed.). New York: Harper & Row.

Maslow, A.H. (1971). The farther reaches of human nature. New York: Viking Press.

Messick, D. M., & Kramer, R. M. (2005) (Ed.). *The psychology of leadership: New perspectives and research.* Mahwah, N.J.: Lawrence Erlbaum Associates.

McSween, T. E. (2001). *The values-based safety process: Improving your safety culture with a behavior-based approach* (2nd ed.). New York: Van Nostrand Reinhold.

Petersen, D. (2001). *Authentic involvement.* Itasca, IL: National Safety Council.

Rotter, J. B. (1966). Generalized expectancies for internal versus external control of reinforcement. *Psychological Monographs, 80,* No. 1.

Ryan, R. M., & Deci, E. L. (2000). Self-determination theory and the facilitation of intrinsic motivation, social development, and well-being. *American Psychologist, 55,* 68-78.

Seligman, M. E. P. (1991). *Learned optimism.* New York: Alfred A. Knopf.

Senge, P. M. (1990). *The fifth discipline: The art and practice of the learning organization.* New York: Doubleday/Currency.

Senge, P., Kleiner, A., Roberts. C., Ross. R., Roth. G., & Smith. B. (1999). *The dance of change.* New York: Doubleday Publishing.

Skinner, B. F. (1971). *Beyond freedom and dignity.* New York: Knopf.

Skinner, B. F. (1981). Selection by consequences. *Science, 213,* 502.

The Arbinger Institute (2006). *Leadership and self-deception: Getting out of the box.* San Francisco: Berrett-Koehler Publishers, Inc.

Watson, D. L., & Tharp, R. G. (1997). *Self-directed behavior: Self-modification for personal adjustment* (7th ed.). Pacific Grove, CA: Brooks/Cole.

Wheatley, M. (1999). *Leadership and the new science.* San Francisco: Berrett-Koehler Publishers, Inc.

Williams, J.H. (2010). *Keeping people safe: The human dynamics of injury prevention.* Lanham, MD: Government Institutes/Scarecrow Press.

ACKNOWLEDGEMENTS

The Motivation to Actively Care is a revision and republication of *When No One's Watching,* published in 2010 by Coastal Training Technologies Corp. and disseminated exclusively at select occupational-safety conferences. Bob Veazie and I are extremely grateful that David Hancock, CEO of Morgan James Publishers, perceived value in a wider distribution of this narrative approach to teaching principles and applications of psychological science relevant for actively-caring-for-people (AC4P) leadership. We also greatly appreciate the competent contributions of the Morgan James publication team led by Margo Toulouse. They prepared our scholarship for publication, from designing the cover to formatting the text and illustrations.

This realistic narrative brings to life the most practical and effective leadership principles included in the seventeen culture-improvement books I've authored, co-authored, or edited since 1996. Thus, this realistic narrative has benefited from the cumulative advice, support and encouragement of literally hundreds of colleagues, teachers, students and safety leaders. My prior books thanked many of these individuals. Here, I recognize those with whom I've worked directly to accomplish this scholarship.

First and foremost, I'm profoundly grateful for the talent, dedication and inspiration of my co-author—Bob Veazie. I first met Bob in 1997 when he invited me to offer workshops to the management team and hourly workers at the Hewlett Packard (HP) facility in Corvallis, Oregon. As a Culture-Change Agent for the 6,000 employees at that plant, Bob exemplified transformational leadership throughout the facility, from commending employees for their competence at doing worthwhile work to offering relevant advice to managers for motivating more engagement, inclusion, and self-accountability among individuals and teams. Indeed, I had never met anyone who was so genuinely dedicated to cultivating an interdependently-motivated work force all day and every day.

Bob took the behavior-based principles I taught and customized practical procedures and accountability systems to enable the Corvallis HP facility to reach record-high levels of safety excellence. And most relevant to this book, Bob was the first practitioner to truly appreciate the innovative and practical potential of the "actively caring for people" (AC4P) dimension of my teaching.

Others have shown interest and appreciation for the notion that one's propensity to actively care—to go beyond the call of duty on behalf of another person's well-being—is influenced by certain person-states that vary as a function of interpersonal communication. However, Bob made these assumptions behavior-based, and recorded instances that supported their validity.

This storybook was Bob Veazie's idea. Convinced of the potency and practical potential of the AC4P concepts and proposals he had learned from my workshops and books, Bob enticed me to collaborate on this challenging venture—the creation of a fun-to-read book that brings to life the essential leadership lessons anyone can use to improve behavior, attitude and organizational performance.

Bob outlined a storyline, and then asked me to link principles with practical applications. We deemed it necessary to use real-world characters and incidents to illustrate lessons and implementations. Bob's experiences at HP were invaluable, as well as my own interactions in the business world. However, one particular safety professional sparked our rhetoric about courage and compassion: Joanne Dean, the Safety Director of the Gale Construction Company, a subsidiary of Mack-Cali.

I met Joanne at a safety conference fifteen years ago, and ever since, I've been impressed with this individual's daily dedication to preventing injuries among hundreds of construction workers and company leaders. I reported her remarkable AC4P behavior in several of my monthly "Psychology of Safety" columns in *Industrial Safety and Hygiene News*. For example, she helped to develop a large consortium of safety leaders from major construction firms throughout New Jersey who meet monthly to share leading-edge strategies and accountability systems for injury prevention; she arranged for the high-school classmates of a victim of ALS (Lou Gehrig's disease) to document their compassion and caring for this talented athlete, coach and community leader in a memorable and heart-warming book; she taught emergency medical response skills to company employees throughout New Jersey; she consistently exemplifies the principles and procedures of AC4P in group meetings and in one-on-one conversations; and as a professional health and fitness instructor for more than 45 years, Joanne has guided and motivated the integration of health-enhancing exercise into the lifestyles of countless individuals. But most notably, Joanne Dean never fails to step to the plate for occupational safety, even when such action puts her at risk for an uncomfortable interaction. Joanne rarely fails at these interpersonal interventions because her courage is always compassionate; she actively cares for people.

Joanne Dean epitomizes the four key leadership concepts illustrated in this book—competence, commitment, courage, and compassion. Her special success as a safety leader verifies the social and societal validity of the life lessons portrayed here. Thus, it's fitting that we named the lead character "Joanne."

The name of another key character in our story was purposely assigned Dr. Pitz, the distinguished professor who teaches Joanne critical leadership lessons that change her life. Dr. Gordon F. Pitz was the chair of both my thesis and dissertation committees in graduate school at Southern Illinois University (SIU) in Carbondale, Illinois. He gave me special coaching in research methodology and data analysis, and refined my skills for professional writing. Most importantly, Dr. Pitz became my mentor at a critical time in my graduate education.

My first year in graduate school, I was assigned to work in the animal research laboratory of a professor with whom I did not get along. He told me I lacked the ability and dedication to become a successful researcher, while I perceived him to be a disorganized individual, more interested in personal fame than teaching.

This assistant professor convinced his research staff I should not be in graduate school, and he spread this perspective to other students and faculty.

With low self-esteem, self-efficacy, personal control, optimism and belongingness in my assigned research environment, I was on the verge of quitting graduate school at the end of my first year. Fortunately, I met Dr. Pitz in the midst of my darkest time since leaving home for my undergraduate education. This professor overlooked the negative talk about my research performance, and awarded me a graduate research assistantship to work in his human information processing and decision-making laboratory. This was a courageous act for a non-tenured, assistant professor. But Dr. Pitz did much more; he actively cared for my successive development as a researcher, teacher and scholar. He helped me recharge those five person-states that had been depleted throughout my first year at SIU, and thereby enabled me to feel competent and committed throughout the remaining four years of my graduate education.

My career as an author of books for the business world has benefited greatly from the talent and insight of Dave Johnson, Editor of *Industrial Safety and Hygiene News*. As a friend and professional colleague since 1999, Dave has taught me how to translate academic theory and research into concise language suitable for public consumption. Dave was the editor of four of my occupational safety books, and my co-author for *People-Based Patient Safety*, a comprehensive treatise of evidence-based and practical methods for preventing human error in healthcare settings.

We were privileged to engage the special skills and talents of Bo Wilson, a highly acclaimed author and playwright. Bo Wilson's artful treatment of our draft chapters distinguishes this book from all other storybooks prepared for human development, organizational enhancement, and/or culture enrichment. More specifically, Bo's prudent modifications of our written expression add vivid reality to the cast of our story and to their various teaching/learning episodes.

Bo's dramatic refinement of our scholarship involved much more than editing. He not only substituted words and sentences to develop our story characters and add drama, he eliminated substantial text that was unnecessary and distracting, and then made significant additions, enhancing realism and incorporating humor. We could not have turned our drafts over to a better-equipped artist. Thank you, Bo Wilson, for making our book the most true-to-life and fun-to-read among the countless other self-help and human development books on the market.

How did we find and employ Bo Wilson? Nancy Kondas made this happen. Indeed, Nancy Kondas was key to the development, production, and marketing of each of my four books published by Coastal Training Technologies Corp. From the initiation of a book plan to the final review of page proofs, I relied on the advice, acumen, vision and supportive management of Nancy Kondas. I'm convinced none of my People-Based Safety books would have seen the light of day without the dedication and leadership of this VP of Creative Product Development for Coastal Training Technologies. Bob and I are indebted to Nancy Kondas for the expected success of this book to make a difference in people's lives. Words are insufficient to express our utmost gratitude. Thank you, Nancy!

Also, I am extremely appreciative for the unique and unvarying support of Ashley Underwood and Brian Doyle, the current Coordinators of Virginia Tech's Center for Applied Behavior Systems which I direct. Not only did Ashley and Brian assume critical leadership roles that enabled me to work on this revision, they helped me prepare the text and illustrations for the publisher.

This brings me to two additional noteworthy contributors to this book—Marshall McClure and George Wills. Marshall McClure applied her creativity and composition skills to qualify our first edition (*When No One's Watching*) for printing. This included the formatting of original artwork by George Wills, a professional illustrator from Blacksburg, Virginia. George has supported my teaching with his imaginative artwork for over 25 years. Since 1990, I have used George's original cartoons, created and customized per my instructions, to illustrate concepts in my university classes and to add humor in my keynote addresses. Indeed, all of my safety and leadership books have been enhanced with George Wills' artistic talents; this book is no exception.

George's illustrations interspersed throughout this book depict his interpretation of our story characters in various situations. We think they add vitality and drama to the printed prose, and thereby enhance readability. We hope you feel the same.

Any book project is a collaborative team effort, and I have identified only the key players here. Many others contributed to this product, including hundreds of colleagues who have provided Bob Veazie and me the teaching/learning experiences and revelations reflected in our story. The synergy from your interdependent support and sustenance bestows a noble legacy—leadership lessons and applications readers can use to improve interpersonal relationships, enhance individual, group and organizational performance, and enrich a culture.

E. Scott Geller

ABOUT THE AUTHORS

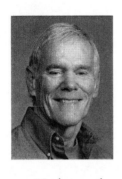 E. Scott Geller, Ph.D., an Alumni Distinguished Professor at Virginia Tech, is co-founder and senior partner of Safety Performance Solutions, Inc., a leading-edge training and consulting organization specializing in AC4P safety since 1995 (safetyperformance.com). For almost five decades, Professor Geller has taught and conducted research as a faculty member and director of the Center for Applied Behavior Systems in the Department of Psychology.

He has authored, edited or co-authored 37 books, 82 book chapters, 39 training programs, 259 magazine articles, and more than 300 research articles addressing the development and evaluation of behavior change interventions to improve quality of life on a large scale. His most recent textbook: *Applied Psychology: Actively Caring for People* defines Dr. Geller's research, teaching, and scholarship career at Virginia Tech, which epitomizes the VT logo: *Ut Prosim*—"That I May Serve".

Dr. Geller is a Fellow of the American Psychological Society, the Association for Psychological Science, the Association of Behavior Analysis International, and the World Academy of Productivity and Quality Sciences. He is past Editor of the *Journal of Applied Behavior Analysis* (1989-1992), current Associate Editor of *Environment and Behavior* (since 1982), and current Consulting Editor for *Behavior and Social Issues*, the *Journal of Organizational Behavior Management,* and the *Journal of Safety Research.*

Professor Geller has received lifetime achievement awards from the International Organizational Behavior Management Network (in 2008) and the American Psychological Foundation (in 2009). And in 2010 he was honored with the Outstanding Applied Research Award from the American Psychological Association's Division of Applied Behavior Analysis. In 2011, the College of Wooster awarded E. Scott Geller the honorary degree: Doctor of Humane Letters.

 Bob Veazie is President of People Powered Leadership (PPL) with a mission to help organizations develop high performance safety cultures through employee inclusion and empowerment. PPL's primary focus is to help organizations develop an injury-free safety culture utilizing a "Commitment-Based" approach. Bob has worked in industry for more than 30 years at Shell Oil Company, Fluor Corporation and Hewlett Packard Company.

Bob Veazie has been a keynote speaker at numerous professional development conferences (ASSE, NSC, VPPPA, BSN, WEI, Alaska Governor's Conference, Industry Week Best Plants and more) and has authored articles in both *Professional Safety* and *Industrial Safety Hygiene News.* Bob has spoken at company management team meetings as well as presented the new paradigm on Commitment Based Safety to corporate leadership teams. Since forming his own safety consulting company eight years ago, Bob has worked with tens of thousands of employees in many diverse industries to apply behavioral solutions to managing risks and reducing injuries in organizations.

Bob earned his Bachelor of Science in Business Management from California Polytechnic State University at San Luis Obispo in 1978 and a Masters of Business Administration from California State University at Long Beach in 1981.

Bob has studied organizational performance with some of the top thought leaders in the field—Dr. Stephen Covey, Peter Senge, Peter Block, Margaret

Wheatley, Ken Blanchard, David Whyte, and many more. Bob has worked and studied key psychological principles under the mentorship of Dr. E. Scott Geller, including applications to reduce injuries in organizations.

OTHER AC4P BOOKS BY E. SCOTT GELLER

The Courage to Actively Care: Cultivating a culture of compassion
(co-authored with Bob Veazie)

Life Lessons from Psychological Science:
How to bring out the best in yourself and others

Applied Psychology: Actively caring for people

Actively Caring for People in Schools: How to cultivate a culture of compassion

Actively Caring for People Policing: Building positive police/citizen relations
(co-authored with Bobby Kipper)

Actively Caring for People's Safety: How to cultivate a brother's/sister's keeper work
culture (co-authored with Krista S. Geller)

Leading People-Based Safety: Enriching your culture

People-Based Patient Safety: Enriching your culture to prevent medical error
(co-authored with Dave Johnson)

People-Based Safety: The source

The Participation Factor: How to increase involvement in occupational safety

The Psychology of Safety Handbook

Understanding Behavior-Based Safety:
Step-by-step methods to improve your Workplace

Beyond Safety Accountability: How to increase personal responsibility

Building Successful Safety Teams: Together Everyone Achieves More

Working Safe: How to help people actively care for health and safety

The Psychology of Safety: How to improve behaviors and attitudes on the job

Morgan James
Speakers Group

We connect Morgan James published
authors with live and online events
and audiences whom will benefit
from their expertise.

CPSIA information can be obtained
at www.ICGtesting.com
Printed in the USA
LVOW11s0243290417
532627LV00004B/4/P